THE
HUMANE
INTERFACE

THE
HUMANE
INTERFACE

New Directions

for Designing

Interactive Systems

JEF RASKIN

ADDISON–WESLEY

Boston • San Francisco • New York • Toronto • Montreal
London • Munich • Paris • Madrid
Capetown • Sydney • Tokyo • Singapore • Mexico City

Many of the designations used by manufacturers and sellers to distinguish their products are claimed as trademarks. Where those designations appear in this book and we were aware of a trademark claim, the designations have been printed in initial capital letters or all capitals.

The authors and publisher have taken care in the preparation of this book, but make no expressed or implied warranty of any kind and assume no responsibility for errors or omissions. No liability is assumed for incidental or consequential damages in connection with or arising out of the use of the information or programs contained herein.

The publisher offers discounts on this book when ordered in quantity for special sales. For more information please contact:

Pearson Education Corporate Sales Division
One Lake Street
Upper Saddle River, NJ 07458
(800) 382-3419

corpsales@pearsontechgroup.com

Visit AW on the Web at *www.awl.com/cseng/*

Library of Congress Cataloging-in Publication Data

Raskin, Jef.
    The humane interface: new directions for designing interactive systems / Jef Raskin.
        p. cm.
    Includes bibliographical references and index.
    ISBN 0-2-1-37937-6
    1. Human-computer interaction. 2. User interfaces (Computer systems) I. Title.
QA76.9.H85 R37 2000
004'.01'9–dc21   00–021300

ISBN 0-201-37937-6
Text printed on recycled paper.
3 4 5 6 7 8 9—CRS—04030201
Third printing, January 2001

We are oppressed by our electronic servants.
This book is dedicated to our liberation.

CONTENTS

PREFACE

I don't know what percentage of our time on any computer-based project is spent getting the equipment to work right, but if I had a gardener who spent as much of the time fixing her shovel as we spend fooling with our computers, I'd buy her a good shovel. At least you can buy a good shovel.

—*Erasmus Smums*

Creating an interface is much like building a house: If you don't get the foundations right, no amount of decorating can fix the resulting structure. *The Humane Interface* reexamines the cognitive foundations of human-machine interaction to elucidate a crucial aspect of why interface designs succeed or fail. One finding is that present-day graphical user interfaces, such as those of the Windows and Macintosh operating systems, which are based on an architecture of operating system plus application programs, are inherently flawed. A different approach is required if computers are to become more pleasant and if users are to become more productive. This book describes some of the fundamental flaws in user interfaces and describes solutions for overcoming those flaws.

Although the techniques covered in *The Humane Interface* apply to a wide range of products—including web sites, application software, handheld personal data managers and other information appliances, and operating systems—this book does not present a survey of the field of human-machine interface design. Rather, this book strikes out in new directions while also reviewing those established parts of interface design that are needed in the development of the new material.

If we are to surmount the inherent problems in present human-machine interfaces, it is necessary that we understand the teachings of this volume; it is not, however, *sufficient*. Many important aspects of interaction design are not included here because they are well covered in the literature. This book is intended to complement existing—or to be a prolegomenon to future—treatments of interface design.

The audience for this book includes

• Web designers and managers who want to give their sites a special ease of use that appeals to audiences and helps customers to find the information they need and to buy what they want

• Product designers and product managers who need to be able to create web sites or products that will win and retain customers by offering ease of use and ready learnability and by having a first-rate feature set

• Corporate managers who correctly insist on making products that have low maintenance and that reduce the need for help desks

• Programmers who do interface design—and who doesn't these days?—and who want to understand more of the factors that make their work most useful

• IT (information technology) managers who need to know which interface features will minimize their costs for training and which interface designs are likely to aid productivity

• Consumers who want to learn what to hope for in terms of pleasant interaction with computers and other equipment, and what is wrong with the way today's software is designed

• Computer science and cognitive psychology students who want to understand what lies behind heuristics of interface design

Finally, this book is for human-machine interface researchers, who may find that they will never again be able to view interfaces in quite the same way they did before reading *The Humane Interface*.

ACKNOWLEDGMENTS

Friendly counsel cuts off many foes.

—*William Shakespeare (*King Henry VI, *Act III, Scene 1)*

To list those who have helped is difficult, because they are so numerous, and the debt is so enormous. Many friends, colleagues, relations, reviewers, and some generous strangers I know only via the Internet have contributed ideas, critiques, suggestions, and detailed editorial work. Please forgive (and inform) me if you've helped and I've left you out or gotten your name or title wrong.

Thanks to the groups at Addison Wesley Longman, whether editors, designers, in PR, marketing, or whatever, all of whom seem to have been chosen not only for their competence, but also for their friendliness and forbearance. On the other hand, the anonymous reviewers they chose were merciless, for which I am also grateful.

Among the following list are friends, acquaintances, colleagues, my brother, my son's horn teacher, a fellow model airplane enthusiast—a seemingly unlikely lot. Only a few are experts in human-computer interface design, but all have read my manuscript and made essential contributions to the book or have contributed over the years to its concepts: David Alzofon (who also drew Quasimodo), Bill Atkinson, Thomas Atwood, Paul Baker, Jerry Barenholtz, John Bumgarner, David Caulkins, William Buxton, Ph.D., Renwick Curry, Ph.D., Robert Fowles, Josh Garrett, Ph.D., Jean-François

Groff, Scott Kim, Ph. D., Kathleen Mandis, Pamela Martin, Troy May, Miriam Meisler, Ph.D., Douglas McKenna, Michael S. Miller, David Moshal, M.D., Andrew Nielsen, Jakob Nielsen, Julie Ososke, Ian Patterson, Michael Raskin, Ph.D., Erasmus Smums, Spider Robinson, Minoru Taoyama, Shay Telfer, Yesso Tekerian, Bruce Tognazzini, David Wing, Terry Winograd, Ph.D., the local chapter (BayCHI) of the ACM's Special Interest Group in Computer-Human Interaction, which has let me preach and debate my theses, and the students at the Center for Computer Research in Music and Acoustics at Stanford University and its director, John Chowning.

I am lucky to have a literate as well as a loving wife, Linda Blum, R.N., who has never cared that writing a technical book is no way to support a family, so long as it was a worthy endeavor. Her attention to the ideas, direction, and details of this book have improved many a page. I can take no credit in choosing my parents, but they deserve much credit for teaching me to value people over things and to relish the arts as well as the sciences, choices that lead directly to this work. My son Aza contributed far beyond what you'd expect from someone of his youth, including ideas, editing, and hard work on the illustrations. He and his sisters were amazingly patient with me as I wrote. Especially important in my life is L. Roland Genise, my best teacher, who, during high school, gave me the twin gifts of intellectual self-confidence and a love of mathematics. Among those who have shared warm friendship, philosophy, and music, and who have been devastating editors of my earlier works, I am lucky to be able to name Brian Howard and Douglas Wyatt. I have disagreed with a few details of the writings of Dr. Donald Norman in this book, but these are minor points as I regard his work as essential reading in the field; without his critiques and teachings this book would not have come about. I am grateful to Bill Verplank, a quiet and agreeable sort whose comments are delivered so gently that you don't realize the rug's been pulled out until you hit the floor. His was one of the voices that convinced me to completely change the tone and orientation of the book, for the better. Another who hammered this book into shape was Lyn Dupré, a fierce and nitpicking professional editor. She wrote *BUGS in Writing,* which you should read. Many concepts, a few of which are cited in the text, came from or were polished during discussions and work done with my friend James Winter, M.D., Ph.D. The delightfully acerbic computer scientist Dick Karpinski, who styles himself aptly as the world's largest leprechaun, has been helpful in manifold ways, whether expounding on a technical point, introducing me to a key person or book, or dropping by with dim sum. And, whom I've saved for last, there's Peter Gordon, a man of wisdom, persistence, and (especially) patience, who was my advocate at

Addison-Wesley. Our correspondence must never be made public as it would reveal a penchant for extended word play and awful puns that would forever besmirch both our names, but which lightened the burden of endless details that must be attended to in putting together even so slim a book as this.

Thanks to Agfa Corporation for supplying the digital camera used in creating some of the illustrations.

Thanks, also, to the following readers, who first offered me particular corrections, or suggested changes, that have now been incorporated into the book: Eric Blossom, Jon Bondy, Paul Cubbage, Peter Jones, G. A. Michael, Cam Mitchner, Rich Morin, Martin Portman, and Elisabeth Riba. The author is also grateful to Rich Morin for supporting the www.jefraskin.com Web site.

INTRODUCTION

The Importance of Fundamentals

One person, one computer.

—*Apple Computer slogan*

Imagine that you have just boarded an airliner resplendent in its livery: fitted with a wide choice of video and audio for every glove-soft, leather-covered, oversized seat; its galleys provisioned with fine food and drink. You take your seat and look out the freshly cleaned large window. With a sigh of anticipation for a particularly pleasant flight, you reach into a small compartment in front of you to see what is there. A not-too-small bottle of your favorite beverage comes to hand first, followed by a little booklet about this remarkable airliner.

As the flight attendants swing the doors shut and you settle in, you read the booklet. You learn that the aircraft is the work of some of the finest interior designers from all over the world, that chefs from five-star restaurants have created the menu and personally prepared the dishes, and that because the internationally acclaimed artists who designed the exterior made the craft look so much faster than any other airliner, there had been no need to include professional aeronautical engineers in the aircraft's development team.

In the small print used for legalese, the booklet warns that the ride tends to be bumpy, even in the absence of turbulence, and that the plane crashes regularly. However, the booklet promises, until any of those events occur, you will be comfortable and well entertained.

Suddenly, the latching of the doors seems menacing instead of promising. Your equanimity is gone; you are trapped. This flight, the only one to your destination, is doomed, and you are on it. At this point, you'd rather be sitting on a hard seat, no drink in your hand and no window by your side but in an aircraft blessed by great engineering.

This absurd situation closely parallels the nature of most human-machine interfaces today. Our computers and cellular telephones have the latest chips and electronics; today's operating systems are a feast for the eyes, with glorious colorful backgrounds and three-dimensional tromp l'oeil effects. You click on a button, and lo! it appears to move most realistically; you hear a digital stereophonic, full-fidelity rendering of a switch clicking, and your ears are enchanted by a resonant harp glissando as a window opens before you.

But when you start to use the system, it begins to poke you with uncomfortable corners of unexpected behavior. You cannot find the command you want among the thousands that the system provides. Simple, routine tasks take forever to do. The program you bought last year does not run under the improved operating system, so you have to buy an upgrade. And, of course, the system crashes regularly.

Some engineering fundamentals that are not widely known underlie good interfaces. And why should those fundamentals be studied? How interfaces should look and work seems well established: They've been incrementally improved for two decades now; we have interface guidelines published by the major software producers to ensure future compliance; development tools allow us to put together interfaces quickly such that they look just like other modern interfaces—just as my mythical airliner *looked just like* a well-designed, safe, and comfortable flying machine.

But consider what these interfaces fail to do for us. When you want to set down an idea, you should be able to go to your computer or information appliance and just start typing: no booting, no opening the word processor, no file names, no operating system. (My definition of an operating system: What you have to hassle with before you get to hassle with the application.) You should not have to learn an entire new application to perform what you know to be only a few simple tasks that you'd like to add to the repertory of your system. Regrettably, the design of interfaces has taken a wrong turn, leading to a level of difficulty unjustified by technological or logical necessity.

Millions of us have a love-hate relationship with information technology: We can't live without it, but at the same time, we find it difficult to live with. The problem of making technology comfortable does have solutions, but we can't buy them now; they will be available to us only if we drop a lot of the baggage of the past. The customary, desktop-based, applications-oriented interfaces turn out to be part of the problem. This book offers some alternatives. After all, computer problems are not like the weather: We *can* do something about them.

Given the prevalence of the Internet and the obvious importance of products that facilitate group interaction, it may seem odd that *The Humane Interface* concentrates on single-user interface design. One reason is that the design of single-user interfaces is not a solved problem. The primary reason is that the quality of any interface is ultimately determined by the quality of the interaction between one human and one system—between you and it. *If a system's one-on-one interaction with its human user is not pleasant and facile, the resulting deficiency will poison the performance of the entire system, however fine that system might be in its other aspects.*

ONE

Background

Nothing is more impossible than to write a book that wins every reader's approval.

—*Miguel de Cervantes*

This chapter explains that the nature of interfaces and of interface design is widely misunderstood. There is more to interfaces than windows, icons, pull-down menus, and mice. The need to take interface design into account early in the design cycle is sometimes overlooked. Another factor often overlooked is the commonality in the cognitive equipment handed out to all of us. We must take into account common factors before we can deal with the differences among individual humans. Unfortunately, the tools widely available for interface construction are inadequate to this task.

I reject the idea that computers are difficult to use because what we do with them has become irretrievably complicated. No matter how complex the task a product is trying to accomplish, the simple parts of the task should remain simple. This chapter ends with a definition of a humane interface.

1–1 Interface Definition

Call our USA number above and test your stamina against the incredible frustration provided by our voice mail system.

—Note at the bottom of an advertisement for Simple-brand shoes

In this book, I usually shorten *human-machine interface* or *human-computer interface* to *user interface* or simply *interface*. Many people assume that the term *user interface* refers specifically to today's graphical user interfaces (GUIs), complete with windows and mouse-driven menus. For example, an article in *Mobile Office* magazine said, "Before too long, you may not have to worry about an interface at all: You may find yourself simply speaking to your computer." As I pointed out in response, a voice-controlled system may have no windows, but neither do telephone voice-response systems, and they often have hellaciously bad interfaces. The way that you accomplish tasks with a product—what you do and how it responds—that's the interface. (See also Raskin 1993.)

1–2 Keep the Simple Simple

Technology is a queer thing. It brings you great gifts with one hand, and it stabs you in the back with the other.

—C.P. Snow (quoted in Jarman 1992)

Despite a burgeoning population of interface designers, few consumers claim that new products, such as an electric, four-button wristwatch, are easier to use than they were a few decades ago. If you point out to me that watches, like computers, now have much greater functionality (true) and that, in consequence, the interfaces have had to become more complex (debatable), I respond by pointing out that even the simple tasks that I used to do easily have become mired in complexity. Complex tasks may require complex interfaces, but that is no excuse for complicating simple tasks. Compare the difficulty of setting the time on your electronic, four-button wristwatch to that of completing the *same* task on a mechanical model. No matter how complex the overall system, there is no excuse for not keeping simple tasks simple.

Of the many absurdities foisted on us by inept interface design, perhaps it is the complication of what should be simple that gives comic strips and comedians the most opportunities. In the movie *City Slickers*, three chums are driving a herd of cattle. Billy Crystal's character tries unsuccessfully—apparently for hours—to explain how to use a VCR to record a show on one channel while watching another. When the friends finally explode in exasperation at the lengthy explanation, Crystal's character cheerfully agrees to drop the subject and offers instead an explanation of how to set the clock on the VCR. This offer enrages his cronies and cracks up the audience. The humor arises from the dissonance between the simplicity of the task and the difficulty of the interface: If the vertical front of a VCR had labeled buttons situated above and below the digits of a clock as shown in Figure 1.1, few people would have any trouble setting the clock.

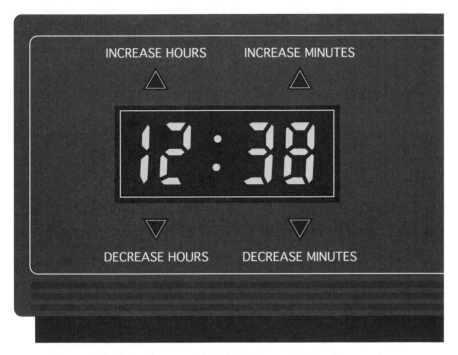

Figure 1.1. An easy-to-set digital clock on a VCR. An even better design would be a clock that set itself based on broadcast time signals.

1-3 Human-Centered Design and User-Centered Design

We have overcomplicated the software and forgotten the primary objective.

—*Jim and Sandra Sundfors*

Not only interface designers but also managers in the electronics and computer industries understand the need for user- or customer-centered design. The first step in meeting this need is to get to know your users, but in commercial practice, getting to know the users usually consists of listening to task domain experts. Domain experts often know the parameters and details of the problem to be solved, but their formal expertise does not usually extend to questions of human psychology. Although users' task-related needs differ, your user population shares many common mental attributes. Before exploring the application or even working to accommodate differences among individuals, interface designers can minimize their work by exploiting what is common to all humans with regard to interface-design requirements. After that is accomplished, the interface designers can accommodate the differences across individuals and groups, and, finally, they can satisfy the varying requirements of their tasks. That crucial first step—making sure that the interface design accords with universal psychological facts—is customarily omitted in the design process. For the most part, interface designers have abdicated that responsibility to "industry standards." All current popular interfaces have been built on underpinnings that flout what we know about human thought and behavior. For example, files with file names are a nearly universal feature in computer systems, yet we all have trouble remembering what file name we used to store a document six months ago. (A solution to this problem will be discussed in Section 5-3.) We want comprehensible software that demonstrates, by its impeccable behavior, that its designers were focused more on usability than on glitz.

1-4 Tools That Do Not Facilitate Design Innovation

Creating fine interfaces can require undertaking intensive and expensive work. Interface-building tools, such as Visual Basic or Visual C++, are marketed as lowering development costs and speeding implementation. In spite of their utility, these tools will not be mentioned often in this book; they enshrine current paradigms and thus unduly limit the scope of what you can do. Similarly, the Macintosh or Windows interface guidelines and a portion of the heuristics presented by books on interface design occasionally give advice that is demonstrably incorrect—often due to the company's need to maintain compatibility with earlier versions of the interfaces and to the misperception that users will inevitably revolt if old, familiar interface methods are abandoned. Where real improvement can be achieved by making major changes, the interface designer must balance the legitimate use of familiar paradigms, which ease the learning process, against the enhanced usability that can be attained by abandoning them. In a situation of rapid turnover of personnel or the customer base, familiarity might be the better design choice. *Where most of the users' time will be spent in routine operation of the*

*product and where learning is only a small part of the picture, designing for productiv-
ity—even if that requires retraining—is often the correct decision.*

1-5 Interface Design in the Design Cycle

Project methodologies often fail to take full advantage of what is
known about interface design. This omission can be the result of bringing in
interface designers long after much of the opportunity for improving the
quality of interaction between user and product has been lost. Designs are
most flexible at their inception. If interface designers are consulted only after
the software has been designed and the software tools chosen or when the
software is nearly complete, the correct advice—namely, to start over—is
unacceptable. The budget and most of the schedule have already been
expended, and the option of throwing away much or all of the design and
the completed code makes the project managers look bad. Even so, as recent
a book on project management as the *UML Toolkit* (Eriksson and Magnus
1998) fails to recognize that the interface has to be part of the requirements
analysis, which is Eriksson and Magnus's first phase of project development.
Contrary to their suggestion, interface design cannot be postponed until the
technical design phase (their third phase). *Once the product's task is known,
design the interface first; then implement to the interface design.* This is an iterative
process: The task definition will change as the interface is designed, and the
implementation will be influenced by the task definition and the interative
design as well. Flexibility on all fronts is needed. The place to start the implementation is to list exactly what the user will do to achieve his or her goals
and how the system will respond to each user action.

*Users do not care about what is inside the box, as long as the box does what
they need done.* What processor was used, whether the programming language was object oriented or multithreaded, or whether it was the proud
possessor of some other popular buzzword does not count. What users want
is convenience and results. But all that they see is the interface. *As far as the
customer is concerned, the interface is the product.*

Your Time Is Sacred; Your Work Is Sacred

I have learned to save my work frequently so that, even in the
event of a system crash, I will not lose much time. I use a keyboard-
operated save command every time I complete a paragraph or even a
few sentences. This command places a copy of my work on the disk,
where it is relatively safe from damage in a crash. Every hour or so, I

further back up my work to a nonvolatile memory card that I physically remove from the computer so that the backup is isolated from the computer and is safe, no matter how the computer runs amok; every week, I back up the whole system on an external disk drive. I am not paranoid, just realistic. Yet these elaborate procedures should be unnecessary. *The system should treat all user input as sacred* and —to paraphrase Asimov's first law of robotics, "A robot shall not harm a human, or, through inaction, allow a human to come to harm" (Asimov 1977, p. 44). The first law of interface design should be: *A computer shall not harm your work or, through inaction, allow your work to come to harm.*

While working on this book, and at the suggestion of my editors, I began to use a facility that allows me to accept or to reject suggested changes. After every few decisions, I used the save command. When the system crashed, I was not worried, because of my continual saves. But when I went to find my most recent changes, they were gone, and I had to redo my work. By trying a few experiments, I finally figured out that when the accept-reject feature is in use, the keyboard save command does not operate. No warning is given. I lost more than three hours in work and in experimenting to figure out what had happened, in the hope of preventing a recurrence. Aside from the sheer complexity of today's computer systems, it is vexing details such as this one that prove the need for better interface design.

For a second interface law, you could do worse than to insist on this one: *A computer shall not waste your time or require you to do more work than is strictly necessary.* Section 4-3 introduces a measure of how much work is necessary to complete a task.

1-6 Definition of a Humane Interface

You can have any combination of features the Air Ministry desires, so long as you do not also require that the resulting airplane fly.

—*Willy Messerschmidt (preeminent World War II German aircraft designer)*

*An interface is **humane** if it is responsive to human needs and considerate of human frailties.* If you want to create a humane interface, you must have an understanding of the relevant information on how both humans and machines operate. In addition, you must cultivate in yourself a sensitivity to the difficulties that people experience. That is not necessarily a simple undertaking. We become accustomed to the ways that products work to the extent that we come to accept their methods as a given, even when their interfaces are unnecessarily complex, confusing, wasteful, and provocative of human error.

Many of us become annoyed, for example, at the amount of time that it takes a computer to start up, or to boot. An advertisement for a computer-based car radio in 1999 assures us that "unlike a home computer, there are no long boot-up times to worry about." A scan through six respected books on the subject of interface design—books that have been written over most of the span of time during which interface design has been a recognized field—finds the topic of booting unmentioned (Shneiderman 1987; Norman 1988; Laurel 1990; Tognazzini 1992; Mayhew 1992; Cooper 1995). I am sure that each of these authors would wholeheartedly agree that reducing or eliminating this delay would improve usability; I have never met a user to whom the delay is not an annoyance. Yet the boot delay is so much a familiar and accepted part of using a computer that it is seldom questioned in the interface-design literature. There has never been any technical necessity for a computer to take more than a few seconds to begin operation when it is turned on. We have slow-booting computers only because many designers and implementers did not assign a high priority to making the interface humane in this regard. In addition, some people believe that the sale of millions of slow-booting computers "proves" that the way these machines now work is just fine.

The annoyance of having to wait for a machine to start up has not been ignored in other product areas. The defunct Apple Newton, the Palm Pilot, and other handheld computers manage to start instantly, and the introduction of a sleep mode—a state in which the computer is using less power than when it is on but from which it can be brought to operational status quickly—on certain computers is a step in the right direction.

Engineering has successfully tackled some more difficult problems. In early television sets, for example, the wait due to the time it took to heat the cathode of the picture tube was nearly a minute. In certain television sets, engineers added a circuit to keep the cathode warm, reducing the wait to reach operating temperature. (Keeping the cathode fully heated would have been wasteful of electricity and would have shortened the life of the tube.) Other engineers designed picture tubes that had cathodes that heated in a few seconds. Either way, the user's needs were satisfied. In the early twentieth century, the failure of the Stanley Steamer, a steam-powered automobile that apparently was a superior vehicle in other aspects, may have been a result of the 20-minute delay between firing it up and its having sufficient boiler pressure to drive.

That a user should not be kept waiting unnecessarily is an obvious and humane design principle. It is also humane not to hurry a user; the more general principle is: *Users should set the pace of an interaction.*

It does not take much technical knowledge to see, for example, that higher-bandwidth communication channels can hasten downloading of web pages. Other relationships are not so evident. It is useful for designers of a human-machine interface to understand the innards of the technology; otherwise, they have no way to judge the validity of assertions—by, say, programmers or hardware designers—that a given interface detail is not feasible.

TWO

Cognetics and the Locus of Attention

He wept and was nothing content, but it booted not.

— Dominic Mancini, speaking not of a dead computer but of Edward V of England. Occupatione Regni Anglie per Riccardum Tercium *(1483). Quoted in Alison Weir,* The Princes in the Tower *(1992).*

As complicated as computers and other products of our technology may be, it is easier to understand the machine side of the human-machine interface than to come to grips with the far more complex and variable human side. Even so, many—perhaps surprisingly many—human performance factors are independent of a user's age, gender, cultural background, or level of expertise. These properties of human learning and performance are directly applicable to the foundations of any interface design. In particular, that we have one locus of attention affects many aspects of the design of human-machine interfaces.

2-1 Ergonomics and Cognetics: What We Can and Cannot Do

Know thyself.

—Inscription at the Delphic Oracle, from Plutarch, Morals

Use a machine or a tool in accord with its strengths and limitations, and it will do a good job for you. Design a human-machine interface in accord with the abilities and foibles of humankind, and you will help the user to not only get the job done but also be a happier, more productive person.

Design guidelines for products that interact with us physically are reasonably straightforward. The sizes and capabilities of the human frame and senses have been well cataloged; these studies form the science of **ergonomics**. Chairs, tables, keyboards, and displays can be designed with a high degree of likelihood that they will work reasonably well for their human users, although thorough testing can never be neglected. You would not design a machine that required one person to simultaneously operate two switches 3 meters apart: We all know that humans are not that large. Mayhew (1992, Chapter 12) discusses computer-relevant ergonomics, a topic outside the scope of this book, in her overview of interface design. Ergonomics takes into account the statistical nature of human variability. You might design a car seat to accommodate only 95 percent of the population, even though you know that 5 percent of the potential car purchasers will find the seat uncomfortable. It might be too expensive or mechanically impossible to give the seat the range of adjustment needed to work with the rare 1-meter midget or the rarer still 2.5-meter giant.

For the most part, the machines that our civilizations have built have been mechanical and have interacted principally with our physical selves. Consequently, our physical limitations are relatively well understood. Increasingly, inventions have come to the aid of intellectual rather than physical pursuits. *We must master an ergonomics of the mind if we want to design interfaces that are likely to work well.* As surprising as it may seem, we are often blind to our own mental limits; we must rely on careful experiment and observation to discover the edges of our own mind's abilities.

The study of the applicable, engineering scope of our mental abilities is cognitive engineering, or **cognetics**. Certain cognetic limitations are obvious: You do not expect a typical user to be able to mentally multiply a pair of 30-digit numbers in 5 seconds, and you would not design an interface that requires such an ability. But we are often not aware of other mental limitations that adversely affect our performance when we use human-machine interfaces, although these limitations are inherent in every human. Remarkably, all of the well-known computer interfaces—and many non-computer human-machine interfaces—are designed as though their designers expect us to have cognitive abilities that experiment shows we do not possess. Much of the difficulty that we have with computers and related devices is due to poor interface design rather than to any complexity inherent to the task or to any lack of effort or intelligence on the part of users.

Just as ergonomics takes into account the statistical nature of human variability, so too should cognetics. However, because there has been so little practical use of what is known of the limits of human cognition that are common to all of us, it seems wise to look first at those limits.

Fortunately—if only because our present knowledge of these topics is uncertain—we do not need to examine the structure of the physical brain. We can design successful interfaces based on a pragmatic and empiric view of what the human mind can and cannot do, of how long the mind and body take to do particular tasks, and of the circumstances that increase the likelihood that we will make mistakes.

2-2 Cognitive Conscious and Cognitive Unconscious

Oh Doctor Freud, Oh Doctor Freud, how we wish that you'd been otherwise employed!

—"Doctor Freud," David Lazar, 1951

It can be difficult to deal with the psychologically, philosophically, and historically laden terms—such as *conscious* and *unconscious*—that we use to describe aspects of the way our minds work. In an engineering context, it is useful to work with the more limited concepts of the **cognitive conscious** and the **cognitive unconscious**. More accurate would be the terms *empirical conscious* and *empirical unconscious,* but Kihlstrom's more euphonic coinage has priority (Cohen and Schooler 1997, p. 137). Understanding that we possess these two distinct sets of limited mental abilities and understanding how they work in relationship to human-machine interfaces is as essential to designing interfaces as is knowing the size and the strength of the human hand when we are designing a keyboard.

Here is a first-cut definition: Unconscious mental processes are those of which you are not aware at the time they occur. The cognitive unconscious is not the seething, mythic creature of Freudian psychology but rather a phenomenon that you can demonstrate with a straightforward experiment, which you will be asked to try shortly. Although a growing mountain of books discusses the questions and paradoxes of consciousness, following the approach taken in Bernard J. Baars's *A Cognitive Theory of Consciousness* (1988)—a book that has broadly informed this chapter—helps us to avoid the dilemmas and to deal only with what we can observe directly and produce concretely. As Baars says in his preface, "one time-honored strategy in science is to side-step philosophical issues for a time by focusing on empirically decidable ones." Cognetics is a practical discipline. Although theoretical studies can be illuminating and eventually may lead to firm and practical results, we avoid them until they do. (Analogously, although a study of human bone growth can inform ergonomics, such a study would fall within the purview of physiology rather than of ergonomics itself.)

Consciousness and Models of the Mind

In following Baars's useful treatment of the cognitive properties of consciousness, it is not necessary also to subscribe to his theory of mind, which uses contemporary digital computer structures as models. I am leery of that approach, especially because throughout the ages, thinkers have borrowed the latest technology as models for understanding humans only to abandon or to limit the models when technology advanced.

Don Norman, a cognitive psychologist who is especially conversant with computers, spoke of the mind in terms of computational units (Norman 1981). J. R. Anderson, beginning in 1976, based his model of mental operations on productions—a tool prominent at the time for describing the syntax of computer languages (Anderson 1993). Although the analogies are usually enlightening, some scholars tend to overapply the metaphor of the moment. I predict a flowering of psychological theories in the next few years with the client/server architecture, the Internet, and the World Wide Web with its hypertext links and browsers appearing as models for how certain aspects of the mind work.

We must monitor this tendency carefully lest we reify the analogies without neurophysiological support. In the seventeenth century, the universe and its denizens were often spoken of in terms of clockwork (Dijksterhuis 1961, p. 495); with our present understanding of both clockwork and organisms, however, this metaphor has become pallid. In the nineteenth century, the metaphor of the steam engine permeated many philosophical musings on human function; now we know that the analogy's value is limited primarily to explaining metabolism, insofar as the metabolic system is a heat engine.

Two popular books that consider the subject of consciousness are Roger Penrose's *The Emperor's New Mind* (Penrose 1989) and Daniel

Dennett's *Consciousness Explained* (Dennett 1991). These treatments, however fascinating to read, unfortunately turn out to be of no use in the design of human-machine interfaces. Without direct evidence of functional parallelism in hand, it is wise to avoid taking computer-brain metaphors too literally.

X.B, !

Because concerns about what is conscious and unconscious usually seem remote from our workaday world, let us tangibly demonstrate their reality in your life by means of a question: What is the final character in your first name? Until you read the previous sentence, you were probably not thinking about this alphabetic character and its relationship to your name. You know—and have long known—what that character is and where in your first name it lies, but you were not paying attention to that knowledge. You were not thinking of it; you were not considering it. Or, to use our preferred terminology, you were not conscious of it. The information was not being accessed, yet you could recover it on demand. We will call that place from which the character was fetched the cognitive unconscious. The cognitive unconscious may not be a physical place, although it must be represented by physical phenomena in the brain. To help dispel the notion that the unconscious or conscious *must* be places in the brain—which is different from the notion that they *might* be—we can think of possible alternative mechanisms. For example, when you became aware, or conscious, of the alphabetic character, this becoming might have been a change of state. Alternatively, perhaps our brains use a pointer mechanism, and a pointer was changed while the memory or thought was left where it was in your brain. It is possible that thoughts and memories could be distributed, like a holographic record of an image.

We could consider other mechanisms or descriptions, but we have no need to do so. For our purposes, all we need is to acknowledge that you were not conscious of the character at one moment and were conscious of it at another moment. I use a positional metaphor from time to time, speaking of a thought as moving from the conscious to the unconscious or back, but you should not think of this verbal convenience as denoting a model of how the brain works. (Research into the physical brain may show such a model to be valid, but that is not our concern here.)

When I use the terms *conscious* and *unconscious* in this book, I will generally intend them as abbreviations for the cognitive conscious and the cognitive unconscious. When you did think about the final character in your first name—a thought triggered by a sentence in this book—that thought became part of your conscious awareness. This change of state of your thought, from unconscious to conscious, demonstrates that you have at least two forms of knowing. To build a science of cognetics, we must banish solipsism and assume that other humans would make the same observations about their mental processes as you just did about yours.

A stimulus, such as reading a particular portion of this book, can trigger the migration of not only an item of information but also a sensation, a feeling, or another aspect of your memory or knowledge from the unconscious, where it is stored, to the conscious, where you are aware of it. Notice how your clothes feel: where they are tight and where they are loose. Until you came across the sentence that directed your attention to your clothes, you probably were not consciously aware of the various pressures that your clothes were putting on portions of your body. You can also call up memories—say, of a recent happy event—and perhaps can even retrieve a bit of the accompanying emotion from your cognitive unconscious and can bring the memories into your cognitive conscious. Now pay attention to the feel of this book in your hand—if you are reading this text in book form—or to the input device that you are using to control your computer—if you are reading from a display. I trust that these experiments on your part have convinced you that you have a cognitive unconscious and a cognitive conscious and that a stimulus can bring a mental construct from the former to the latter.

By definition, you cannot experience, or be conscious of, any unconscious process. An unconscious process, such as the one that monitors your bladder pressure, can be a stimulus, whereupon the need to relieve yourself becomes conscious.

A bothersome philosophical question in connection with the previous sentence is: Who is the "you" about whom I am talking? Can I distinguish between you and your conscious? Taking an engineering perspective, I sidestep this question, saying simply that the "you" in this case is the union of your physical self and all of the physical and mental phenomena that your physical self manifests. We do not have to address the question of the possible distinctions among you, your conscious, and your unconscious to understand interface-design principles.

It seems likely that memories or keys to memories are stored in physical places in the brain, because in some cases, direct electrical stimulation of parts of the brain, as is sometimes done during brain surgery, can evoke a memory—that is, can make that memory conscious. Stimulating one place may reproducibly call up a particular memory, feeling, or sensation; stimulating another place may reproducibly evoke a different experience. Studies of the brain performed with such techniques as magnetic-resonance imaging (MRI) and positron-emission tomography (PET) are helping researchers to elucidate the physical correlates of various mental activities. These technologies are mentioned because they may, at a future time, be directly helpful in the design—and, especially, in the testing—of interfaces. For example, there is an inverse correlation between a person's localized glucose uptake—an indicator of how much energy the brain is using in a particular physical structure—and the ease with which that person uses a tested interface feature. Interface testing in the future may well make increasing use of direct measures of brain activity, but a further exploration of these methods lies outside the scope of this book.

Our examples so far have followed mental constructs from unconscious to conscious. Here is an example moving the other way: A sudden noise or other unexpected event can pull your attention away from what you are doing—for example, reading this book—and to the question of what caused the sound; the sound of a lamp falling from a shelf (what was your cat doing up there?) is an example. After you return to reading, your knowledge of the event will move from the cognitive conscious to the cognitive unconscious.

There are borderline cases, and there is much that we do not understand about the conscious and the unconscious. For example, you sometimes feel that someone's name is on "the tip of your tongue"; you can almost think of the name, but you cannot quite do so. Sometimes, the memory becomes fully conscious and you recall the name. Other times, the memory remains elusive. Is there a state between the conscious and the unconscious? Have we caught the mind in the middle of "moving" the information about the name from one region of the brain to another? Is an almost remembered name evidence for a link partially formed or intermittently connected, sputtering like a loose electrical contact? Such open questions are interesting, but we do not need to answer them, just as in cosmology, we can understand that the universe is expanding, without having a clue about what happened before the expansion started, that is, before the big-bang event that most cosmologists believe was the raising of the curtain on our universe.

As I have said, I do not want to reify any particular metaphor of how the brain works. However, we cannot avoid building mental models of our brain: We build these models of our brain in our brain, a mind-boggling thought. For the time being, then, picture the conscious and the unconscious as separate compartments. These compartments are more than just different places or states for storing thoughts or memories: They have different ways of interacting with the world and with concepts. As has been elucidated by cognitive psychologists over the past century, the cognitive conscious and the cognitive unconscious have properties beyond our awareness and unawareness of them.

Table 2.1 summarizes the differences between the cognitive conscious and the cognitive unconscious. The table tells us that the cognitive conscious is brought into play whenever you encounter a situation that seems new or threatening and whenever you have to make a nonroutine decision—that is, one based on what is happening in the here and now. Only when you are conscious of a proposition can you determine whether it is logically consistent. The cognitive conscious operates sequentially and can consider only one question or control only one action at a time. You can be conscious of only between four and eight distinct thoughts or things at once. Your conscious memory fades in, at most, a few seconds.

The conscious is invoked in branching tasks. It is sometimes difficult to distinguish a branching task from a nonbranching task. For example, braking for a traffic light may be either. It is nonbranching—and is handled by the cognitive unconscious—if you are simply reacting to a red light by pressing the brake pedal. However, if a light that you are approaching turns yellow, such that you have to decide whether to continue through the intersection without pause or to stop, your cognitive conscious comes into play. While you are learning a task, you may see and react to it as a branching event requiring conscious attention. With repetition, your execution of the task may become nonbranching and automatic. In Section 2-3, we start looking into these properties and their implications for interface design.

TABLE 2.1. PROPERTIES OF THE COGNITIVE CONSCIOUS AND THE COGNITIVE UNCONSCIOUS

PROPERTY	CONSCIOUS	UNCONSCIOUS
Engaged by	Novelty	Repetition
	Emergencies	Expected Events
	Danger	Safety
Used in	New circumstances	Routine situations
Can handle	Decisions	Nonbranching tasks
Accepts	Logical propositions	Logic or inconsistencies
Operates	Sequentially	Simultaneously
Controls	Volition	Habits
Capacity	Tiny	Huge
Persists for	Tenths of seconds	Decades (lifelong)

2-3 Locus of Attention

You have a degree of control over making unconscious thoughts conscious, as you demonstrated when you brought the final character of your first name "into mind." You cannot deliberately make conscious thoughts unconscious, however. "Don't think about an elephant," a girl whispers to a boy, knowing that the boy cannot comply. But in a few moments, unless the conversation stays on elephants, the animal will fade into the boy's unconscious. When that happens, the boy is no longer paying attention to the thought of an elephant: The elephant is not his locus of attention.

I use the term *locus* because it means *place,* or *site.* The term *focus,* which is sometimes used in a similar connection, can be read as a verb; thus, it conveys a misimpression of how attention works. When you are awake and conscious, your **locus of attention** is a feature or an object in the physical world or an idea about which you are intently and actively thinking. You can see the distinction when you contemplate this phrase: "We can deliberately focus our attention on a particular locus." Whereas *to focus* implies volition, we cannot completely control what our locus of attention will be. If you hear a firecracker unexpectedly exploding behind you, your attention will be drawn to the source of the sound. *Focus* is also used to denote, among the objects on a computer display, the one that is currently selected. Your attention may or may not be on this kind of focus when you are using an interface. Of all the world that you perceive through either your senses or your imagination, you are concentrating on at most one entity. Whatever that one object, feature, memory, thought, or concept might be, it is your locus of attention. Attention, as used here, includes not only the case of actively paying attention but also the passive case of going with the flow, or just experiencing what is taking place.

You see and hear much more than whatever is the locus of your attention. If you go into a room to look for a misplaced item, what you seek may be plainly in view but remain unnoticed. We can demonstrate through optical considerations that the image of the sought object was on your retina; it might even have been within the 5-degree cone of your foveal vision. We know through experiments in neurophysiology that a signal representing the object was being generated and transmitted over the optic nerve, yet you do not notice it, because it never became your locus of attention. If I listen for them, I notice that the fluorescent lights in the hall near my office buzz annoyingly, but otherwise I do not hear them. The sound is there, as a tape recording can demonstrate, even when I am unaware of it. I most often notice the sound when I turn the lights on or off. The sudden start of the buzzing calls my attention to it; the sudden stop makes me realize—amazingly, because it is after the fact—that I had been hearing it. Indeed, what seems to be a full-fidelity recollection of the sound I had just been hearing suddenly becomes my locus of attention. Experiments show that direct perceptions—the contents of what psychologists call perceptual memory—seem to persist for a brief period: The well-known phenomenon of the persistence of vision is what makes the discrete frames of a movie appear to flow in continuous motion. In particular, visual perceptions decay in typically 200 milliseconds (200 msec), with a range of 90 msec to 1,000 msec; auditory perceptions decay in typically 1,500 msec, with a range of 900 msec to 3,500 msec (Card, Moran, and Newell 1983, pp. 29–31). I cannot now, sitting at my desk, recreate the buzz in that same vivid, immediate way as I did right after it had stopped and my attention had been directed by the sudden onset of silence to the previous presence of the sound. Now, hours later, the perception is long gone, and only a relatively pale memory—one having the character more of a description than of a sensation—remains of the annoying fluorescent buzz.

Perceptions do not automatically become memories. Most perceptions are lost after they decay. One implication for interface design of the rapid decay of sense perceptions is that you cannot assume that, because someone has seen or heard a particular message 5 seconds earlier, that person will remember its wording. If that particular wording is important or if there is an important detail—for example, if the message is, "Report error type 39-152," with the critical detail being the particular number—either you must keep the message displayed until it is no longer needed (the best strategy), or the user must be able to apply the information immediately—that is, before memory of it decays. As the information becomes the locus of attention, it moves into short-term memory, which we define in Section 2-3-4; it will persist there for as long as 10 seconds.

2-3-1 Formation of Habits

Anything worth doing is worth doing badly—at first.

—*Dick Karpinski*

When you perform a task repeatedly, it tends to become easier to do. Juggling, table tennis, and playing piano are everyday examples in my life; they all seemed impossible when I first attempted them. Walking is a more widely practiced example. With repetition, or *practice*, your competence becomes *habitual*, and you can do the task without having to think about it. Lewis Thomas (1974), whose writings on biology are always a joy to read, expanded lyrically on the subject.

> Working a typewriter by touch, like riding a bicycle or strolling on a path, is best done by not giving it a glancing thought. Once you do, your fingers fumble and hit the wrong keys. To do things involving practiced skills, you need to turn loose the systems of muscles and nerves responsible for each maneuver, place them on their own, and stay out of it. There is no real loss of authority in this, because you get to decide whether to do the thing or not, and you can intervene and embellish the technique any time you like; if you want to ride a bicycle backward, or walk with an eccentric loping gait giving a little skip every fourth step, whistling at the same time, you can do that. But if you concentrate your attention on the details, keeping in touch with each muscle, thrusting yourself into free fall with each step and catching yourself at the last moment by sticking out the other foot in time to break the fall, you will end up immobilized, vibrating with fatigue. (p. 64)

When an observer suggested that a baseball player should think about his technique as he was hitting, baseball star Yogi Berra echoed Lewis's theme but with characteristic brevity: "How can you think and hit at the same time?" (Kaplan 1992, p. 754).

Any habit is a surrender of detail control, but habits are essential to the earth's higher life forms. At the other extreme, life is entirely possible— for example, in microbes—in the absence of any consciousness whatever, at least as far as we know or have any reason to believe. We also use the term *habit* in a pejorative sense. Despite Lewis's claim that there is no real loss of authority, bad habits do develop. Habits can be so strong as to approach addiction, sometimes reaching the point of a total loss of conscious control. (I am speaking not of physiological addictions here, such as to nicotine or opiates, but rather of undesired learned habits, such as nail biting.) Insofar as our conscious selves are who we are, I am reminded of Unamuno's observation: "To fall into a habit is to begin to cease to be" (Unamuno 1913). Unamuno was, perhaps, warning us against the pernicious aspects of habit formation; when it comes to the routine aspects of everyday life, however, you want your conscious attention to "cease to be."

You can readily imagine how difficult it would be to drive your car if you had to think, "Uhh, I want to stop. Let me see now: The engine needs to slow down, so I have to take my foot off the accelerator. Now I have to dissipate my car's kinetic energy into heat by pressing on the brake pedal. . . ." Fortunately, as an experienced driver, you perform the operation habitually. Similarly, you have developed many small habits that help you to use your computer, watch, alarm clock, telephone, and every other device that has an interface.

Persistent use of any interface will cause you to develop habits that you will find yourself unable to avoid. Our mandate as designers is to create interfaces that do not allow habits to cause problems for the user. We must design interfaces that (1) deliberately take advantage of the human trait of habit development and (2) allow users to develop habits that smooth the flow of their work. *The ideal humane interface would reduce the interface component of a user's work to benign habituation. Many of the problems that make products difficult and unpleasant to use are caused by human-machine design that fails to take into account the helpful and injurious properties of habit formation.* One notable example is the tendency to provide many ways of accomplishing the same task. Having multiple options can shift your locus of attention from the task to the choice of method (a topic explored in Section 3-7).

You cannot often break a habit by an act of volition. As often or as fiercely as you tell yourself that you will not perform the habitual action, you may not always be able to stop yourself. Say that, for example, next Sunday your car will interchange the functions of the brake and accelerator pedals. A red light will illuminate on your dashboard to warn you of this change. You might manage to drive a few blocks successfully with the pedals reversed, but most of us would not get out of the driveway without making an error. As soon as your locus of attention is pulled away from the novel arrangement—for example, if a child runs into the street—your habitual reaction will make you stomp on the wrong pedal. The red light will be of no help at all. I emphasize that you cannot undo a habit by any single act of willpower; only a time-consuming training process can undo a habit. A designer can lay—or create inadvertently—a nasty trap by permitting to run, on one computer, two or more heavily used applications that differ in only a handful of often-used details. In such a circumstance, the user is guaranteed to develop habits that will cause him errors when he attempts to use in one application a method appropriate to only the other.

2-3-2 Execution of Simultaneous Tasks

In the language of cognitive psychologists, any task that you have learned to do without conscious thought has become *automatic*. Automaticity enables you to do more than one activity at a time: All but at most one of the tasks that you perform simultaneously are automatic. The one that is not automatic is, of course, the one that most directly involves your locus of attention. When you do two tasks simultaneously, neither of which is automatic, your performance on each task degrades—a phenomenon that psychologists call *interference*—compared to your performance on each task alone, because the two tasks compete for your attention. The more predictable, automatic, and unconscious a task becomes, the less it will degrade or compete with other tasks (Baars 1988, p. 33).

We humans apparently simulate the simultaneous accomplishment of tasks that require conscious control by alternating our attention between tasks, attending now to one, then to the others (Card, Moran, and Newell 1983, p. 42). You achieve true simultaneity when all but at most one of your tasks become automatic. For example, you can, at the same time, eat a snack without choking, walk without tripping, and think through a mathematics problem to a satisfactory conclusion. (You may also be working on another math problem unconsciously, but by the definition of the cognitive unconscious, you wouldn't notice that you were. I am claiming only that you cannot simultaneously work *consciously* on two different math problems.) For most people, all of the tasks, except for finding the solution to the mathematics problem, are so well learned that they undertake these tasks on autopilot. However, if you were practicing these simultaneous activities and suddenly discovered a nasty-tasting morsel in the snack, you would become conscious only of what you were eating. You would no longer be conscious of the mathematics problem.

Equally important as the fact that you cannot be conscious of more than one task at any moment is the realization that humans cannot avoid developing automatic responses. This idea is important enough to bear repetition: No amount of training can teach a user *not* to develop habits when she uses an interface repeatedly. That we form habits is part of our fixed mental wiring; habit formation cannot be prevented by any act of volition. If you have ever unintentionally driven toward your normal workplace on a Saturday morning when you intended to go somewhere else, you've been had by a habit that formed through repetition of a fixed sequence of actions. When you learned to read, at first you sounded out and paid attention to each letter and syllable; now (I hope) you read without conscious attention to the process of translating marks into words.

Any sequence of actions that you perform repeatedly will, eventually, become automatic. A set of actions that form a sequence also becomes clumped into a single action; once you start a sequence that takes less than 1 or 2 seconds to complete, you will not be able to stop the sequence but will continue executing the actions until you complete that clump. You also cannot interrupt sequences that take longer than a few seconds to execute unless the sequence becomes your locus of attention. Thus, after you take the wrong turn on Saturday, you may suddenly realize that you intended to drive in the opposite direction; this realization makes your navigation your locus of attention, and you can interrupt the automatic sequence of actions that would have led you to your workplace.

When you repeat a sequence of operations, making *and keeping* what you are doing your locus of attention is the only way to keep a habit from forming. This is very difficult to do. As expressed in a common phrase, our attention wanders.

The inevitability of habit formation has implications for interface design. For example, many of us have used computer systems that, before they will perform an irreversible act, such as deleting a file, ask, "Are you sure?" You then must type, say, a *Y* for yes or an *N* for no in response to the question. The idea is that, by making you confirm your decision, the system will give you a chance to correct an otherwise irrecoverable error. This idea is widely accepted. For example, Smith and Duell (1992), addressing a nursing environment, say, "If you inadvertently delete part of the permanent record (which is hard to do because the computer always asks if you're sure) . . ." (p. 86). Unfortunately, Smith and Duell are unrealistic in their assessment: You can readily make an accidental deletion even when this kind of confirmation is required. Because errors are relatively rare, you will usually type *Y* after giving any command that requires confirmation. Due to the continual repetition of the action, typing *Y* after deleting soon becomes habitual. Instead of being a separate mental operation, typing the *Y* becomes part of the delete-file action; that is, you do not pause, check your intentions, and then type the *Y*. The computer system's query, intended to serve as a safety measure, is rendered useless by habituation; it serves only to complicate the normal file-deletion process. The key idea is that *any confirmation step that elicits a fixed response soon becomes useless.* Designers who use such confirmations and administrators who think that the confirmations confer protection are unaware of the powerful habit-forming property of the cognitive unconscious (see Section 6-4-2).

A more effective strategy is to allow users to undo an erroneous command, even if they have performed intervening actions since issuing it. You cannot protect against a user developing a habit of confirming without reestablishing the decision as the locus of attention, even by making the required confirmation action unpredictable. For example, have the computer specify that the user must type either twice or backward—that choice being presented at random—a word displayed, also chosen randomly, in the dialog box.

> The action that you have requested cannot
> be undone. It will cause permanent loss of
> the information in the file. If you are sure
> you wish to delete the information forever,
> type backward the tenth word in this box.

Requiring this kind of confirmation is as draconian as it is futile. Any attempt at an effective confirmation process is necessarily obnoxious because it prevents the user from forming a habitual response and from ever becoming comfortable with it. If, for legal or other reasons, a file should never be deleted by the user, it should be made impossible for such a deletion to be performed. Such measures also create a new locus of attention; the user is not attending to the correctness of their prior response, thus frustrating the purposes of both the confirmation and the user.

No method of confirming intent is perfect. Even having the user type in the reason for a deletion—a technique especially useful in a situation that carries legal implications—will soon lead to the user's supplying one of a few stock answers. If the rationale for performing an irreversible act was flawed from the outset, no warning or confirmation method can prevent the user from making a mistake.

Trapped in the Pitfall of Automaticity

I was trapped in the pitfall of automaticity while I was writing this chapter: I italicized a word, then tried to unitalicize it. In most Macintosh word processors, pressing and holding the key marked with a drawing of an apple (called the Command key) and then pressing and releasing the key marked with the letter T (Command-T) returns the text to normal status. In Microsoft Word, however, Command-T alters the paragraph format. If you had asked me— if you had thus made it my locus of attention—I would have told you that I was using Word, yet I reached (automatically!) for Command-T, typed it, and mangled the paragraph formatting. The only way to prevent such errors is through interface designs that take into consideration the inevitability of habit formation.

2-3-3 Singularity of the Locus of Attention

I can't think about X *if I'm thinking about* Y.

—Chris, *a character on the television show* Northern Exposure, *31 October 1994*

For our purposes, an essential fact about your locus of attention is that there is but one of them. This observation underlies the solution of numerous interface problems. Many people do not believe that they or others have only one locus of attention, but experiments, described in the cited literature, strongly support the hypothesis that we are unable to attend to multiple simultaneous stimuli. This notion, which parallels our discussion on the limitations of the cognitive conscious, is sufficiently surprising to justify examining the support for it.

As Roger Penrose (1989) noted, "A characteristic feature of conscious thought . . . is its 'oneness'—as opposed to a great many independent activities going on at once" (p. 398). Bernard Baars (1988), a widely recognized leader in the study of the cognitive conscious, explains that when people are "asked to monitor a demanding stream of information [they are] largely unconscious of alternative streams of information presented at the same time, even to the same sensory organ. Similarly, in absorbed states of mind, when one is deeply involved with a single train of information, alternative events are excluded from consciousness" (p. 33). The alternative events are not loci of your attention.

Common parlance recognizes this observation. For example, we may have a thought, and we may have many thoughts, but we speak of our attention only in the singular. We never speak of a person's *attentions* except in unrelated usages, such as *unwanted attentions.* Although you are unconscious of all but the one line of thought—the single conceptual thread that you are following—an unexpected or surprising event can pull your attention from that thread. I have described how surprising events trigger conscious attention. What is salient here is that you have acquired a new locus of attention and lost the old; it is not the case that a second locus has been brought into play.

An interrupting event does not need to be external: A sudden pain or the realization that it is time for an appointment may break into your cognitive conscious, derailing your current train of thought and putting it on a new track.[1] However, if outside or internal events are routine and unpress-

---

1. Considerable attention has been paid to the biological mechanisms that allow animals to synchronize with external time cycles, but I am unaware of any work regarding how we set and respond to internal alarm clocks.

ing, your unconscious recognizes that status, and you ignore those events—without being conscious that you are ignoring them. In other words, in the presence of the ordinary, your attention is not pulled away. You can train yourself to scan the environment consciously from time to time to notice events to which your attention would not be otherwise called. To illustrate, pilots are taught to scan their instruments regularly, without outside stimuli to initiate scanning. A scan allows pilots to detect, for example, an instrument that subtly shows an abnormal condition. (Not every instrument in an aircraft has an alarm associated with it.) Nonetheless, pilots regularly fail to perform their scan when events force their attention to a particular locus.

Absorption Kills 101 People

An extreme example is an accident that killed 101 people in December 1972. Normally a green indicator in the airliner's cockpit lights to signal that the landing gear is down and ready for landing. When the indicator failed to light, the pilot decided to circle at an altitude of 2,000 feet, and the copilot put the aircraft on autopilot to maintain the altitude. All three crew members then tried to change the bulb, but it stuck and they could not get it out. Perhaps due to their moving around and working on the bulb, they accidentally turned off the autopilot; in any case, it became disengaged. Soon, as the cockpit recording later showed, an automatic warning sounded; a 0.5-second chord warned them that they had gone 250 feet below their assigned altitude. A yellow warning indicator also lit up. The crew, absorbed in the problem with the green bulb, failed to notice either warning. A little later, while still struggling with the bulb, the copilot noticed that the altimeter indicated 150 feet, alarmingly low. He then asked the pilot, "We're still at two thousand, right?" The pilot replied, "Hey, what's happening here?"

As the pilot spoke, a low-altitude warning horn went off. "And even with the altimeter approaching zero, an amber light on the altimeter indicating they were off their assigned altitude, the radio altimeter approaching zero, and a radio altimeter warning horn beeping, everyone in the crew was so sure they were at 2,000 feet that no one could bring himself to act and eight seconds after the first officer noticed the altimeter, the aircraft crashed into the Everglades." (Quoted material from Garrison 1995.)

You can be more or less absorbed in the task that involves your locus of attention. The more intensely you are focused, the more difficult to transit to a different locus of attention, and the greater the stimulus needed to effect such a change. In the extreme case, when we are completely absorbed by a task, we cease to monitor our environment. You have probably experienced the absorbed state when you are reading a book, are thinking deeply about a problem, or are in the midst of a crisis that, as the expression goes, demands your attention. The use of a computer is often so stressful and difficult that a user will become absorbed in working on the computer system, and therefore distracted from the completion of tasks. Our goal is to leave the task as the locus of the user's attention.

Absorption in a task or a problem decreases the ease with which a person can change her locus of attention. On the other hand, such absorption—if it is confined to the task and if the system does not pull attention to itself—is essential to productivity. Systems should be designed to allow users to concentrate on their jobs. Interfaces should be designed as though the user will be so absorbed in her task that she may not respond to your attempts to communicate with her. An interface must work, whatever the user's state of absorption. For example, interface designers sometimes assume that the user's locus of attention is the cursor and that changing the cursor's shape will inevitably command the user's attention. The cursor location is a good place to put indicators, but even there, the indicator can go unnoticed; the shape of the cursor is not the locus of attention; rather, the place or object to which it is pointing may well be. An example is given in Section 3-2.

Many examples of absorption seem unbelievable until you experience a similar incident or until you have seen so many reports that you become convinced of the strength of absorption's grip. Because aviation accidents are often well researched and carefully documented, they are a good source for case studies. Here is another (Garrison 1994). A well-known pilot was flying an aircraft unfamiliar to him, one that required him to lower the retractable landing gear as he made his descent. As a reminder, a buzzer sounds when this particular model of aircraft is a certain distance from the ground and the gear has not been lowered. "I landed gear-up at one point, having persuaded myself that the insistent buzzer I kept hearing as I approached the gravel runway had something to do with the airbrakes. (This was one of my early lessons in the bizarre mental mix-ups that can lead to accidents)" (Garrison 1994). But there was no bizarre mental mix-up: Garrison was concentrating on making a good landing, one of the most difficult tasks that a pilot must accomplish and one that requires a great deal of concentration.[2]

The human ability to tune out disturbances is not necessarily an all-or-nothing response, as in the previous examples; it can be proportional to the level of absorption and the degree of disturbance. As stress increases, "people concentrate more and more on but a few features of their environment, paying less and less attention to others" (Loftus 1979, p. 35). Thus, *if the computer behaves unexpectedly while you are using an interface, you become less likely to see hints, help messages, or other user aids as you become increasingly agitated about the problem.*

The more critical the task, the less likely it is for users to notice warnings that alert them to potentially dangerous actions. A computer warning message is most likely to be missed when it is most important for it not to be missed; this sounds like a humorous corollary of Murphy's law,[3] but it is not. One way we can help is to *make sure that users cannot make interface operation errors, or that the effects of any actions are readily reversible rather than simply notifying users about the potential consequences of their actions.* Most interface situations can be designed such that error messages are unnecessary. A forceful diatribe against using error messages appears in *About Face* (Cooper 1995, pp. 421–440).

2-3-4 Origins of the Locus of Attention

That we have only one locus of attention may seem odd. Let us explore how we may have come to have this trait. Baars (1988) speaks eloquently to the question; he seeks a biological rationale for our having evolved in this limited fashion, asserting that

> consciousness and related mechanisms pose a great challenge to functional explanations because of the paradoxical limits of conscious capacity. Why can't we experience two different "things"

---

2. An interface designer might wonder why, if the aircraft could sound the buzzer, could it not also automatically lower the landing gear? This book is not the forum for a discussion of the details, but at times, automatically lowering the landing gear could be dangerous to the occupants. Therefore, it is always left up to the pilot to choose whether to lower the gear.

3. If anything can go wrong, it will. The first corollary is, If nothing can go wrong, it will anyway.

at one time? Why is Short Term Memory[4] limited to half a dozen unrelated items? How could such narrow limits be adaptive? Reasoning naively, it would seem wonderful to be able to consciously read one book, write another one, talk to a friend, and appreciate a fine meal, all at the same time. Certainly the nervous system seems big enough to do all these things simultaneously. The usual answers, that the limitations are "physiological" or that we only have two hands and one mouth to work with, are quite unsatisfactory because they simply move the issue one step backwards: Why have organisms blessed with the most formidable brain in the animal kingdom not developed hands and mouths able to handle true parallel processing? And why does our ability to process information in parallel increase with automaticity, and decrease with conscious involvement? (p. 348)

Baars suspects that the answer lies in there being only one "whole system": There is but one "I" in each of us. But to say that there is one personhood per human being begs the question. That is, why are there not multiple personhoods per mind-body ensemble? I am speaking not of changes that occur serially,[5] but rather of true simultaneous and independent minds in a single, connected physical entity. It may simply be that having a single personhood is a biological accommodation to the linearity of time or results from an accident of evolution rather than from a functional adaptation. Nevertheless, it seems more likely that our single personhood is adaptive: an accommodation to the purely physical impediments to having multiple simultaneous persons in one body. Given our evolved body plan, both personalities would not be able to speak at once or to turn the head in different directions simultaneously. Even if our eyes could have evolved to operate as independently as a gecko's, would they be able to serve two independent curiosities? I can imagine—to mention just one possible catas-

---

4. Short-term memory, often abbreviated STM in the literature, describes the behavior of memory with respect to stimuli just seen, heard, or otherwise sensed. If we do not make use of the memory or make it our locus of attention, STM fades in 10 to 20 seconds, or far less if we pay attention to new events. As Baars notes, STM is not only short but also of very limited capacity, and new events will drive out the old irretrievably. For a nontechnical and eminently readable account of the structure of human memory, see Loftus (1980).

5. Continuing change of personality is a human constant: We grow and change all the time. These changes, as well as the changes called multiple-personality disorder, are not what is being discussed.

trophe—that any multiple-mind mutation was eaten when it tried to escape a predator by deciding to run in two different directions at once.[6]

Siamese twins and two-headed animals do occur from time to time, and they have two independent minds, but they are developmental accidents, a mismatching or a misreading of the genetic code. They are not successful from an evolutionary standpoint and are not products of natural selection. In the wild, such sports of nature rarely survive and reproduce.

2-3-5 Exploitation of the Single Locus of Attention

We have examined the effects and the possible origins of having a single locus of attention. The next step is to make use of that singularity. We can redesign neither our own internal wiring nor that of other users, but we create products that have interfaces that accommodate these cognitive capabilities.

That people have a single locus of attention is not always a drawback. Magicians exploit this characteristic shamelessly. A good magician can fix the attention of an entire audience on one hand so that not a single spectator will see what the other hand is doing, although that hand is in no way concealed. If we know where the user's attention is fixed, we can make changes in the system elsewhere, knowing that the changes will not distract the user. This phenomenon was exploited in designing the Canon Cat (Figure 2.1). When a user stopped working, the Cat stored a bit-for-bit image of the screen—exactly as the display appeared when she stopped—on the first track of the disk. When the user again loaded her disk, the Cat placed the most recently viewed image on the screen, in only a fraction of a second. It takes about 10 seconds for a person to switch contexts or to prepare mentally for an upcoming task (Card, Moran, and Newell 1983, p. 390), but it took only 7 seconds for the Cat to read into memory the rest of the disk. So while the user was staring at the static screen image, recalling what she had been doing and deciding what she was going to do next—her locus of attention being the preparations for the coming task—the system finished loading. Only

---

6. I have often seen my cat poised between curiosity and fear, its senses intently trained on an unfamiliar object, its body tensed for immediate flight. I have acted the same way myself. Sometimes, what is learned by not fleeing is of value, and sometimes the delay is fatal: whence the expression "curiosity killed the cat." This occasional "being of two minds," as the idiom goes, is an internal sequential dialogue rather than two independent simultaneous processes.

then did the screen become active, although it did not change appearance, except that the cursor began to blink. Only a handful of users ever noticed this trick. Most Cat owners thought that the product magically managed to read in the whole diskette in the fraction of a second that it took to display the first screen. Presto!

Many people do not believe that it takes a person approximately 10 seconds to switch contexts; the time is measured between the final command executed in the previous context and the first command issued in the new context. The hiatus is not noticed because the minds of the users are occupied; they are not aware of the passage of time. However, this phenomenon should be used carefully when designing an interface. If the work flow is such that a user makes a particular context switch repeatedly, so that it becomes habitual, the user will make the switch in far less time.

Time delays can be masked; for example, a card game that takes time to create a new deal will feel faster if a card-shuffling noise is played during the delay. The value of masking was vividly demonstrated when such a game had its sound turned off inadvertently and the players suddenly found the delay annoying (Dick Karpinski, personal communication 1999).

Figure 2.1. The Canon Cat. Note the two LEAP keys below the space bar.

2-3-6 Resumption of Interrupted Work

Usually, after dealing with an interruption to a task, you then return to the interrupted task. If the interruption lasts only a few seconds—within the decay time of short-term memory—no further stimulus is required to signal you to return to the prior task. After a longer break, however, your return to the interrupted task must be triggered, often by seeing your incomplete work lying before you. Such cueing is as common in daily life as it is when using a computer: A banana peel left on the kitchen table by your 4-year-old child becomes a cue to dispose of the peel.

A metaphor that permeates personal computers and derivative technologies is that of a central, neutral dispatch area, or desktop, from which you can launch a variety of applications. When computers are turned on, most of them present the desktop, although some of them can be set to launch a fixed set of applications. When you quit an application, you are usually returned to the desktop. This interface strategy is inefficient and nonhumane. The reason is straightforward: When you quit an application, you (1) want to either return to the previous task on which you were working or (2) start a new task.

In current desktop-based systems, you must *always* navigate to the task. *This is the same as the worst case for an interface that always returns you to what you were last doing, because in the case of wishing to return to the task from which you left off, you have to do no work at all.*

Similarly, when you return to an online site, such as a web page, it would generally be better to return you to where you last were than to a home page that, if the site is well designed, is always available with a single click. The same reasoning suggests that *when you open a document in an application, such as a word processor, you should be returned to the place where you were working when you last closed or saved it.*

The Canon Cat had the property of always returning you to the previous task when you started to use it; moreover, it presented exactly the same screen appearance, including cursor placement, as when it was last used. Many users reported that seeing the same display helped them to remember what they had been doing when they had last used the machine, which made returning to the Cat a more pleasant experience than returning to a computer that boots into a desktop. More recently, the Apple iBook has taken a similar approach, saving the current state to disk and whisking it back in when you turn the machine on.

Designers of digitally tuned radios and televisions make sure that their products retain the most recently tuned station and volume settings, a requirement that adds to the complexity and cost of those products in the form of nonvolatile memory that otherwise would be unnecessary. For computer designers, who work with products that already have substantial nonvolatile memory, such as a hard disk, the hardware needed to do this is already in place, and there is no excuse.

THREE

Meanings, Modes, Monotony, and Myths

There is no progress without struggle.

—*Frederick Douglass*

So that we can discuss interface with precision, a few definitions and conventions of notations are introduced here. We use these tools, building on the notion of locus of attention from Chapter 2, to understand modes and their harmful effects on interface design. We introduce a beneficial property of interfaces, called *monotony*, which leads to a critique of interfaces that have beginner and expert modes.

3-1 Nomenclature and Notations

The world is divided into people who think that they're right.

—*Diedre McGrath*

Content is the information that resides in a computer or other information-processing device and that has meaning and utility for you. Creation or alteration of content is the task that you intend to accomplish with the device. If you are a writer, the content is those of your writings that are stored in the system. If you are an artist, your graphics are the content of the system. Where the system is a computer, the menus, the icons, and other paraphernalia of the computer are not your content—unless you are an interface designer or a programmer. We can now paraphrase Asimov's first law of robotics from Chapter 1 in terms of content: Any system shall not harm your content or, through inaction, allow your content to come to harm.

A **graphical input device** (GID) is a mechanism for communicating information, such as a particular location or choice of object on a display, to a system. Typical GID examples are mice, trackballs, lightpens, tablet pens, joysticks, or touchpads. The **GID button** is the principal button on any GID—for example, the left button on a two-button mouse. In general, you use the graphical input device to control the position of the cursor, which is an arrow or other graphical emblem on the display to indicate the system's interpretation of where you are pointing. Because we can pay attention to only one cursor at a time, systems should not display more than one cursor for each graphical input device on the system. The rationale for the one-button mouse is discussed in Appendix A.

A **tap** is the act of pressing and releasing a key or switch without any intervening action. *Tap* applies only to keys on a keyboard or to other momentary contact switches that, when released, automatically return to their original position and electrical state.

To **click** is to position the GID and then to tap the GID button. Thus, "click the word *alligator*" indicates that you are to move the cursor such that it points to *alligator* and then, while the cursor remains stationary, tap the GID button. This operation constitutes "clicking on *alligator*." To **drag** is to press the GID button at one location and then to move the GID before releasing the GID button at a new location; this action is sometimes called *click and drag*. To **double click** is to position the GID and then to tap the GID button twice quickly, without any intervening motion of the GID or other user action. (In practice, a small amount of GID motion is allowed, because it will usually move slightly when the button is pressed.) Triple- and higher–order clicks have been used in interface design.

The usual notations for the overlapping keystrokes that are used to control most software are sometimes ambiguous. For example, the act of pressing and holding the Control key and—while holding it—pressing and holding Shift and—while continuing to hold them both down—tapping the letter *t*, is often written *Control-Shift-t* or *Control+Shift+t* in manuals. However, these encodings of keyboard operations are indistinguishable from the conventional notations for the sequences of keystrokes *Control, hyphen, Shift, hyphen, t*; and *Control, plus, Shift, plus, t*, respectively.

This ambiguity can cause errors. For example, while I was writing this manuscript, I looked up a key combination for a command I needed; the manual listed it (at the end of a sentence) as

Control +.

So I pressed Control and, while holding it, typed a plus sign. Due to the manual's ambiguous notation, my interpretation was wrong: The manual was trying to direct me to press and hold Control and, while holding Control, to tap the period key.

Furthermore, the usual notations do not allow you to notate pressing and holding down, say, both the Shift and Command keys, and—while holding them both down—typing multiple alphabetic characters, releasing Shift but not Command after the first two alphabetic characters have been typed. The alternative that I have just used—expressing the operation in natural language—is clumsy albeit unambiguous.

To denote keyboard operations with precision and brevity, I use a downward-pointing arrow immediately after the name of a key to indicate that the key has been pressed and is to be held; for example, *Shift↓* signals that the Shift key is to be pressed and held. An upward-pointing arrow after the name of a key indicates the release of that key: *Shift↑*. A tap of a single key—for example, *t*—is rigorously notated *t↓ t↑*. The tap of a single key can be abbreviated, where the shorthand is unambiguous, as *t↓↑* or, where it will not cause confusion, simply *t*.

A space separates the notation of consecutive actions. A tap of the space bar is represented by the notation

Space

This convention does not introduce any ambiguity with typing the word *space,* because typing the letters of the word *space* is represented by letters separated by spaces, namely,

s p a c e

When there is a risk of misinterpretation, or when exactly what is being typed requires emphasis, I use the full notation:

s↓ s↑ p↓ p↑ a↓ a↑ c↓ c↑ e↓ e↑

Arbitrary combinations of keys can be represented linearly in this notation. For example, pressing and holding Shift and then tapping *n*, pressing and holding Control while Shift is still held and then tapping *k*, releasing Shift while still holding Control and then tapping *w* before releasing Control is written as follows:

Shift↓ n Control↓ k Shift↑ w Control↑

The release of any of the keys currently being held—if the order in which they are released is immaterial to the functioning of the interface—is denoted by an up arrow for each key being held. This convention allows us to denote typing the word *space* this way:

s↓↑ p↓↑ a↓↑ c↓↑ e↓↑

Here is a more useful example: To reset parameter RAM on a Macintosh computer, you use the following sequence of commands:

Command↓ Control↓ Power↓ ↑↑↑ Command↓ Option↓ p↓ r↓

Hold these keys and wait until a chime sounds

↑↑↑↑

(In English: Press and hold the Command key—the lack of an up arrow means that you should not release the key immediately. Rather, while you are holding it, press and hold the Control key. There is no up arrow here either, so while you are holding both of those keys, you press the Power key. There have been no up arrows, so now you are holding down three keys. The three up arrows that follow mean that you should release all three keys in any order or all at once. Next, you are instructed to press and hold the Command key, press and hold the Option key, press and hold *p*, and then press and hold *r*, such that, eventually, you are holding down four keys at once. You hold these keys until after the chime and then let all four keys go.)

If a typed sequence has special time dependencies, they should be noted in accompanying text. For example, for the user to type a single letter *t*, we use this sequence:

t↓ t↑

With most keyboards, however, if a delay, usually of at least 500 msec, occurs between *t↓* and *t↑*, extra instances of the letter *t* will be produced at a rate of approximately one every 100 msec. This feature is often called autorepeat. Delays, such as the one that triggers autorepeat, cause problems in interfaces. The use of delays in interfaces and an improved way to implement autorepeat are described in Section 6-4-4.

3-2 Modes

Since humans are more pliable than computers, it can be easier to make a human fit the computer's limitations than to design the computer to fit the human's needs. When that happens, the human becomes a prisoner trapped by the computer rather than liberated by it.

—Karla Jennings

Modes are a significant source of errors, confusion, unnecessary restrictions, and complexity in interfaces. Many of the problems modes cause have been widely recognized; nonetheless, making systems truly mode-less is an underused tactic in interface design. Before we can discuss methods for eliminating modes, we must understand them in detail, especially because even interface professionals have disagreed about what constitutes a mode (Johnson and Englebeck 1989).

To understand modes, we must first define a gesture. A **gesture** is a sequence of human actions completed automatically once set in motion. For example, typing a common word, such as *the*, is a single gesture for an experienced typist, whereas the typing of each letter would be a separate gesture for a beginning typist. Combining a sequence of actions into a gesture related to the psychological process is called **chunking**: the combining of separate items of cognition into a single mental unit, a process that allows us to deal with many items as though they were one (Buxton 1986, pp. 475–480; Miller 1956).

Most interfaces have multiple interpretations of a given gesture. For example, at one moment, tapping Return inserts a return character into the text, whereas at another time, tapping Return causes the text typed immediately prior to that tap to be executed as a command.

Modes are manifested by how an interface responds to gestures. *For any given gesture, the interface is in a particular mode if the interpretation of that gesture is constant.* When that gesture has a different interpretation, the interface is in a different mode. This definition gives us a useful initial view of what constitutes a mode; we will refine the definition later.

A flashlight that is operated via a push-button toggle can be either on or off, assuming that it is in good operating condition. Pressing the button turns the light on if the present state is off, and turns the light off if the present state is on. The two states of the flashlight correspond to two modes in the interface: In one mode, tapping the button turns the light on; in the other mode, tapping the button turns the light off. If you do not know the present state of the flashlight, you cannot predict what a press of the flashlight's button will do. If your flashlight is deep in a duffel bag where you cannot see it, you cannot check by feel whether the light is off or on, assuming that it does not get detectably warm; if your intent is to make sure that it is off, you will have to take it out. Your inability to determine the state of the flashlight is a classic problem caused by an interface that has modes; you cannot tell by inspecting the controlling mechanism what operation you need to perform to accomplish your goal. If you operate the controlling mechanism without separately verifying the state of the system, you cannot predict the effect that the operation will have.

Toggles are difficult to label. For example, in an interface I was shown, an on-screen button was labeled *Lock*. When users first encountered the button, they understood that they had to click on it to lock the data in that window. When they did so, the button's label changed to *Unlock*, to indicate that operating that button would unlock the data. Later, most of the users wondered why the data was unlocked, a conclusion they came to because the button said *Unlock*. As often happens when toggles are used on buttons or in menus, users read the label as an indicator of state. And they are justifiably confused: The button said *Lock* when the data was unlocked and *Unlock* when the data was locked. Obviously, you cannot solve the problem by interchanging the labels and having the button say *Unlock* when the data is unlocked and *Lock* when it is locked.

What can help is to use a check box rather than a button and to use the word *Locked* rather than *Lock* on it. This is usually understood correctly: When the box is checked, the data is locked. When the box is not checked, the data is not locked. The labels do not change. You can make more complete labels, such as "Click this button to unlock the data" or even "The data is currently locked; click this button to unlock the data." But it is difficult to put full explanations on a button, alongside a check box, or in a menu, unless a zooming interface is available, as discussed in Section 6-2.

Check boxes can leave the user guessing what the alternative is. For example, if a check box labeled "Save to archive on closing" is checked, the data will be saved to an archive when the window is closed, but the label gives little clue as to what will happen if the box is not checked. Will the data be saved somewhere else, not saved at all, or will another option appear when you close the window? Often, the best solution is to use a set of radio buttons (Figure 3.1); they are not modal, and the user can clearly see not only the current state but also the alternative(s). Whether check boxes or radio buttons are used, it is important to label them with adjectives, which describe the state of the object affected, rather than verbs, which describe an action, in which case the user does not know whether the action has taken place or is yet to take place.

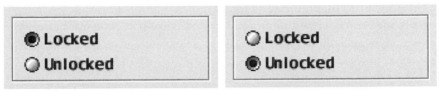

Figure 3.1. A pair of radio buttons labeled with adjectives. The option chosen has the dot in the circle; the left image reflects the locked state and the right image the unlocked state. Confusion is unlikely, and the user is aware of the available options.

For one-of-many choices, radio buttons are already the standard, and there is rarely reason to use other mechanisms. *Use radio buttons rather than toggles; toggles work reliably only when the value of the state controlled by the toggle is your locus of attention and is visible, or is in short-term memory.*

Except when the state is the locus of attention—and it is usually not—toggles will at times cause users errors. The kinds of errors caused by toggles are usually transient, and recovery is easy, but this is no reason to overlook them in interface design. To work in interface design without attending to details at this level is like trying to play a violin concerto, only occasionally forgetting to play a sharp or a flat given in the key signature. The errors annoy by pulling the listener's attention away from the continuity of the music. Similarly, occasional little "gotchas" in an interface impede the user's work flow.

Another troublesome aspect of modes—one that causes computer users considerable exasperation—is exemplified by the way that the Caps Lock key, found on most keyboards, functions. Often, your first indication that this key has become engaged accidentally is that you notice that the sentence you have typed is set in all uppercase letters, and only then do you also notice that the Caps Lock key's light is on, if it has such a light. "It is no accident that swearing is denoted by #&%!#$&," writes my colleague, Dr. James Winter; it is "what a typewriter used to do when you typed numbers when the Caps Lock was engaged" (personal communication 1998).

Decades ago, Larry Clark observed that modes cause problems because they make habitual actions have unexpected effects (Clark 1979).[1] The most commonly prescribed remedy for mode errors is to indicate

---

1. I am not sure for how long the term *mode* has been used in describing interfaces. An internal Xerox report on the Gypsy Typescript System boasted, "There are no 'modes' in Gypsy" (Tesler and Mott 1975). There were, in fact, modes in Gypsy, but some of the more problematical ones of contemporary word processors had been eliminated. The term *mode* was new enough in 1975 that the authors felt it necessary to put it in quotes.

prominently to a user the state of the system. Dr. Donald Norman characterized mode errors as resulting from inadequate feedback, the feedback being provided by an indicator of system state (Norman 1983). The real culprit, however, is not inadequate feedback but that the user's locus of attention is not the provided indicator.

An especially clear example of the failure of using an indicator to provide feedback of system state to the user occurs in the generally excellent interface to the computer-aided design (CAD) package Vellum (Ashlar 1995). To anybody who is designing a drawing package, I strongly recommend a study of Ashlar's Drafting Assistant; it represents an extraordinarily good interface, one that is more productive and pleasant than that of the better-known AutoCAD.[2] One of Vellum's time-saving functions is a tracer that can follow the inside or the outside of a geometrical figure, selecting the border as it travels. To enable the tracer, you click on a palette item that turns the standard cursor ⬉ into a distinct shape, the tracer cursor ▸. After you finish tracing, you often forget to switch back to the standard cursor. As I click to select an object after I have executed a trace operation—selecting by clicking being an action that I do so often that it long ago became automatic—instead of succeeding in making the selection, I sit surprised as the tracer goes off on its rounds. I have been making this mistake for years, as have other users with whom I have spoken. Although I sometimes catch myself in time, I never will learn—I never *can* learn to always catch that I am in tracer mode—because clicking to make a selection is, for me, automatic. My locus of attention is the object I am selecting, not the cursor shape. Vellum's changing cursor shape is one example of many that confirm that feedback and indicators of system state are not sufficient to guarantee the elimination of mode errors, even if the indicators are physically colocated with your locus of attention. They may be in your high-resolution foveal field, and, in this case, you are even using the indicator as your cursor, yet because it is not your locus of attention, you are not aware of the message it is trying to convey. Essential topics for future research include quantifying the frequency of mode errors and understanding the conditions that affect the frequency with which these errors occur.

Expertise is no protection against modes; an expert has developed firm habits. Naiveté is also no protection. In the example of Vellum's cursors, the beginner has not yet established in his mind that it is necessary to change the cursor back after tracing. By the time a beginner has learned to do this step without having to think about it explicitly, he is an expert with respect

---

2. In fact, AutoCAD licensed this technology while this book was being written.

to this feature and is subject to the habituation problem. If the current state of the interface is not the user's locus of attention and if an interface has modes, the user will sometimes make errors because his locus of attention is not the current mode.

Here is another example: On some popular computers, many programs give you a new, clean form when you type

Command↓ n↓↑ ↑

The *n* stands for *new*. In the America Online electronic mail package, in contrast, you obtain a new, blank e-mail form by typing

Command↓ m↓↑ ↑

I presume that *m* stands for *mail*. The error that is repeatedly made when a user wants to start a new electronic mail message is to use

Command↓ n↓↑ ↑

The interface state that gives rise to a mode in this example consists of having a particular application active. The problem occurs when users employ the *Command↓ n↓↑ ↑* command habitually. A beginner would probably make this same error for a different reason; he would assume that *Command↓ n↓↑ ↑* operates identically across applications and thus would make the error from excusable ignorance.

Norman (1983) lists three ways to minimize mode errors.

1. Do not have modes.

2. Make sure that the modes are distinctively marked.

3. Make sure that the commands required by different modes are not the same, so that a command issued in the wrong mode will not lead to difficulty.

Of these three, only the first always prevents mode errors. As we have seen, the second works sporadically. The third does not decrease the number of errors, but it does reduce the penalty for erring.

Extreme techniques will usually draw a user's attention to a mode indicator, but by their intrusive strength, they redirect the user's locus of attention to the current state of the system and not on what he is trying to accomplish—a result that is as undesirable as the mode error that the indicators might prevent. Norman defined mode errors as mistakes that occur when a user misclassifies, or when the user makes an erroneous analysis of a situation (Norman 1981). The terms *misclassifies* and *analysis* hint at active, conscious participation on the part of the user and therefore apply while she is unfamiliar with a command but do not apply after her use of it has become automatic.

3-2-1 Definition of Modes

If the definition of a mode is based exclusively on the design of the interface, as our definition has been up to now, all users would make the same errors, albeit with different frequencies. They do not. A given interface feature can be modal for one user and not modal for another. A more complete definition of modes must incorporate how the user views the interface: *A human-machine interface is* modal *with respect to a given gesture when (1) the current state of the interface is not the user's locus of attention and (2) the interface will execute one among several different possible responses to the gesture, depending on the system's current state.*

An interface can be modal with respect to one gesture and not modal with respect to a second gesture. *For an interface as a whole to be classified as not modal, it must not be modal for any gesture.*

A measure, Q, of how modal a particular interface is can be given by classifying each of the gestures in an interface as modal or not modal. Then, given the probability, $p(N_i)$, that a particular nonmodal gesture, N_i, is used, measured for a given user or averaged over a population of users, $Q = \sum_i p(N_i)$. Q ranges from 0, completely modal, to 1, completely nonmodal.

Both parts of the definition of a modal gesture are necessary to decide whether, for example, the gesture of pressing the Backspace key is modal. In most computer interfaces, assuming you are in the process of entering text, the Backspace command erases the most recently typed character. If that character was an *e*, the key erases an *e*. If that character was an *x*, the key erases an *x*. That is, sometimes Backspace is an *e* eraser, and sometimes it is an *x* eraser. Considering only the second part of the definition, the use of Backspace is modal because what it erases depends on the character most recently typed; content is part of system state. However, when you realize that your locus of attention is the object that you are erasing, it is the first part of the definition that explains why the operation is not modal and why you do not make mode errors when you use the Backspace key to erase characters in text or any other kind of object that you can select and delete in the same way.[3]

A command that sets whether the Backspace key operates as a forward or a reverse erase, on the other hand, does make the interface modal.

---

3. On the Macintosh, the key is, more accurately, labeled *Delete*.

The setting of erase direction, made earlier, is usually not your locus of attention when, subsequently, you use Backspace, so sometimes you will erase in the unexpected direction.

Preventing (Aircraft) Crashes by Eliminating a Mode

Due to simple interface design error, both remote-piloted vehicles (RPVs), as used by the military, and civilian radio-controlled model aircraft are occasionally destroyed. To understand the error and a method of solving it, you must first know something about how these devices work.

To fly an RPV, the operator, who stays safely on the ground, moves a small joystick embedded in a control box (Figure 3.2). Typically, you push the stick to pitch down the nose of the RPV, pull on the stick to pitch the nose temporarily upward, and move the stick to the left or right to cause the RPV to roll to the left or right, respectively. Moving the stick causes a proportional motion of a device called a servo in the RPV. The servo is linked mechanically to a control surface, such as the elevator in the rear of the RPV, that controls pitch.

Figure 3.2. A commercial RPV controller. Note the many controls scattered across the face and the top of the device.

A servo has no standard direction of motion with respect to a stick motion, so it is convenient and conventional to have a switch, located on the controller, that allows the user to choose which direction of stick motion corresponds to which direction of servo motion. This clearly modal convention runs into conflict, as modes usually do, with a habituated reaction on the part of the user. Often, one controller is used with multiple different RPVs. Each may have different servo directions corresponding to the actions of the aircraft.

When changing between different RPVs, the user must operate the switches that choose servo direction so that a given stick motion corresponds to the appropriate RPV action.

It is nearly impossible to train a pilot to operate the control sticks in reverse fashion when a servo reversal is unexpected. For example, consider that the pilot about to perform a takeoff with the RPV is unaware that the switch that controls the direction of the roll is in the wrong position. Taking off is a critical maneuver that requires rapt attention. It is common for the RPV to spontaneously roll slightly to the left or the right just after leaving the ground, and the expert pilot will automatically apply a small opposite control input to compensate for the roll; the reaction is so fast that, with a good pilot, a nonpilot observer will not detect the incipient roll. With a reversed-direction control switch, the roll, of course, will get worse, because the servo is moving in the wrong direction. On seeing this, a well-trained pilot will apply a stronger compensating stick motion that, because of the servo reversal, exacerbates the roll, and the RPV will, at this point in the flight, usually be demolished as soon as the wingtip contacts the ground or the RPV rolls entirely on its back. (This entire sequence can take a fraction of a second.) I have never seen a pilot successfully figure out the problem and reverse reactions in time to complete the takeoff. This kind of crash has happened to me on two occasions, in spite of a well-trained ritual of checking that control surface motion is in the correct direction before each takeoff. Checking control direction, after its having been done dozens of times, also becomes a habit, to the point that you don't always verify that the directions in which the control surfaces move are correct. (If they don't move at all, that is sufficiently surprising to alert you to the presence of a problem.) During these checks, I have more often than not caught reversed servos on RPVs I was going to fly. However, when under pressure or with other things on my mind, I, like hundreds of other pilots, have missed the reversal.

Interestingly, this error does not usually occur on a new aircraft's first flight, during which you are especially alert for potential problems. It is only after flying the particular craft has become "second nature," or habitual, that the problem strikes.

This is an example of a mode that cannot be removed from the world. Modes are inherent in the nature of servos and control sticks.

Yet the problem can be greatly ameliorated. The solution: Put the servo reversal switch in the aircraft, perhaps as part of the servos, and have no servo reversal switches on the controller. The interiors of RPVs are not normally accessible: The switches would be set during assembly of the RPV. Correct direction of operation would be checked by the assemblers, rechecked by inspectors, and checked again (usually) by the pilot prior to the first flight. This method does not eliminate the possibility of a crash, but once the first flight is completed, servo reversal on that RPV will not be a problem, no matter how many different RPVs the controller is used with in the interim. To the operator of the RPV, the mode is gone.

Nearly all model aircraft controllers have servo reversal switches. Crashes due to having the controller in the wrong mode are not uncommon. Worse still is the "feature" of many controllers to have other modes set by long-handled paddle switches, easily knocked to the wrong position by accident. On the controller I designed for my own use, all such switches are of a design such that the switch levers have to be pulled away from the controller against spring tension before they can be moved (Figure 3.3) I have never had an accident due to a switch being unknowingly pushed to the wrong position. Sometimes, the solution to a mode problem is mechanical.

Figure 3.3. These switches on an RPV controller cannot be operated accidentally; the handle must be pulled out before the switch can be operated.

Modes also restrict your scope of activity. If a gesture *g* invokes action *a* in mode *A* and action *b* in mode *B*, you must, if you are in mode *B* and want to invoke action *a*, first leave mode *B* and reset the interface into mode *A*. Only then can you use the gesture *g* to invoke *a*. The division of an interface into bounded areas is a necessary consequence of modes; the set of states in which the gesture *g* has a particular interpretation can be called the

range of *g*. Software sold as an application—for example, a spreadsheet—usually consists of one or more overlapping ranges. Certain ranges are relatively large. For example, the following sequence performs a cut in nearly all applications on both the Macintosh and Windows platforms:

> *Command↓ x↓*

Other ranges are tiny. The following sequence in a certain computer game opens a treasure chest only when the chest is visible:

> *Command↓ h↓*

Grouping commands into separate ranges, or what we usually call *applications*, can be an aid to understanding and using a complex interface, but there are ways to organize an interface that are less restrictive than are modes. *A fully humane interface would consist of exactly one range.*

When an interface is controlled by another machine, you might think that modelessness is of no importance, because machines have no problem remembering state; they just model it internally with a state of their own. However, if an interface is modal and the program operating it does not initially know the current state of the interface—for example, if it connects to the system after the system is already running—the program, prior to operating any modal control, must be provided with a means for testing that state. Interface toggles are particularly troublesome in this regard, where consecutive invocations of the toggling mechanism cycle the control through a number of states before returning to the initial state (the cycle then repeats).

This discussion of programs that operate interfaces is relevant to human-machine interface design because you might want to construct a set of stored commands that can be played back with a single gesture, a *macro*, which is a rudimentary form of computer program. A macro cannot set a toggle into a specific state unless the macro first interrogates the system to determine the system's current state. We saw this problem in the example of the flashlight in the duffel bag. One solution is to have any multiple-option switch always reset to a specified initial state immediately after it is operated. Then, counting the number of invocations of the switch always informs the operator of the switch's current state. More than about five states is excessive if the switching is to be done by a person. As mentioned earlier, another solution is to use radio buttons.

We have not yet exhausted what harm modes do. Modes can put the computer, instead of the user, in charge of an interaction. This aspect is especially noticeable when you are forced to stop what you are doing to reply to a message box. Certain designers consider forcing the user to stop and to work in lockstep with a planned sequence to be an interface advantage, in that the system is "guiding" the user. There may be circumstances under which it is imperative that the user make a particular decision—if there is no user decision, there is no need for a dialogue at all—by a certain time or before doing another step in the sequence. In the first case, put up a count-down clock, but do not restrict the user from doing other operations with the system. In the second case, have a message stating that the decision must be made before the next step will be presented, but the system should not prevent the user from performing other operations that are not part of the programmed sequence. For example, what if the user needs to look up something in a file or do a calculation in order to answer the question? Guidance should be offered modelessly, so that the user remains in control of as much as possible of the system.

3-2-2 Modes, User–Preference Settings, and Temporary Modes

Facilities for setting user preferences constitute an example of modes and are a major source of user frustration. Ironically, these features are usually touted as a user benefit. Present interfaces are often so difficult to use that a user may feel an urge to rearrange them. Microsoft (1995, p. 4) specifically recommends that such facilities be provided: "Users, because of their widely varying skills and preferences, must be able to personalize aspects of the interface . . . such as color, fonts, or other options." On the other hand, a user of Microsoft Word described the effect of setting a preference as being like dropping a time bomb into the word processor. She needed to build a list in a format different from the one she usually used, so she looked up how to make the changes and chose new settings. The next time she wanted to build a list, she used the familiar List command and, of course, unexpectedly obtained the one she had reset Word to give her rather than the one she was used to. It took her more than an hour to figure out what had happened and to fix it. (Her first impulse was to believe that there was something wrong with the program or in her use of the command, and she repeated the command many times before she remembered that she had reset the preferences.)

Bob Fowles, of the Pennsylvania State University Computer Center, observed:

> People not aware of the complexity of Word can really get into trouble when they accidentally press Command, Option, or Control plus

another key while they are typing rapidly. My wife got into a problem yesterday that took me quite a few minutes to figure out. Every time she pressed Return, she got a bullet. Looking at the Edit pull-down menu, I saw "undo Autoformat." After several minutes of searching and using Help, I found where Autoformat could be turned on or off and turned it off. Somehow, she had typed a keyboard shortcut that had turned it on. (personal communication 1998)

This user was injured by a customization, a mode, an invisible keyboard shortcut, and excessive design complexity all at once.

Customizations are software design changes that are not reflected in the documentation. For example, when I was using Word, I tried to turn off a feature that was unfamiliar to me. The Help facility instructed me simply to click a certain button on the standard toolbar; however, a previous user had modified this toolbar using a user-preference setting, so that the button was not there. It took me a long time to figure out how to make the program behave. More important, the incident pointed out another fundamental problem of having user preferences: How do you test for interface quality or even succeed at documenting a system whose configuration the designers and writers cannot know in advance? In my case, the previous user's mode change rendered the documentation wrong.

Allowing the user to change the interface design often results in choices that are not optimal, because the user will, usually, not be a knowledgeable interface designer. Typically, a user will choose the method closest to one with which he is already familiar or a customization needed only temporarily. Some designers have argued that applications for high-level users should have many preference settings so that a user can tailor the system as much as possible. However, high-level users have no special claim to being good interface designers and, being habituated to their software, have an especially strong need for a stable system so that their habits will not be rendered useless by changes, even changes they themselves make.

By providing preferences, we burden users with a task extraneous to their job function. A user of, say, a spreadsheet has to learn how to use not only the spreadsheet but also the customizing facilities. *Time spent in learning and operating the personalization features is time mostly wasted from the task at hand.* Managers complain about the time workers waste "playing with" the system preferences. Most users just want to get their jobs done and care not whether the numbers in the spreadsheet default to Palatino in purple, Garamond in green, or Bodoni Semibold Extended Italic in bellwether blue.

Personalizing an interface in a shared environment is an invitation to disaster, as it means that the interface can change without notice. The right action yesterday—say, clicking the red button—is clicking the blue button today, because someone thought it looked better in blue. Your training and habits are undermined. Especially over the telephone or via e-mail, it is also more difficult to help the user of a system that has preferences.

Customization sounds nice, democratic, open-ended, and full of freedom and joy for the user, but I am unaware of any studies that show that it increases productivity or improves *objective* measures of usability or learnability. Adding customization certainly makes a system more complex and more difficult to learn. I suspect that if you were to take a user survey, more people than not would be in favor of lots of personalizable features. But then, when GUIs were first coming in, a majority of users said that they'd never want to use one. It is also important to recognize that users will customize an interface in such a way that it appeals to their subjective judgment. As has been observed in a number of experiments, *an interface that optimizes productivity is not necessarily an interface that optimizes subjective ratings*. (For an example, see Tullis 1984, p. 137.)

The central point of this issue is that if we are competent user interface designers and can make our interfaces nearly optimal, personalizations can only make the interface worse. Therefore, we must be sparing and deliberate in offering user customizations. If a user can, by a few judicious choices, really improve the interface, we probably have done a poor job.

On the other hand, if a program's interface is as dismal—to voice an opinion—as that of Microsoft Word 97/98, the situation is reversed. Almost any change the user makes is an improvement, to exaggerate only slightly. However, Word's interface is not the kind of goal toward which we should be striving.

Modes that vanish after a single use cause fewer errors than do those that persist, if for no other reason than that they have less time to cause havoc. In the Vellum cursor example, fewer user errors would result if the cursor, after performing its trace function, reverted in form and function to its normal state. If you use a temporary mode immediately after setting it, the fact that you set the mode may not have evaporated from your short-term memory, and you will not make a mode error; you may even incorporate setting the mode as part of the gesture that carries out the command, which makes the situation completely nonmodal for you. However, if you set the interface mode for a command, and, prior to using the command, are delayed or distracted, you are likely to make a mode error.

To avoid a mode, the Canon Cat was designed without a power switch.[4] The reason was that products react to gestures differently, depending on whether they are on or off, and a power switch therefore introduces a mode. To save energy, the Cat went into a low-powered sleep state if it was not used for five minutes. To make sure that sleep was not a mode, any user action or incoming message turned on the Cat without perceptible delay; furthermore, the user action that turned it on was not lost but took effect just as if the machine had not been in the sleep state.

In many systems, computers come out of sleep mode at the touch of a key, but the keystroke that turns them on—and any keystrokes made subsequently but before the system is fully awake—are lost. Not losing any keystrokes turned out to be an elegant feature. For example, if you had a sudden inspiration or had to take a note during a telephone call, you could just start typing without worrying about the state of the Cat or even looking at the display. It is a characteristic of modelessness that, once you become habituated, you do not have to think or plan before you act; your attention stays on the content of your work. (If you happened to put your note in the midst of something else, you'd just select the note and move it after you were done memorializing your inspiration or finishing your telephone call.)

Occasionally, designers claim that modes are necessary because the number of desired software functions exceeds the number of gestures that a user can make with a keyboard and a graphical input device, making gesture reuse necessary. However, display-based commands, such as menus, and typed multiple-character commands, as in command line–driven systems, offer an unlimited number of commands and thus avoid that difficulty. (How you make sure that the various commands in a command line system are visible, rather than having to be memorized, will be discussed later.)

The bottom line on modes is this: *If you design a modal interface, users will make mode errors except when the value of the state that is controlled by the mode is the user's locus of attention and is visible to the user or is in the user's short-term memory. The burden is on the designer to demonstrate that a mode is being used under the appropriate condition or that the advantages of a particular modal design outweigh its unavoidable disadvantages.* It is always safe to avoid interface designs that have modes.

---

4. I was startled to find a power switch on the back of the Cat when the first units came back from Japan. I pointed out that the design specifications said that there was to be no power switch, and I had gone over the rationale for this repeatedly with the engineers. "We thought the specifications had an error," I was told.

Buttons that Change in the Night

Some aircraft have pushbuttons that contain a dot-matrix display used to change the legend that appears on the button. This change is done under the aircraft's computer's control so that the buttons can be relabeled on the fly. The advertising copy for one brand of these buttons made some human factors claims. For one thing, fewer buttons would be needed in the limited cockpit area. For another, avionics and other system changes could be effected without having to rewire the cockpit.

From the perspective of cognitive science, good labels enhance visibility. Assuming that the person choosing the labels bothers to test the wording, to make sure that the chosen labels are effective and unconfusing, it is, on the face of it, a good idea.

But more careful thinking reveals a number of potential pitfalls to the product: All legended buttons get obscured—by the very finger you are using—just as you are about to press them, obviating a last-second check that you are pressing the right button. But this is a minor problem, for normally you have looked at the legend before you press the button—if you have looked at all. (I am certainly not looking at the legends on the keycaps of my keyboard as I type this.)

Then there is the deeper problem of the disappearing button. You want to enable, say, the manual controls on the cabin air conditioner. There is, you recall, a button labeled MANUAL AIR, but it is nowhere to be found. The reason is that it now says COMM BACKUP. You have to figure out how to get that button to light up the way it did before. Perhaps a switch or a button somewhere else changes the legends on the buttons. Or perhaps the legends are context-sensitive and won't allow you to change the air conditioning right now. Whatever the cause, when a button has variable legends, the button you want will perhaps have vanished because the system is in a different mode.

But the gravest problem has to do with habituation. Imagine the experienced pilot reaching up and pressing a button. The radio's not working; something's wrong. A communications problem: Time to enable COMM BACKUP. She jabs out expertly at the COMM BACKUP button. Click! Too bad. The copilot was adjusting the cabin temperature in response to a passenger complaint, and the buttons are now in climate-control mode. The pilot has just achieved complete manual control over the air conditioning system.

Variable-legend buttons could be useful, for instance, if several people use the same console, each using it in such a way that the buttons do not change meaning for any one user. But this is a situation seldom encountered. Soft keys, whereby a display has changable legends that affect on-screen buttons or buttons adjacent to the display, have the same liability as do variable-legend buttons. A similar problem exists with the use of function buttons, labeled F1 through F12 on many computers. If their functions are unchanging, the labeling is unmnemonic. If their functions change, you cannot use them automatically. In either case, they are a poor design.

Are Fewer Buttons Better?

Figure 3.4. Fluke scopemeter: powerful and rugged, zillions of functions, a paucity of keys, but difficult to learn and sometimes slow to get to the function you need. On the other hand, its color-coded leads eliminate a traditional source of confusion about which lead does what. (See color insert.)

A portable Fluke[5] oscilloscope I recently tested (Figure 3.4) is incredibly sturdy and capable. Its 35 buttons control a bounteous multitude of modes and functions. The device was difficult to learn and has proved impossible to operate quickly when trying to work with many of its features.

5. I am grateful to John Fluke Manufacturing Co. for providing the sample unit.

Figure 3.5. The Tektronix oscilloscope has a myriad settings, but although initially intimidating, it is quick and easy to operate. All knobs that can uncalibrate the unit are in red. (See color insert.)

A Tektronix oscilloscope (see Figure 3.5) with its myriad settings that seem so daunting at first glance, is easier both to teach and to use. The number of switches and knobs is about the same as on the digital scope, but many of the knobs have multiple settings that you can access immediately, and the settings are marked on the face of the product, so that they are visible rather than hidden in a menu that must be summoned to be seen. Fluke's product offers much greater functionality but at the cost of making some tasks that were previously easy more difficult. The rotating knobs are each far more powerful than each of the Fluke's buttons. Fluke also went further than necessary in creating submenus of excessive depth.

Operation of the oscilloscopes parallels the relative ease of use of two radios I own. My truck radio (Figure 3.6) has 18 preset stations, arranged in three groups of six. One button cycles through the three groups, and a linear arrangement of six buttons chooses the station within each group. An LCD panel shows the group number (1 through 3). Seven buttons suffice to select among 24 stations.

Figure 3.6. The radio in my truck is difficult enough to use as a radio, and I find it impossible to remember how to set the clock.

My other radio is the electronically superb Sony 2010 (see Figure 3.7), which has 32 presets on 32 identical buttons in four rows of eight buttons each. At first sight, this radio looks more complex, but as interviews with owners and long personal use have proved to me, this design makes it easier to find a preset station, especially in the

Figure 3.7. The Sony 2010 short-wave radio has many buttons but a fast, readily learned operation. (See color insert.)

dark; just count down and over to the button you want and tap it. The Sony 2010 stores all parameters of the station, such as whether the station is AM, short-wave, FM, or aircraft band, and any other settings you have chosen. Tap one of the 32 buttons, and everything needed to play that station is set automatically and at once. I put the most frequently accessed stations near the upper-left corner of the array.

The truck radio sacrifices usability to obtaining a low button count and small panel size. The worst part of the design is that you are forced to take your eyes from the road to know which set of presets you are using, or you can be distracted fishing for the station you want. (If you are switching from AM to FM or vice versa, you must find and tap two buttons; with the Sony, it is always one tap to select any preset.)

It is only slightly hyperbolic to suggest that it should be illegal to have a toggling, modal interface in a motor vehicle. Clearly, my truck radio has an unsatisfactory interface for selecting stations; even less satisfactory is its invisible method for setting the clock. I have to look it up every time: Press and hold the DISP button for 2 seconds; let it go. Turn the tuning knob counterclockwise to advance hours; turn it clockwise to advance minutes; press the DISP button to finish setting the clock. (The DISP button is the volume-control knob.) On the plus side, at least my radios have real volume-control knobs, unlike the pair of volume-control buttons on some more modern equipment. Volume-control buttons suffer from making it take too long to get to the desired loudness and from the fact that the current setting is neither visible to the eye nor accessible to the sense of touch. In a recent user survey that I conducted, every subject ($n = 55$) preferred a knob in this role.

Fewer buttons and simpler-looking controls are not always better. The lesson applies to screen design as well as to instruments and appliances.

3-2-3 Modes and Quasimodes

Using the Caps Lock key to type uppercase letters and holding the Shift key to the same effect are significantly different. The first case establishes a mode; the second case does not. A set of experiments at the University of Toronto confirmed that the act of holding down a key, pressing a foot pedal, and any other form of physically holding an interface in a certain state does not induce mode errors (Sellen, Kurtenbach, and Buxton 1992). Other studies revealed the neurophysiological roots of this phenomenon: Most of our nervous system operates such that a constant stimulus yields signals that, in time, decrease in their ability to capture our attention. This decrease continues until our cognitive system receives no signal at all. However, the signals that report back to us whether our muscles are actively producing a force do not fade.

Activating and holding a control while performing another user action has been referred to as a *spring-loaded mode* and a *spring-locked mode* (Johnson and Engelbeck 1989). But this terminology is inappropriate because no physical spring may be involved, the key or button is not locked, and holding a control does not cause mode errors. The phrase *user-maintained mode* (Sellen, Kurtenbach, and Buxton 1992) for this action is accurate but makes it difficult to frame a corresponding adjective. I have come to use the term *quasimode* and its adjectival form, *quasimodal*, to denote modes that are maintained kinesthetically. (See Figure 3.8.)

Figure 3.8. The hunchback of Notre Dame.

Quasimodes are very effective in eliminating modes (Raskin 1989); however, excessive use of quasimodes can lead to absurd interface conventions that require the user to remember dozens of commands, such as *Control↓ Alt↓ Shift↓ Esc↓ q↑↑↑↑*. The limit for the number of effective quasimodes is probably between four and seven. But one quasimode can solve a multitude of varied problems (see Section 5-4).

A typical problem that is readily solved by the use of quasimodes occurs when an interface presents you with a set of choices, such as the Macintosh's pull-down menus. In this application of quasimodes, you press and hold down the graphical input device button when, on the name of the menu, the other choices appear for as long as you are holding down the button. You move the cursor to the desired item and release on that item to make your menu choice.

Another use of quasimodes is to cycle through a set of options. So long as the cycle starts on the same element in the set and proceeds in the same order, and so long as there are not too many elements, a fixed number of taps chooses the option. For example, in the design of the Canon Cat, the user could change a selection to any of four paragraph styles: left-aligned, centered, right-aligned, and justified. Paragraph styles were chosen by repeatedly tapping the key that had on its front the legend

¶ STYLE

To access a key with a front legend on the Cat, you held down a special Shift key that was marked on its top Use Front (Figure 3.9). In general, the Use Front key allowed you to execute the function indicated by the legend on

Figure 3.9. Canon Cat's Use Front key and some of the command keys. The words USE FRONT are light blue, as are the legends on the fronts of the keys that are enabled by the Use Front key. (See color insert.)

the front of a key. Because paragraph style was a quasimode (you had to hold down Use Front while tapping the Paragraph Style key), the Cat knew how many times you had tapped it. As a consequence, you soon learned that one tap left-aligned the selection, two taps right-aligned the selection, and so forth. Had the software cycled from wherever you left off, as many interfaces do, there would have been no way of making your use of the paragraph style command habitual; you always would have had to look at the display to know what was happening. Note that a paragraph style button that did not require holding down Use Front would not have worked as well; it was the establishment of the quasimode, when you pressed the Use Front key, that allowed the system to know when to start counting.

A habituating feature is often one that can be operated successfully by a blind user. Following the principles in this book will often result in interface methods that can be used by the blind. We are all blind—in a very real sense—to the world outside of our locus of attention.

Some menus or palettes take the most-used or the most recently used item and position it at the top of the menu or in the palette: a simple example of an *adaptive menu* or an *adaptive palette.* A menu or a palette is made adaptive on the assumption that having the favored item available, without having to pull it down, will speed your use of the system. It is useful to compare two approaches: The first approach is to *remove* the chosen item from the list that has been pulled out and place that item in the main palette or menu; the second approach is to *duplicate* the chosen item into the main palette or menu (Figure 3.10).

It might seem that the first strategy is better. For one thing, there is one less choice in the list that has been pulled out. It also takes less screen space. But you also have to stop and check whether the tool you want is in the main palette or in the pulldown, especially if it has been more than a few seconds since you last used the tool. But it is the second alternative, whereby you can adopt the simple strategy of always using the *n*th pulldown for a desired task, that is usually faster. It is certainly easier from a cognitive standpoint. If you remember that a certain option is now in the main menu, you save having to pull down the complete list. But if you don't remember, you can use the pulldown as you always do.

Vellum (Ashlar 1995) is an example of a product interface with adaptive palettes done correctly (Figure 3.10). In Vellum, the palette is adaptive, *and* each tool can also be found in its accustomed place. However, an experienced user might ignore the adaptive feature, going automatically to the accustomed tool position. An additional aspect of providing multiple ways of invoking a feature will be discussed in Section 3-5.

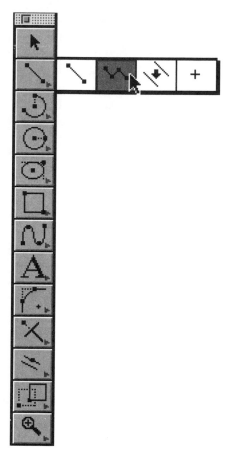

Figure 3.10. Ashlar pull-out palette. Note the duplication of the first icon on the pulled-out group, so that the pullouts are always in the same order; their use can, therefore, become automatic.

It has been suggested that interfaces should adapt to accommodate the user's emotional state, and some products, such as Microsoft's Bob, attempt to tailor the interface to the personality of the user. It is not clear how an interface can adapt to the user in these ways without upsetting habituation. But even if we can, someday, reliably detect a user's emotional needs and use that information to improve the performance of an interface without interfering with our learned and automatic responses, our interfaces must still first satisfy the user's unchanging cognetic needs. The principles outlined in this book will still apply and will probably need to be applied prior to any adjustment for emotional needs.

Fundamentally, there are only two kinds of inputs you make to your computer or information appliance: creating content or controlling the system. The rule of thumb adopted here is this: *Quasimodes are reserved for control functions. Operations you perform when no quasimode is engaged create content.* It is this way rather than the other way around because it is more difficult to operate a system while a quasimode-establishing button is being held, and it is hoped that users will spend more time creating and working with content than in using commands.

3-3 Noun-Verb versus Verb-Noun Constructions

A large class of commands involve applying an *action* to an *object*. In operating a word processor, for example, you might take a paragraph and change its typeface; in this case, the object is the paragraph, and the action is the selection of a new font. The interface can allow you to sequence the operations in two ways. You choose either (1) the *verb* (change font) first and then select the *noun* (the paragraph) to which the verb should apply or (2) the noun first and then apply the verb. At first glance, it would seem that the situation is symmetrical and the order is of no importance, but in most interface designs, the situation is not symmetrical, and the order (either noun-verb or verb-noun)[6] makes a significant difference in usability.

Most interface guidelines correctly recommend noun-verb interaction (Apple 1987, Hewlett Packard 1987, IBM 1988, Microsoft 1995). A locus-of-attention analysis shows the benefits.

- *Error reduction.* Verb-noun style sets up a mode. Once you have chosen a command in this style, it will take effect on the next selection you make. If there is a delay or a distraction between issuing the command and making the selection, the ensuing action may be surprising when you next make a selection. With noun-verb construction, commands are executed when issued, when your locus of attention is the command.

- *Speed.* You do not have to shift your attention away from your content—which is what triggered the need to perform an operation—to the command and then back to find your place in the content again to make the selection. With noun-verb construction, you make the selection—your locus of attention—and then switch your attention to the command. There is one less change of locus of attention.

---

6. The terminology *object-action* versus *action-object* is also used.

- *Simplicity and reversibility.* In the verb–noun paradigm, you need to have an escape or a cancel feature associated with the command; if you issue a command and then decide against it, you are in a mode where the system expects you to make a selection, so a mechanism must be provided so that you can signal the system that you do not want to make a selection, you want to issue another command. In noun–verb construction, if you decide to change your selection, you simply make another selection. No Cancel button or cancel method is necessary.

Every interface guideline I have seen that advocates noun–verb construction also permits the verb–noun style of commands. The Microsoft manual states that verb–noun style is necessary for palettes, such as those for the various brush styles in paint programs (Microsoft 1995). This is not strictly true. A pure noun–verb model is possible: You draw in a default set of attributes, such as a thin black line, and then apply color, width, texture, or whatever via commands. However, we really want to see the full effect of each stroke as we make it—with all of its attributes in full flower.

The conventional method, whereby you first select the attributes from one or more palettes—much as you dip a real brush into this or that paint and then make your mark—does lead to the mode errors we have come to expect in such situations. It also makes sense to let the mode you have chosen persist until you deliberately change it. Therefore, it will happen that you start to draw and find unexpected attributes appearing. Fortunately, the appearance of what you are drawing is your locus of attention; if the software is humane, you will be able to immediately undo the offending mark, change the attributes to those desired, and continue working. The mode errors are annoying, and it would be gratifying to find a noun–verb or other nonmodal method that would be effective in this situation, but to the best of my knowledge, nobody has as yet found a solution to this particular problem.

In general, the noun–verb paradigm is preferred. Verb–noun methods should be limited to palette selections intended for immediate use.

Case Study of a Noun–Verb Fix to a Verb–Noun Problem

Workers in various departments of a multinational corporation used a computer system to requisition products. This example illustrates one way to change a seemingly natural verb–noun situation to a noun–verb one. In practice, this change eliminated the errors that the initial design had caused and also speeded the requisitioning process.

The original process had three steps.

1. Choose the department from which the order was originating. This consisted of clicking on a check box alongside a department name. One of the check boxes was prechecked as a default. The default was the department in which the computer was situated.

2. Choose the desired items from a scrollable list of items, each item having an associated text box into which you could type the desired quantity for each item.

3. Click on one of two buttons at the bottom of the display: either Cancel Order or Confirm Order.

The first problem was that users failed to select their department when they were ordering from other than their usual computer station. A solution that had been suggested by the company's designers was to provide no default, forcing the user to select a department first, every time. Then, they pointed out, the only possible error would be to choose the wrong department. This solution, however, is annoying to users, who usually work at a specific station and thus might be irritated at having to supply information already available to the system.

The problem was a disguised verb–noun situation: You first entered what you wanted to do (deliver these items to the department) and then chose what you wanted to have delivered. When you entered the requisitioning screen, the item or items you needed were, or recently had been, at your locus of attention.

Part of the solution was to put the checklist of items at the top of the requisition display. Thus, the user would start by selecting the desired items. The location list, previously unlabeled, was given a descriptive label: "To which department do you want the requisitioned items delivered?"

If the system could determine—from the user's log-on information—the user's department, a new item was automatically added to the top of the list of departments. It was labeled "My Department" and, like the other items on the list, had a check box.

The rest of the list contained all of the departments in alphabetical order and a check box for each. When the user placed a check in one of the boxes, a message appeared: "Your items have been requisitioned." The message automatically disappeared at the user's next action.

With the redesigned interface, choosing a department represented an action—a verb—namely, to cause the previously selected items to be sent. Psychologically, it was now an act of closure rather than a preliminary step. Also, note that at this point, the requisition form had been filled in; the user's attention was no longer on the desired items but rather on having them delivered. The work flow now accorded with the path that the user's locus of attention would ordinarily follow.

No default location was needed, because the interface supplied psychological closure by indicating that the user had finished with choosing items and wanted them sent. The initial design also had required a confirmatory click, whereas the new design did not impose an additional click on the user; the key-click count had typically decreased by one. With the new design, users could still form a habit of choosing their usual location from the location list and, on the rare occasions this option was desired, might sometimes forget to specify that they wanted the order sent elsewhere. However, even with this potential fault, the new design was a major improvement over the previous one.

3-4 Visibility and Affordances

On a clear disk you can seek forever.

—*Source unknown*

Whether a product is a handheld two-way radio or a computer's desktop, it is not always clear what functions are available, what they do, or how they are accessed. You should be able to use your senses to easily discover both what abilities are available and how they are to be operated.

An interface feature is **visible** if it either is currently accessible to a human sense organ—usually the eyes, although this discussion applies also to other sensory modalities—or was so recently perceived that it has not yet faded from short-term memory. If a feature is not visible, we say that it is **invisible**. For an interface to work well, "[j]ust the right things have to be visible: to indicate what parts operate and how, to indicate how the user is to interact with the device. Visibility indicates the mapping between intended actions and actual operations" (Norman 1988, p. 8).[7] If an interface forces you to memorize the fact that a feature exists, that feature is invisible. If you are forced to root around in the interface until, by luck and perseverance, you reach a sequence of actions that activates a feature, such a feature is not visible. If you have to use a help system to discover how to perform an operation, the methods for invoking that operation are invisible. Many computer games are, essentially, undocumented interfaces in which the controls, or their mapping to desired effects, are invisible. Add documentation and these games become trivial. *Most people do not want to play games when they are trying to get work done. It is up to the designer of an interface to make every feature of a product visible.*

In designing to accommodate visibility, each function and the method of operating it would be apparent—to most people in the culture for which it is intended—by merely looking at it. A control that has this attribute has come to be called an **affordance** (Norman 1998, p. 123). "Affordances provide strong clues to the operations of things. . . . Knobs are for turning. Slots are for inserting things into. Balls are for throwing or bouncing" (Norman 1988, p. 9). If you, as a designer, put a knob such as is used in volume controls on a product, people will attempt to turn that knob. Put on something that looks like a pushbutton, and people will push it. Whether a feature is or is not an affordance depends on the experience and the background of the people who will be using the product and the context in which the feature appears.

In analyzing interfaces, we should always ask how the user knows that an action is possible, and we should always require that each visible feature provide a recognizable affordance. Icons are often considered the epitome of visible affordances, but they do not always serve this function, as we discuss in Section 6-3.

Visibility is more than just detectable existence. An object may be visible in the sense that it is there, but it might be too small to be noticed, or it may have too little contrast to be readily distinguished from the background. Optimizing the perceptual qualities of an interface is an important ergonomic consideration, but the concern here is with the cognitive properties of interfaces.

---

7. This book, *The Psychology of Everyday Things,* is not to be missed.

Affordance Avoidance: BART

It is the interface to its ticket machines that brings Bay Area Rapid Transit (BART) into this book. The machines at a local station are the result of the transit authority's ignorance of 25 years of experience with the old ticket-dispensing robots. As I stand in line at one of the two machines not presently out of service, I watch person after person baffled by the machine's layout. Although experienced with the machines myself, I still fumble at the unnatural sequence of operations that they require.

The obvious way to start the interaction, and what nearly everybody whom I've observed tries at first, is to put in money or an old ticket, which is a money-equivalent. That's how vending machines work: Put in money, make choice, get stuff. It is a cultural paradigm.

The BART ticket-vending machines must have been designed on another planet. First, you choose between BART and BART-MUNI buttons. (A pamphlet, available nowhere in the vicinity, explains the subtle difference.) These buttons are at the top of the wall of the machine face: a reasonable place to start but an unreasonable transaction with which to start. The slots into which you then put your ticket (to the left), coins (in the middle), or bills (lower right) are widely separated instead of being clustered. The LCD display is up high at top center, where short people cannot easily read it; in any case, it is far enough from the rest of the interface that many people do not notice it at all. Maybe it's good they do not see it, in that its response time is so slow that people who do watch it either repeat their actions in hope of forcing a response or stand there wondering whether the machine is broken, which it often is.

Then there's the "correction" button, labeled as though it is to be used in case you've made a mistake that has to be corrected. In fact, you do not use this button for correcting a mistake: You use it if you want the ticket to be issued for less than the total amount of money that you have put in. That is, it simply tells the machine you want some change back.

Another indication that the new machines are badly designed is the bright, colorful, large numbers "1, 2, 3, 4" and the big arrows presumably placed to guide you. If the front of the machine were well laid out, you wouldn't need crutches. The numbers do not help

tremendously anyway, because you must remember what step you
are executing (say, step 2) while you put in your money ($5), know-
ing that you only want to get a $3 ticket so you must hit the correc-
tion button in the next step (step 3), keeping in mind that you'll
want to count your change ($2) that will come in the form of quar-
ters (eight of them). Hurry! You can hear the 7:06 train coming!
What step did you say you were on? When you find a computer
interface that requires bright colors and myriad explanatory legends
to guide you, you can guess that the design has gone astray.

Here is one way in which the BART machines could work.
Remember, however, that were you consulting to BART, you
would request user testing of your proposed design to verify that
people will use it as you have predicted.

On the left—because English and Spanish are written from left to
right—is the slot for old tickets, a horizontal slot for bills, and a small
vertical slot for coins, grouped together and well labeled. The display—located at average eye level—reads: "Put in money OR your
old BART ticket OR both." As you put in each, the total value
accrued appears *immediately* in the LCD display with this message:

> You now have put in $4.55.
>
> If you want a ticket for more than $4.55, put in more money or
> another old ticket
>
> If you want a ticket for less than $4.55 press:
>
> <u>Change Ticket Amount</u>
>
> If you want a ticket for $4.55, press one of these buttons:
>
> <u>Issue BART Ticket</u>
> <u>Issue MUNI-BART Ticket</u>

If the user selects "Change Ticket Amount," he is asked to type in
the amount for which he wants the ticket issued and to press the
large ENTER button that is under the numeric key pad. The user is
returned to the display that shows the current total and asks him to
increase it, decrease it, or OK it. When the ticket is issued, any
change due the user is returned. For the experienced traveler with
the right amount of money in hand, this interface reduces six
actions to these two: put in money and then press an Issue-Ticket
button.

3-5 Monotony

Man is an over-complicated organism. If he is doomed to extinction he will die out for want of simplicity.

—*Ezra Pound*

Designers of interfaces often present users with a choice of methods. For example, both a menu item and a keyboard shortcut may execute the same command. In most word processors, you can move a contiguous portion of the text by either (1) the three steps of selecting, cutting, and pasting or (2) the two steps of selecting and dragging. Also, the selection process itself can be invoked in more than one way. The user has a smorgasbord of methods.

One justification for having multiple methods to do a given task is that some users prefer one method and other users prefer a different method. For example, a novice user might find menus easier to learn, although an expert user might rather keep her hands on the keyboard and issue commands by typing them (see Section 3-6). Another justification is that one method—for example, selecting, cutting, and pasting—is useful between distant portions of a document, and the other method—selecting and dragging—is effective only when the source and destination are both visible on the display. Another reason for a plurality of methods is that each of them is sanctioned by custom, and the developers felt it wise to accommodate as many previously developed skills as possible.

This last reason, called *backward compatibility*,[8] is the weakest and can lead to absurd interfaces that are an accumulation of incompatible methods. When I was grounded and waiting for the weather to improve during a long flight by commercial jet, I went to the cockpit, where I studied an autopilot that had no fewer than five ways of entering coordinates and similar numbers of methods for performing most of its other functions. When I asked the pilot for the rationale, she said that it had been built to functionally resemble, as closely as possible, autopilots from other aircraft that pilots might have trained on and thus avoid the need for expensive retraining. The question was whether the tactic was successful and whether the old units had been duplicated exactly. As she explained, the pilots not only had to learn the small but annoying differences between their old system and the emulation of their old system on the new autopilot but also were required to learn the four other ways of using the autopilot. A pilot must be familiar with *every* aspect of *every* piece of equipment in the cockpit; besides, many of the newer features of the autopilot were

---

8. I usually suggest that if the word *compatibility* is eliminated from this phrase, its true meaning becomes apparent.

available in only some of the emulations; those of the earlier autopilots did not have those features because the autopilots being copied had not had them.

The tactic of portmanteau interface design, or just toss every method you can think of into the bag, increased training time, produced a harder-to-use autopilot, and, as the pilot noted, increased cockpit confusion and opportunities for errors. She did not say so, but it also probably increased the cost and complexity of the product, the manuals, and the cost of maintenance. The same is true for any interface that is a conglomeration of disparate design philosophies, accumulated over time; this includes the Macintosh and Windows.

I use the term *monotonous*, tongue partially in cheek, to describe an interface having only one way to accomplish a task (See Appendix B; Alzofon and Raskin 1985, p. 95). **Monotony** is the dual of modelessness in an interface. In a modeless interface, a given user gesture has one and only one result: Gesture g always results in action a. However, there is nothing to prevent a second gesture, h, from also resulting in action a. A monotonous interface is one in which any desired result has only one means by which it may be invoked: Action a is invoked by gesture g and in no other way. An interface that is completely modeless and monotonous has a one-to-one correspondence between cause (commands) and effect (actions). The more monotony an interface has for a given task space, the easier it is for the user to develop automaticity, which, after all, is fostered by not having to make decisions about what method to use.

Another cause of nonmonotonous design is managerial indecision. Given two or more choices of interface methods and no rational method of choosing one above the others, I have seen the problem "solved" by expediently putting in *all* of the proposed methods. This is rationalized as giving the user a choice, as if the user were an interface expert and will make the most productive choice.

A common myth, discussed in more detail in Section 3-6, is that beginners and expert users of a system require radically different interfaces. Designers speak in terms of "the tradeoffs between ease of learning and speed of execution in a system" (Card, Moran, and Newell 1983, p. 419). This may be true of particular interface designs, but I have seen no demonstration that it is necessarily a property of all interface designs; in particular, it is not a property of the kinds of designs discussed in this book. *Present desktop GUIs are a compound of at least two distinct interfaces, a relatively visible and learnable but time-consuming menu-based system and an incomplete keyboard-based collection of hard-to-learn and unmemorable shortcuts. Two wrongs do not make a right.*

When you have to choose among methods, your locus of attention is drawn from the task and temporarily becomes the decision itself. This is a primary reason for choosing to design a monotonous system. If the conditions for making the decision are sufficiently clear and distinct, the path you take in each case can become habitual, and you have monotonized the situation. It still behooves the designer to seek an efficient monotonous solution to gain benefits, including ease of learning, simplicity of implementation, minimization of documentation, and lowered maintenance costs. These benefits are either free to the implementers or can be had for the relatively small one-time cost of careful design and testing. Monotony does not mean that the same content cannot be arrived at in many ways but that there should not be multiple gestures to invoke the same command.

Monotony happens spontaneously. Many users monotonize the interfaces they use by choosing one method and sticking to it, ignoring alternatives whatever the situation. Computer gurus who pride themselves on knowing every wrinkle of a system often decry such users as amateurs; nonetheless, the "amateurs" may be using the interface more efficiently than the gurus do. From the point of view of an implementer, such users are wasting features; from the point of view of the users, it is the implementers who are wasting resources.

I believe that an interface that is both modeless and, insofar as possible, monotonous—all other design features being of at least normal quality for a modern interface—would be extraordinarily pleasant to use. A user would be able to develop an unusually high degree of trust in his habits. The interface would, from these two properties alone, tend to fade from the user's consciousness, allowing him to give his full attention to the task at hand. The psychological effects of totally (or near totally) modeless and monotonous systems is an area of interface design ripe for experimental study.

If I am correct, the use of a product based on modelessness and monotony would soon become so habitual as to be nearly addictive, leading to a user population devoted to and loyal to the product. Its users would find moving to a competitor's product psychologically difficult. Unlike selling illicit drugs, marketing an addictive interface is legal, and the product is beneficial to its users; in another way, it is just like selling illicit drugs: extremely profitable.

3-6 Myth of the Beginner-Expert Dichotomy

We're humans first, beginners or experts second.

—*Clifford Nass, CBC "Quirks and Quarks" radio program, 23 January 1994*

Psychologist Clifford Nass's point is similar to one that this book makes: Our interface designs must begin by accommodating universal human frailties and exploiting universal human strengths. We must make sure that every detail of an interface matches both our cognitive capabilities and the demands of the task (not that those two objectives exhaust our concerns). His comment also reflects the common assumption that users can be grouped into two classes: beginners and experts, perhaps with a few temporarily in transition. This dichotomy is invalid. As a user of a complex system, you are neither a beginner nor an expert, and you cannot be placed on a single continuum between these two poles. You independently know or do not know each feature or each related set of features that work similarly to one another. You may know how to use many commands and features of a software package; you may even work with the package professionally, and people may seek your advice on using it. Yet you may not know how to use or even know about the existence of certain other commands or even whole categories of commands in that same package. For example, a user of a photo-processing application who produces only online images may never need, or even learn of, that same application's facility for doing color separations, a feature needed primarily by commercial printers.

Interface designers have tried various approaches to accommodate the premise that users can be separated into beginners and experts. Because this premise is false, the approaches have failed. Adaptive systems that shift automatically from beginner mode to expert mode when they judge that your competence has reached a certain level are a good example. If you are using such a system in beginner mode and it suddenly shifts into expert mode, you will find yourself on unfamiliar ground, at least with regard to a portion of the system. A system that shifts piecemeal, feature by feature, is no better. It will feel unstable and unsettling, because the habits that you were developing as a novice yesterday become useless when the feature shifts into expert mode today.

One web-based program I studied promoted you to expert status after you had used it once successfully. The program put you back into beginner mode when you had not used it for six months. Any such arbitrary schedule may not accord with a user's personal rate of learning and memory decay. If a program that promoted you switches to beginner mode after too short a time, you will feel annoyed at being forced to use the tedious beginner method. If the program does not switch back to beginner mode in time, you will be faced with features that you have forgotten how to use. Given present technology, a system cannot know when you have forgotten how to use a given feature, so it cannot know when it should shift back to beginner mode. A program that quizzed you from time to time to assess your level of expertise would be obnoxious.

Most attempts to make interfaces adaptive are ill-advised; whenever a system changes automatically, even if the change is as small as, say, a reordered set of items on a menu, your expectations are upset and your habituation is frustrated. (Microsoft features adaptive menus in its Windows 2000 operating system.[9]) On the other hand, there is no theory that tells us that the same fixed interface cannot work well over the full span of a person's experience with it, from novice to old timer. It seems best not to have to shift paradigms during your use of a product, and no elaborate analysis is needed to reveal the advantage in having to learn only one interface to a task.

It is easy to fall into the trap of designing different interfaces for different classes of users, because by doing so, you can make sweeping assumptions that simplify the design process. Few such assumptions are likely to be true of every user in any reasonably large class of users that you specify. The antidote is to view an interface not from the perspective of a class of users but rather through the eyes of an individual. Every person who uses software over a long period goes through a relatively brief period of learning for each feature or command and a far longer period of routine (and, we hope, automatic) use. We do need to design systems that are easy to learn and understand, but it is more important that we make sure that these systems can be efficiently used in the long run. The exceptions are applications that will be used only briefly, so that every user is a novice, and habituation is not an issue. One example of such an interface is that for a computer-driven kiosk at an exhibition.

The learning phase of working with a feature involves your conscious attention. Therefore, simplicity, clarity of function, and visibility are of great importance. The expert phase is predominantly characterized by unconscious use of the feature; such use is enhanced by such qualities as aptness to the task, modelessness, and monotony. These sets of requirements are not in conflict; therefore, *a well-designed and humane interface does not have to be split into beginner and expert subsystems.*

This is not to say that an interface must not be split on these lines. However, if you find yourself designing an interface and are tempted to provide "expert" shortcuts, consider whether you should instead redesign the existing method so that it satisfies the needs of all users with one mechanism.

---

9. Windows 2000 was a new product as this section was being written, and I was able to interview only a few users. A typical remark was, "Adaptive menus seemed like a cool idea, but the first time a menu changed on me, I found it upsetting. I don't like the idea any more."

FOUR

Quantification

The harmony of the world is made manifest in Form and Number, and the heart and soul and all the poetry of Natural Philosophy are embodied in the concept of mathematical beauty.

—*D'Arcy Wentworth Thompson,* On Growth and Form *(1917)*

A number of methods for analyzing interface details quantitatively are available. However, explicit directions on how to use them are rare. This chapter gives an easy-to-use treatment and fully worked-out examples of Card, Moran, and Newell's keystroke-level GOMS model, Raskin's measures of efficiency, Hick's Law, and Fitts' law.

4-1 Quantitative Analyses of Interfaces

He fingered and fingered the computer—it simply amazed Melrose that the machine supposed to take the pain out of all sorts of niggling jobs took more time to perform a simple one than it would have taken Bub to do by hand ten times over.

—*Martha Grimes,* The Stargazey *(a detective novel)*

Many qualitative methods and heuristics are useful for analyzing and understanding interface design. These methods form the majority of the content of most books on the subject, including those cited in the references for Shneiderman, Norman, and Mayhew. For example, what an experienced interface designer can learn from passively observing a test of a new interface with a few subjects can be as valuable as what she can learn from any quantitative analysis. My concentration on quantitative methods is not meant to denigrate the importance of qualitative techniques but rather to help even the balance by emphasizing the numerical and empirically testable methods that are not yet widely used. Quantitative methods can often reduce argument to calculation; a further, and most important, benefit is that *understanding* why *the quantitative methods work guides us to understanding important aspects of how humans interact with machines.*

One of the best quantitative analyses of interface design is the classic model of goals, objects, methods, and selection rules (GOMS), which first gained attention in the 1980s (Card, Moran, and Newell 1983). GOMS modeling allows you to predict how long an experienced worker will take to perform a particular operation when using a given interface design. After discussing the GOMS model, I present quantitative methods for determining interface efficiency, cursor movement speed, and the time cost of decision making.

4-2 GOMS Keystroke-Level Model

The aim of exact science is to reduce the problems of nature to the determination of quantities by operations with numbers.

—James Clerk Maxwell, On Faraday's Lines of Force *(1856)*

I will introduce only the simplest—yet nonetheless valuable—aspect of the GOMS method: the keystroke-level model. We designers who know GOMS rarely use a detailed and formal analysis of an interface design, but that is due, in part, to our having absorbed the fundamentals of GOMS and of other quantitative methods such that our designs inherently incorporate GOMS teachings. We do bring formal analysis into play when choosing between two approaches to interface design in which small differences in speed can have significant economic or psychological effects. We can sometimes benefit from the impressive accuracy of the more complete GOMS models, such as critical-path method GOMS (CPM-GOMS) or a version called natural GOMS language (NGOMSL), which takes into account nonexpert behavior, such as learning times. We can, for example, predict how long it will take a user to execute a particular set of interface actions to within an absolute error of less than 5 percent. In these advanced models, almost all predictions fall within 1 standard deviation of the measured times (Gray, John, and Atwood 1993, p. 278). In a field in which religious wars are waged over interface designs and in which gurus often have widely varying opinions, it is advantageous to have in your armamentarium quantitative, experimentally validated, and theoretically sound techniques. For a good overview and bibliography of the various GOMS models, including her own CPM-GOMS model, see John 1995.

4-2-1 Interface Timings

Numerical precision is the very soul of science.

—*D'Arcy Wentworth Thompson,* On Growth and Form *(1917)*

When they developed the GOMS model, its inventors observed that the time it takes the user-computer system to perform a task is the sum of the times it takes for the system to perform the serial elementary gestures that the task comprises. Although different users might have widely varying times, the researchers found that for many *comparative* analyses of tasks involving use of a keyboard and a graphical input device, you could use a set of typical times rather than measuring the times of individuals. By means of careful laboratory experiments, they developed a set of timings for different gestures. In giving the timings, I follow the original nomenclature, in which each of the times is designated by a one-letter mnemonic (Card, Moran, and Newell 1983):

$K = 0.2$ sec   Keying: The time it takes to tap a key on the keyboard

$P = 1.1$ sec   Pointing: The time it takes a user to point to a position on a display

$H = 0.4$ sec   Homing: The time it takes a user's hand to move from the keyboard to the GID or from the GID to the keyboard

$M = 1.35$ sec   Mentally preparing: The time it takes a user to prepare mentally for the next step

R Responding: The time a user must wait for a computer to respond to input

In practice, these numbers vary widely; K can be 0.08 sec for a 135-wpm highly skilled typist, 0.2 sec for a more typical 55-wpm skilled typist,

0.28 sec for a 40-wpm average unskilled typist, or 1.2 sec for a beginning typist. Typing speed is not independent of what is being typed: It takes most people about 0.5 sec to type a random letter, given a set of randomly chosen letters to type. Typing messy codes—for example, e-mail addresses—takes most people about 0.75 sec per character. The value K includes time it takes the user to make corrections that he has caught immediately. Shift is counted as a separate keystroke.

The wide variability of each measure explains why we cannot use this simplified model to obtain absolute timings with any degree of certainty; by using the typical values, however, we usually obtain the correct *ranking* of the performance times of two interface designs. If you are evaluating complex interfaces that include overlapping time dependencies or if you must generate accurate absolute times, you should use the more complete models, which are not discussed in this book, such as CPM-GOMS.

Double Dysclicksia

The interface technique called double clicking, that is, tapping the GID button twice within a small time window and without any significant cursor movement between the taps, as an interface technique suffers from problems. You cannot always predict what objects on the display will or will not respond to a double click, and it is not always clear what will happen if there is a response. There is no indication on displayable items that double clicking is supposed to produce a response: The functionality is invisible. The way that double clicking is used in many current interfaces, the user must remember not only *which* items are double clickable but also how different classes of interface features respond to this action.

The first two burdens on the user could be at least partially alleviated by new screen conventions. The act of double clicking is, however, itself problematical. Double clicking requires operating a mouse button twice at the same location or at two locations in very close and, in most cases, within a short time, typically 500 msec. If the user clicks too slowly, the machine responds to two single clicks rather than to one double click. If the user jiggles the mouse excessively between clicks, the same error occurs. If the user taps the GID button twice in too short a time period, as when trying to select text within a word while working within certain word processors, the machine considers the two taps as a double click and selects the whole word.

A problem arises when the user is trying to select a graphical item that can be repositioned with the GID. Because the GID is likely to move when the user is pressing the GID buttons quickly, graphical applications, instead of reading a double click, may read a drag-and-drop and change the item's position. Similarly, to change the text in a text box, the user may find it necessary to reposition the accidentally moved box and to make the text edit originally intended.

Some of us are unaffected by dysclicksia: These lucky people never miss with the mouse; they single and double click with insouciance and panache, do not suffer from side effects of clicking, always remember what will and what will not respond to double clicking, and can shoot a flying bird with a .357-caliber revolver while driving along a twisty mountain road. But we can't assume that all users are so lucky. We must design for the dysclicksic user and remain aware of the problems inherent in using double clicks in an interface.[1]

The duration of the machine response time, R, can have an unexpected effect on user actions. If a user operates a control and nothing appears on the display for more than approximately 250 msec, she is likely to become uneasy, to try again, or to begin to wonder whether the system is failing.

We cannot build products that can complete any operation within human reaction time, but our interfaces can always, within that time, give feedback that the input has been received and recognized. Otherwise, user actions—often flailing at the keyboard, trying to get a response—during a delay can start the system off on unintended activities, causing further delay or damaging the user's content. For example, if you try to download a file while accessing America Online from a browser, such as Netscape's, there is often a long delay. No feedback lets you know that progress is being made; a small, static message far from the locus of attention says only that the computer is awaiting reply. After a few seconds, inexperienced users start clicking at buttons on the display, which stops the download—again without feedback.

It is important that interfaces provide feedback if delays are unavoidable; display a progress bar (Figure 4.1) that accurately reflects the time remaining. If you cannot predict how much time an operation will take, say so! Do not lie to or misinform users.

---

[1] The term *dysclicksia,* a disease for which the only permanent cure is good design, was coined by Pam Martin (personal communication 1997).

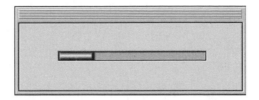

Figure 4.1. A progress bar. It is important that it represent time linearly. A textual statement of time remaining, if accurate, is also a humane feature when delays are unavoidable.

4-2-2 GOMS Calculations

We begin the calculation of the time it takes to perform a method, such as "move your hand from the graphical input device to the keyboard and type a letter," by listing the operations from the GOMS list of gestures (see Section 4-2-1) used in this method, in this case HK. Listing the gestures (K, P, and H) is the easy part of creating an instance of GOMS models. The more difficult part of developing an instance of a keystroke-level GOMS model is figuring out at what points the user will stop to perform an unconscious mental operation: the mental preparation (M) times. The basic rules—following the methods of Card, Moran, and Newell 1983, p. 265—for deciding where mental operations occur in a method are presented in Table 4.1. In Section 4-2-3, we look at how these rules are applied in practice.

In these rules, a **string** is a sequence of characters. A **delimiter** is a character that marks the beginning or the end of a meaningful string of text, such as a natural-language word or a telephone number. For example, spaces are the delimiters for most words; a period is the most common delimiter at the end of a sentence; parentheses delimit parenthetical remarks; and so on. The operators are K, P, and H. When a command needs information, such as when you use the command that sets the time for an alarm to go off and have to supply the time, the information you supply is an **argument** for that command.

4-2-3 GOMS Calculation Examples

An interface design usually begins with a task or a set of tasks that need to be accomplished. A statement of the task and the means available for implementing a solution are often formulated as a requirement or specification. In this example, the user is personified as Hal, a laboratory assistant.

TABLE 4.1. HEURISTICS FOR PLACING
MENTAL OPERATORS

Rule 0 Initial insertion of candidate *M*s

Insert *M*s in front of all *K*s (keystrokes). Place *M*s in front of all *P*s (acts of pointing with the GID) that select commands, but do not place *M*s in front of any *P*s that point to arguments of those commands.

Rule 1 Deletion of anticipated *M*s

If an operator following an *M* is fully anticipated in an operator just previous to that *M*, then delete that *M*. For example, if you move the GID with the intent of tapping the GID button when you reach the target of your GID move, then you delete, by this rule, the *M* you inserted as a consequence of rule 0. In this case, *PMK* becomes *PK*.

Rule 2 Deletion of *M*s within cognitive units

If a string of *MK*s belongs to a cognitive unit, then delete all the *M*s but the first. A cognitive unit is a contiguous sequence of typed characters that form a command name or that is required as an argument to a command. For example, *Y*, *move*, *Helen of Troy*, or *4564.23* can be examples of cognitive units.

Rule 3 Deletion of *M*s before consecutive terminators

If a *K* is a redundant delimiter at the end of a cognitive unit, such as the delimiter of a command immediately following the delimiter of its argument, then delete the *M* in front of it.

Rule 4 Deletion of *M*s that are terminators of commands

If a *K* is a delimiter that follows a constant string—for example, a command name or any typed entity that is the same every time that you use it—then delete the *M* in front of it. (Adding the delimiter will have become habitual, and thus the delimiter will have become part of the string and not require a separate *M*.) But if the *K* is a delimiter for an argument string or any string that can vary, then keep the *M* in front of it.

Rule 5 Deletion of overlapped *M*s

Do not count any portion of an *M* that overlaps an *R*—a delay, with the user waiting for a response from the computer.

Requirement

Hal works at a computer, typing reports; he is occasionally interrupted by one or another of the researchers in the room, and is asked to convert a temperature reading from degrees Fahrenheit (F) or Celsius (C) to degrees C or F, respectively. For example, Hal might be asked, "Please convert 302.25 degrees from Fahrenheit to

Celsius." Hal must use the keyboard or GID to enter the temperature provided; voice or other input means are not available. Conversions from C to F and from F to C are approximately equally likely to be required. About 25 percent of the temperatures called out are negative, although the digits are unpredictable and equally distributed, and only 10 percent of the temperatures have integer values, such as 37 degrees. The numerical result must appear on the display; no other output means are available. Hal reads to the researcher the converted value from the screen. The input and the output must allow for at least ten digits on each side of the decimal point.

In designing an interface for a system that allows Hal to do his job, your goal is to minimize the time it takes Hal to do the conversion. Speed and accuracy must be maximized; screen real estate is not limited. The window, or area of the display in which the temperature conversion takes place, is already active and waiting for Hal's input via GID or keyboard. The way Hal interacts with the interface to return to his typing on the computer is not your concern; your job is finished as soon as the result is displayed.

In estimating the time it takes Hal to use the interface, assume an average of four typed characters in an entered temperature, including any decimal point and sign. Also assume—unrealistically, but for simplicity's sake—that Hal's typing is perfect; error detection and notification are not needed.

Now, I would like you to stop reading so that you can design an interface for this simple example. It will not take long to write down your proposed solution, along with sketches of the display that Hal will see; do not just think about this problem but rather write about it as well. (You will be tempted to read on without honoring my request. Please reconsider. The next few sections will make much more interesting reading if you have already tried to solve the problem yourself.) After designing your interface, read the two GOMS analyses that follow. Then you will be ready to analyze your own interface.

4-2-3-1 Hal's Interface: Solution 1, Dialog Box

The instructions in Figure 4.2 are reasonably clear; from them we can write down the method that Hal must use in terms of the gestures of the GOMS model. The GOMS representation is shown growing incrementally as each new gesture is added to the method.

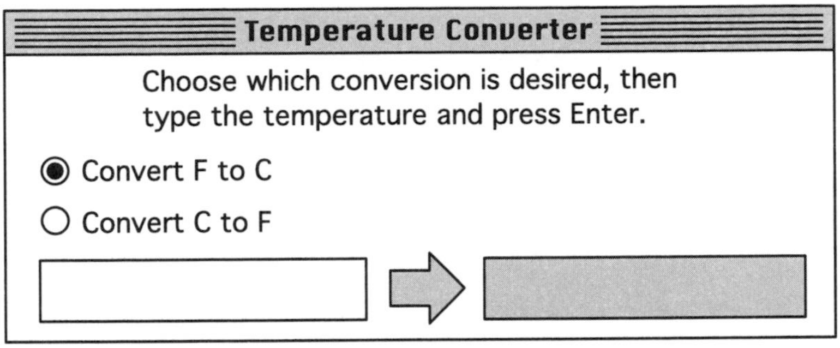

Figure 4.2. A dialog box solution with radio buttons.

- Move hand to the graphical input device:

  H

- Point to the desired radio button:

  H P

- Click on the radio button:

  H P K

Half of the time, the interface will already have the correct conversion chosen, and Hal will not need to click on the radio button. We consider first the case in which it is not the one already chosen.

- Move hands back to the keyboard:

  H P K H

- Type the four characters:

  H P K H K K K K

- Tap *Enter:*

  H P K H K K K K K

The keystroke for the tap of the Enter key completes the method portion of the analysis. Using rule 0, we add *M*s in front of all of the *K*s and *P*s except those *P*s that point to arguments, of which there are none in this example:

H M P M K H M K M K M K M K M K

Rule 1 tells us to change *P M K* to *P K* and to eliminate any other fully anticipated *M*s, of which there are none in this example. Rule 2 eliminates

*M*s in the middle of strings, such as in the string that represents the temperature. Applying these two rules leaves

$H\,M\,P\,K\,H\,M\,K\,K\,K\,K\,M\,K$

The *M* before the final *K* is required by rule 4. Rules 3 and 5 do not apply in this example.

The next step is to add the times represented by the letters. (Recall that $K = 0.2$, $P = 1.1$, $H = 0.4$, and $M = 1.35$):

$H + M + P + K + H + M + K + K + K + K + M + K =$

$0.4 + 1.35 + 1.1 + 0.2 + 0.4 + 1.35 + 4 \star (0.2) + 1.35 + 0.2 = 7.15$ seconds

In the case in which the correct conversion is already selected, the method is

$M\,K\,K\,K\,K\,M\,K$

$M + K + K + K + K + M + K = 3.7$ sec

By the requirements document, these two cases are equally likely. Thus, the average time it will take Hal to use this interface for one conversion task will be $(7.15 + 3.7) / 2 \approx 5.4$ seconds. But, because the two methods that Hal has to use are different, it will be difficult for him to operate this interface automatically. One of the open problems in the quantitative analysis of interfaces is how to estimate error rates from a given interface design.

Next, we explore a graphical interface that makes extensive use of a familiar metaphor.

4-2-3-2 Hal's Interface: Solution 2, GUI

The interface shown in Figure 4.3 uses realistic representations of thermometers to indicate temperature. Hal can lower or raise the pointer on each thermometer in Figure 4.3 by using the drag method with the GID. Hal indicates which conversion he wants by moving the arrow on either the Celsius or the Fahrenheit thermometer. He does not type any characters; he simply selects the temperature on the input thermometer. As he moves one of the pointers, the pointer on the other thermometer moves to the corresponding temperature. To set the required precision, Hal expands and contracts the scales; he can also change the range. When Hal changes the scale or the range on one thermometer, those on the other thermometer change automatically to cover approximately the same set of temperatures. Numeri-

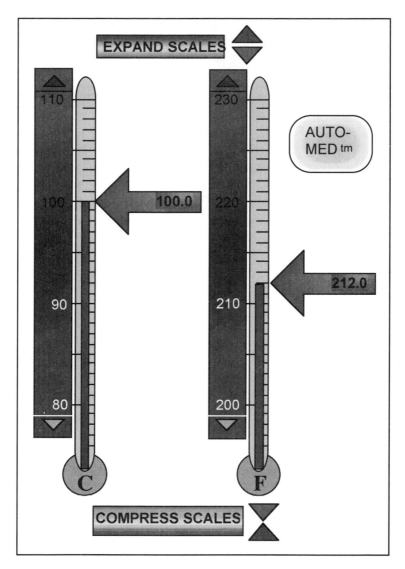

Figure 4.3. A GUI for Hal's interface. (See color insert.)

cal readouts are provided on the movable arrow. The temperature is indicated both numerically and with a bar, so Hal can use either the graphical or the character-based representations of the data to accommodate his learning style or personal preferences. The Auto-Med feature changes the ranges such that they are centered on 37 degrees Celsius and 98.6 degrees Fahrenheit, in case someone in the lab is working with human body temperatures; this feature is designed to save time.

Clicking on Expand Scales or Compress Scales increases or decreases by a factor of 10 the values at tick marks on the vertical thermometers. To get quickly to a far-distant temperature, Hal expands the scale and scrolls up or down until the desired range is in view, puts the arrow near the desired temperature, and then compresses the scale, adjusting the arrow if necessary, until the desired precision is attained.

A GOMS keystroke-level analysis of this graphical interface is complex because the method Hal uses depends on where the converter is presently set and what range and precision Hal needs. We look first at the fastest case, in which the range and the precision of the C or the F thermometer happen to be already set as Hal wants them to be. This analysis will give us the minimum time needed to use this interface.

- Write down the gestures Hal uses as he moves his hand to the GID and clicks and holds down the GID button on the desired arrow:

  H P K

- Continue listing gestures as Hal moves the arrow until it points to the correct value and then releases the GID button:

  H P K P K

- Place *M*s according to rule 0:

  H M P M K M K

- Eliminate two *M*s according to rule 1:

  H M P K K

There are no cognitive units, no consecutive terminators, and no other reasons to apply rules 2 through 5. We find the total time by adding the times for each gesture:

$$H + M + P + K + K$$

$$0.4 + 1.35 + 1.1 + 0.2 + 0.2 = 3.25 \text{ seconds}$$

This calculation applies to the lucky case in which the input thermometer was preset to the appropriate range and resolution. Now consider the case in which Hal wants to expand the scale factor so that he can see the desired temperature, change the range, compress the scale factor to get adequate resolution, and then move the arrow. I will write down the method Hal uses, without going through a step-by-step derivation. (I assume that Hal is a perfect user and does not have to juggle back and forth to find the right places on the thermometer.) Hal has to use the arrows to scroll several times. Each scrolling operation may require several gestures; the computer then animates the scrolling operation, which takes time. To estimate scrolling times for the analysis, I built a similar interface and measured scrolling times, which were all 3 seconds or longer. Using S to represent the scrolling times, we can write the sequence of gestures that Hal uses as follows:

$H P K S K P K S K P K S K P K K$

Using the rules to place Ms, we get

$H + 3(M + P + K + S + K) + M + P + K + K$

$0.4 + 3 \star (1.35 + 0.2 + 3.0 + 0.2) + 1.35 + 0.4 + 0.2 + 0.2 = 16.8$ seconds

Except for the rare case in which the thermometer scales are correctly set at the beginning of the problem, a perfect user will need more than 16 seconds to accomplish a temperature conversion using this method. A real—imperfect—user would jog the scales and the arrows back and forth and thus take even longer.

4-3 Measurement of Interface Efficiency

Every tool carries with it the spirit by which it has been created.

—*Werner Karl Heisenberg*

We have looked at two interfaces, one of which will take about 5 seconds to operate and the other of which will take more than 15 seconds to operate. It is clear which of the two better satisfies the requirement. The next question that we ask is how fast an interface that satisfies the requirement can be.

Given a design for an interface, you can use GOMS and its extensions to calculate how long a user will take to accomplish any well-defined task with that interface. But analysis models do not answer the question of just how fast you should expect an interface to be. To answer this question, we can use a measure from information theory. In the following discussion, *information* is used in the technical sense of a quantification of the amount of data conveyed by a communication, such as when two people have a telephone conversation or when a human sends a message, such as a click of the GID button when the cursor is at a certain location, to a machine. Before dealing with the technical details of measuring the amount of information a user must provide to accomplish a task, we establish the need for such a measurement.

To make a reasonable estimate of the time that the fastest possible interface for a task would take, we can proceed by first determining a lower bound on the amount of information a user has to provide to complete that task; this minimal amount is independent of the design of the interface. If the methods of a proposed interface require an input of information that exceeds the calculated lower bound, the user is doing unnecessary work, and the proposed interface can be improved. On the other hand, if the proposed interface requires the user to supply exactly the amount of information that the task requires, you cannot make a more information-efficient interface for this task. In this latter case, there may yet be ways of improving—and there are certainly many ways of ruining—the interface, but at least this one efficiency goal will have been met.

Information-theoretic efficiency is defined similarly to the way efficiency is defined in thermodynamics; in thermodynamics we calculate efficiency by dividing the power coming out of a process by the power going into that process. If, during a certain time interval, an electrical generator is producing 820 watts while it is driven by an engine that has an output of 1,000 watts, it has an efficiency of 820 / 1,000, or 0.82. Efficiency is also often expressed as a percentage; in this case, the generator has an efficiency of 82 percent. A perfect generator—which by the second law of thermodynamics cannot exist—would have an efficiency of 100 percent.

The **information efficiency** E of an interface is defined as the minimum amount of information necessary to do a task, divided by the amount of information that has to be supplied by the user. As is true of physical efficiency, E is at least 0 and is at most 1. Where no work is required for a task and no work is done, the efficiency is defined as 1. (This formality is necessary to avoid the case of 0 divided by 0, as in responding to a transparent error message. See Section 5-5.)

E can be 0 when the user is required to provide information that is totally unnecessary (Figure 4.4). Surprisingly, a number of interface details achieve the dubious honor of having $E = 0$. A dialog box that allows the user only one possible action, such as clicking the box's OK button, is such an example. (JavaScript has a command, *Alert*, solely for creating such unneces-

Figure 4.4. A dialog box with an information theoretic efficiency of 0.

sary boxes: The designers were wise enough to remove *goto* from the JavaScript language to force structured code, but they failed to provide similar guidance on the interface side.)

E takes into account only the information required by the task and that supplied by the user. Two or more methods may have the same *E*, yet have different total times. It is even possible that a first method has a higher *E* yet is slower than a second method—for example, $MKMK$ versus $MKKK$. In this example, only two characters have to be entered when the first method is used. In the second method, three characters are required, yet it takes less time to perform the task. It is difficult to construct many real-life situations that exhibit this inversion of speed and information efficiency.[2] For the most part, the more efficient interface is also the more productive, more humane interface.

Information is measured in bits; a single bit, which represents a choice between two alternatives—such as 0 and 1, on and off, or yes and no—is the unit of information.[3] For example, a choice made among four objects would require 2 bits of information: If the objects are A, B, C, and D, the first bit could choose either A and B, or C and D; once that choice was made—say C and D—the second bit would choose either C or D. Two binary choices, or 2 bits, suffice to separate one item from a set of four. To choose among eight alternatives, you need 3 bits; to choose among sixteen items, you need 4 bits; and so on. In general, given *n* equally likely alternatives, the amount of information communicated by all of them taken together is the power of 2 equal to *n*:

$$\log_2 n$$

And the amount of information in any one of them is

$$(1/n) \log_2 n \tag{1}$$

If the probabilities among the alternatives are not necessarily equal and the *i*th alternative has probability $p(i)$, the information associated with that alternative is

$$p(i) \log_2 (1 / p(i)) \tag{2}$$

The amount of information is the sum (over all alternatives) of expression (2), which reduces to expression (1) in the equiprobable case. It

---

2. It is possible to design more sophisticated measures of efficiency; for example, the *M* operator does not enter into our calculation. However, the simple measure defined here suffices for the purposes of this book.

3. *Bit* is mathematician John W. Tukey's contraction of the words BInary digiT (Shannon and Weaver 1963, p. 9).

follows that the information content of an interface that allows only the tap of a single button is 0 bits; not tapping the button is not permitted:

$$1 \log_2 (1) = 0 \tag{3}$$

It would seem, however, that the required tap of a single button can, for example, cause the ignition of dynamite used to demolish a building. Would this tap of the button then convey information? It would not, because not tapping the button was not an alternative; the interface "allows only the tap of a single button." If, however, the button was not tapped during, say, a five-minute time window in which the demolition was permitted, the building would not be demolished, and the tap or nontap would convey up to 1 bit of information because there were, in this case, two possible messages. From expression (2), we know that the calculation involves the probability, p, that the building will be exploded. The probability that it will not be exploded is therefore $1 - p$. From expression (2), we can calculate the information content of this interface:

$$p \log_2 (1 / p) + (1 - p) \log_2 (1 / (1 - p)) \tag{4}$$

When $p = \frac{1}{2}$, expression 4 evaluates to

$$\frac{1}{2} \times 1 + \frac{1}{2} \times 1 = \frac{1}{2} + \frac{1}{2} = 1$$

Expression (4) evaluates to less than 1 if $p \neq \frac{1}{2}$. In particular, it evaluates to 0 when $p = 0$ or $p = 1$, as in expression (3).

This example illustrates an important point: We can measure the information embodied in a message only in the context of the set of possible messages that might have been received. To calculate the amount of information that has been conveyed by the reception of a message, we must know, in particular, the probability of that message having been sent. The amount of information in any message is independent of other messages past or future, is without reference to time or duration, and does not depend on any other events; similarly, the outcome of the flip of a fair coin is unaffected by previous tosses or by what time of day it is tossed.

As explained in Shannon and Weaver (1963), it is also important to keep in mind that

> information should not be confused with meaning . . . information is a measure of one's freedom of choice when one selects a message. . . . Note that it is misleading (although often convenient) to say that one or the other message [when just two are possible] conveys [1 bit of] information. The concept of information applies not to the individ-

ual messages (as the concept of meaning would), but rather to the situation as a whole, the unit information indicating that in this situation one has an amount of freedom of choice in selecting a message, which it is convenient to regard as a standard or unit amount. (p. 9)

However, a user's actions in performing a task could be modeled with greater accuracy as a Markoff process, whereby the probability of a later action depends on earlier actions taken by the user, but the single-event probabilities discussed are sufficient for the purposes of this book; messages are assumed to be independent and equiprobable.

The amount of information conveyed by nonkeyboard devices can also be calculated. If your display is divided into two regions—one labeled Yes and the other labeled No—a single click in one or the other region would supply 1 bit of information. If there are n equally likely targets, with one click, you supply $\log_2 n$ bits of information. If the targets are of unequal size, the amount of information given by each does not change, but it does take longer to move the GID to smaller targets—by an amount that we shall show how to calculate presently. If the targets have unequal probability, the formula is the same as that already given for keyboard inputs with unequal probabilities. There is a difference in that a user can operate a keyboard key in 0.2 sec, whereas it will take 1.3 sec to operate an on-screen button, on average, ignoring homing time.

For our purposes, we can calculate the information content of voice input by treating speech as a sequence of input symbols, rather than as a continuous phenomenon with a certain bandwidth and duration.

This treatment of information theory and its relationship to interface design is a simplified account. Yet even in this rudimentary form, information theory—used in a manner analogous to our use of the simplified GOMS keystroke-level model—can give us first-order guidance in evaluating the quality of our interface designs.

4-3-1 Efficiency of Hal's Interfaces

Accurate reckoning: The entrance into the knowledge of all existing things and obscure secrets.

—*Rhind Papyrus, c. 1650 B.C.*

It is useful to go through a detailed example of a calculation of the average amount of information required for an interface technique. I will again use the temperature-conversion example. According to the requirement, the input needed by the converter consists of an average of four typed characters; a decimal point occurs once in 90 percent of the inputs and not at all in the other 10 percent, and the negative sign occurs once in 25 percent of the inputs and not at all in the other 75 percent. For simplicity, and because there is no need for 1 percent precision in the answer, I will assume that all of the other digits occur with equal frequency, and I will ignore the 10 percent of the inputs that have no decimal point.

We need to determine the set of possible messages and the probability of each. Five forms are possible, where d denotes a digit:

1. −.dd
2. −d.d
3. .ddd
4. d.dd *and*
5. dd.d.

The first two each occur 12.5 percent of the time, and there are 100 of each of them; the final three each occur 25 percent of the time, and there are nearly 1,000 of each.[4] The probability for either of the first two types of messages is $(0.125 / 100) = 0.00125$; the probability for any one of the final three types of messages is $(0.75 / 3000) = 0.00025$. The sum of the probabilities of the messages is, as it must be, 1.

The amount of information of each message, in bits, is given by expression (2)[5]:

$$p(i) \log_2 (1 / p(i))$$

This expression evaluates to approximately 0.012 for the negative values and to 0.003 for the positive values. Calculating $200 \times 0.012 + 3000 \times 0.003$ gives a total of 11.4 bits for each message.

Taking the probabilities into account can be important. If we took a simple-minded approach and assumed that all of the 12 symbols (minus, decimal point, and the 10 digits) were equally likely, the probability of each would be $\frac{1}{12}$, and the information contained in a four-character message would be approximately

$$4 \log_2 (12) \approx 14 \text{ bits}$$

4. The "nearly" comes from the fact that the temperature of 0 degrees will not be entered as 0.00 or 00.0.

5. To get logs to the base 2 on a calculator or a computer that has only natural logs (ln), use: $\log_2 (x) = \ln (x) / \ln (2)$.

It is a theorem of information theory that the information is at a maximum when all symbols are equally likely. Therefore, making the assumption of equiprobable messages will give you a value that is equal to or greater than the amount of information in each message. Obviously, this assumption also makes estimating the information content of a message easier to compute. If the resultant value of the approximation is smaller than the amount of information your interface requires the user to supply, you do not yet need to bother with the more refined calculation.

We have just calculated that the task requires that Hal supply an average of about 11 bits of information each time he has to convert a temperature. We can—and will, presently—divide this quantity by the amount of information the interface requires him to supply. The result will be the efficiency of the interface.

Another simplification for quick analysis is to find the amount of information in a keystroke or a GID operation and then to count the various gestures. When a keystroke delivers information to a computer, the amount of information delivered depends on the total number of keys available—for example, the number of keys on the keyboard—and the relative frequency with which each key is used. Thus, keystrokes can be used as a rough measure of information. If a keyboard had 128 keys, each of which had the same frequency of use, each key would represent 7 bits of information. In practice, the frequency of use varies tremendously—for example, space and *e* are common, whereas *j* and \ are rare), and the information per keystroke is closer to 5 bits in most applications. The requirement stated that the average length of the input that specifies the temperature was four keystrokes.

For this analysis, it is easier to use a measure simpler than information-theoretic efficiency but that often achieves the same practical effect. **Character efficiency** is defined as the minimum number of characters required for a task, divided by the number of characters the interface makes the user enter.

Achieving an interface that required four keystrokes, on average, would give us a character efficiency of 100 percent. If we add a keystroke to decide which conversion is desired and then another to delimit the answer, our average length of input will grow to six keystrokes, and our keystroke efficiency will drop to 67 percent. If Hal has as his input device only a 16-key numeric keypad, the information provided by a single keystroke would be 4 bits, and the interface would be more efficient. (The requirements, however, do not permit us to use this option.)

Because any task in a GOMS analysis requires at least one mental operator, the most keystroke-efficient interface for the temperature-conversion problem will have, in theory, an average time of

$$M + K + K + K + K = 2.15 \sec$$

Thus, it will be considerably faster than either of the two interfaces already discussed. However, typing four characters on a standard keyboard supplies at least 20 bits of information, whereas only 11 bits are required—an information-theoretic efficiency of 55 percent—so we know that there is room for improvement. As we have seen, using a standard numeric keypad instead of a full keyboard drops the input information per four keystrokes to 16 bits, raising the efficiency to about 60 percent. A dedicated numeric keypad—one that has only the digits, the minus sign, and a decimal point— will permit a slightly higher score, of about 70 percent efficiency. We raise the score again by using special encodings of temperature information and novel input devices, but training difficulties and excessive costs begin to loom with these extreme approaches, so I will stop here and accept 70 percent information-theoretic efficiency. Theoretical limits may or may not be reached by a practical interface, but they do give us a star by which to steer.

4-3-2 Other Solutions for Hal's Interface

In Section 4-3-1, we stopped trying to improve information-theoretic efficiency when we reached 70 percent. We achieved that efficiency with an unspecified, theoretical interface that somehow managed to have 100 percent keystroke efficiency. Let us see how close we can come to this ideal with a standard keyboard and a GID.

Consider an all-keyboard interface. In this interface, a note appears on the display:

```
To    convert    temperatures,    indicate    the
desired  scale  by  typing  C  for  Celsius  or  F
for  Fahrenheit.  Type  the  numeric  tempera-
ture;  then  press  the  Enter  key.  The  con-
verted  temperature  value  will  be  displayed.
```

A GOMS analysis finds that the user must make six keystrokes. Following the rules for placements of *M*s gives us

$$MKKKKKMK$$

The average time is 3.9 seconds.

We can decrease this time if we can use the C or the F itself as a delimiter. That is, consider an interface in which the following instructions appear:

> To convert temperatures, type the numeric
> temperature, followed by C if it is in
> degrees Celsius or F if it is in degrees
> Fahrenheit. The converted temperature will
> be displayed.

In this example, the Enter key is not used. Some primitive interface-building tools demand that the user tap Enter and will not permit us to use C or F as a delimiter; such tools are inadequate for building humane interfaces.

The GOMS analysis of the C/F-delimiter interface yields

M K K K K M K

The average time is 3.7 seconds. If we did not have an analysis that showed that the theoretical minimum time is 2.15 sec, this solution might strike us as satisfactory. It is considerably more efficient than the ones that we discussed previously, so we might stop here. Tempted by that theoretical minimum, however, we ask whether there is an even faster approach. Consider the interface depicted in Figure 4.5; we might describe it as *bifurcated:* One input will give us two outputs.

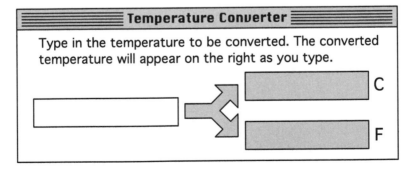

Figure 4.5. An interface that does not require a delimiter. A more efficient interface is made possible by taking advantage of character-at-a-time interaction, and by performing both conversions at once.

Under the bifurcated interface, no delimiter is required. Furthermore, the user does not have to specify which conversion is desired. The GOMS analysis for the average input of four characters is

MKKKK

The bifurcated interface achieves the minimum 2.15 seconds and has 100 percent character efficiency.

If, as in our example, the output sometimes changes when a character is typed, the flickering of the output does not distract you, because your locus of attention is the input. The continually changing output is often beneficial: The user will notice it only peripherally after the first few times that he uses the feature, at which point it will provide him feedback that the system is responding to his input. For single-character interaction to be effective, the system must respond quickly; in particular, the interaction must keep up with the user's typing speed. Only a slow network connection should exhibit this problem.

Although not part of the requirement, you might ask how this converter is "cleared" for the next operation. Does the clear operation add a keystroke? Not necessarily. For example, we could design the interface such that, whenever the operator returns to his background task or goes on to another task, the values in the converter are automatically grayed and the converter becomes inactive. The values shown are not cleared at this time, so that they can be referred to again if necessary. The next input to the converter does clear the old values.

Just because it has optimal speed of operation and is highly efficient, the bifurcated converter is not necessarily the best interface of those discussed or of those possible. Parameters other than speed also are of importance, such as error rate, user learning time, and long-term user retention of the way to use the interface. We should be especially concerned about the error rate of the bifurcated converter, due to Hal's possibly reading the wrong output box, especially because he may have just heard, for example, the word *Celsius* and thus be required to read out the Fahrenheit line. Nonetheless, the bifurcated converter would definitely be on the short list of interfaces to be tested for the temperature-converter application, and a few others that we have seen— solutions that might otherwise have seemed worth a try had we not learned how to do a GOMS analysis—would not make the cut.

Whether we use it in a simple keystroke-timing analysis or in a detailed information-theoretic extravaganza, a quantification of the theoretical minimum-time, minimum-character, or minimum-information interface can be a useful guide for our designs. *Without a quantitative guide, we are only guessing at how well we are doing and at how much room there is for improvement.*

4-4 Fitts' Law and Hick's Law

It behooves us to place the foundations of knowledge in mathematics.

—*Roger Bacon*, Opus Majus *(13th century)*

Various quantitative laws relating to interface design have sound cognetic underpinnings and have been validated repeatedly. These laws often give you additional data on which you can base interface-design decisions. Fitts' law quantifies the fact that the farther a target is from your current cursor position or the smaller the target is, the longer it will take you to move the cursor to the target. Hick's law quantifies the observation that the more choices of a given kind you have, the longer it takes you to come to a decision.

4-4-1 Fitts' Law

Consider that you are moving a cursor toward an on-screen button. The button is the *target* of the move. The length of a straight line from the position at which the cursor started to the closest point on the target is the *distance* used in the statement of Fitts' law. Given the size of the target and the distance to be moved, **Fitts' law** gives you the average time it takes a user to succeed in getting the cursor to the button.

In the one-dimensional case, in which the target's size, measured along the line of motion, is S and the target is at a distance D from the starting position (Figure 4.6), Fitts' law states that

$$\text{Time (in msec)} = a + b \log_2 (D / S + 1)$$

(The constants a and b are determined experimentally or are derived from human performance parameters.)[6] The time that you calculate begins when

---

6. Mathematics, supposedly a paragon of clarity, clings yet to that old-fashioned style whereby undefined variables appears in a formula before you know what they stand for. For example, you will see such statements as

$A = \pi r^2$,

where r is the radius of a circle and A is its area.

This can be confusing, forcing you to read ahead and then go back, especially if the equation is a long one with lots of as-yet-unexplained variables. Far better, from a reader's viewpoint, is to follow the obvious dictum to define terms *before* you use them:

A circle with radius r has an area A, given by:

$A = \pi r^2$

Figure 4.6. Distances used in Fitts' law to determine the time to move a cursor to a target.

the cursor is at the starting point and after the user has chosen the target. The logarithm to the base 2 gives a measure of the difficulty of the task in terms of the number of bits of information it takes to describe the (one-dimensional) path of the cursor.

The units of distance do not affect the calculated time, because D / S is the ratio of two distances and is therefore dimensionless. It follows that, even though we might move the pointing device a distance smaller or larger than the distance the cursor moves on the display, the law still works when the distances are measured on the display, assuming a linear relationship between GID and cursor motion. Fitts' law applies only to the kinds of motions we make when we are using most human-machine interfaces: motions that are small relative to human body size and that are uninterrupted, that is, movements that can be made in one continuous motion. For back-of-the-envelope approximations, I use $a = 50$ and $b = 150$ in the Fitts' law equation.

An extension of Fitts' law to more complex constraints, such as tracking a cursor between straight or curved walls, has been developed and tested empirically (Accot and Zhai 1997). For a two-dimensional target, you can usually obtain a reasonable approximation of the time needed to move the cursor to the target, using the smaller of the horizontal and vertical dimensions of the target for the value of S (Mackenzie 1995).

Fitts' law explains, for example, why it is much faster to move the cursor to an Apple Macintosh–style menu (Figure 4.7) that is on the edge of a display than to a Microsoft Windows–style menu (Figure 4.8) that floats away from an edge. The size S of the Windows menu on my display is 5 mm. The effective size of the Macintosh target is large because you do not have to stop within the confines of the menu bar but rather can continue to move the GID any comfortable distance beyond that needed to put the cursor in the menu: The cursor stops at the edge of the display.

A series of tests I performed determined that users typically stop within about 50 mm of the edge of the display on the Macintosh, so we can use 50 mm as S for the Macintosh. On a 14-inch flat panel display, the aver-

Figure 4.7. The Macintosh menu, at the top edge of the screen, effectively increases its size compared to a menu that floats away from the edge. (See color insert.)

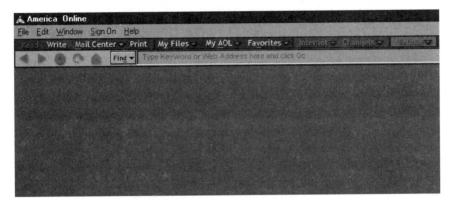

Figure 4.8. The Windows menu is below the top edge of the screen; you have to place the cursor more carefully to pull down a submenu. (See color insert.)

age distance the cursor must be moved to reach the menu bars is 80 mm; thus, the calculated time to move the cursor to a menu item on the Macintosh is

$$50 + 150 \log_2 (80 / 50 + 1) = 256 \text{ msec.}$$

This result is far less than the calculated time it takes to move the cursor to a corresponding menu item on a Windows-style menu:

$$50 + 150 \log_2 (80 / 5 + 1) = 663 \text{ msec.}$$

These calculations apply only to the time it takes the user to move the cursor. Clicking on the target to indicate that you believe that the cursor has reached its goal adds another 0.1 sec on average. ($K = 0.2$ in the GOMS model includes both the downstroke and the release of the button, whereas this timing is stopped by the downstroke.) In a typical experimental situation, you have to add the human reaction time of about 0.25 sec at the start of the cursor movement. When we take these factors into account, we get times that agree with what I have observed: It takes about 0.6 sec, on average, for a user to open an Apple menu, whereas it takes a user more than 1 sec to open a Windows menu. This analysis makes it clear why menus were deliberately placed at the edge of the display when the Macintosh interface was developed.

4-4-2 Hick's Law

Before you move the cursor to a target or take any one action with a multiplicity of choices, you must first choose the target or action. **Hick's law** says that when you have to choose to take one among n alternative actions and when the probabilities of taking each alternative are equal, the time to choose one of them is proportional to the logarithm to the base 2 of the number of choices, plus 1. When put this way, Hick's law looks just like Fitts' law:

$$\text{Time (in msec)} = a + b \log_2 (n + 1)$$

If the probability of the ith choice is $p(i)$, then, instead of the logarithmic factor in the equation, you use

$$\sum_i p(i) \log_2 (1 / p(i) + 1)$$

The coefficients in Hick's law are strongly dependent on many conditions, including how the choices are presented and how habituated to the system the user has become. (If the choices are presented in a confusing manner, both a and b can increase; habituation decreases b.) These dependencies will not be discussed here; all we need to consider is that making decisions takes time, that making complex decisions takes more time than making simple ones, and that the relationship is logarithmic. In the absence of better information, we can use the same coefficients a and b as for Fitts' law to make off-the-cuff or relative estimates.

Whatever positive, nonzero coefficients we use for a and b, it follows from Hick's law that giving a user many choices simultaneously is usually faster than is organizing the same choices into hierarchical groups. Making choices from one menu of eight items is faster than is making choices from two menus of four items each. Assuming that the items are equally likely to be chosen—and ignoring the time it takes to open the second menu, which, if taken into account, would make the time taken for the two-menu interface even longer—we compare the time to select one item of eight, $a + b$

$\log_2 8$, with the time to select one item of four twice, $2 (a + b \log_2 4)$. Because $\log_2 8 = 3$ and $\log_2 4 = 2$, and because both $a < 2a$ and $3b < 4b$, we see that

$a + 3b < 2 (a + 2b)$

This accords with experiments on menu structures (see, for example, Norman and Chin 1988).

Our discussion of Fitts' and Hick's laws is incomplete. For example, it is no accident that they have the same form as the Shannon–Hartley theorem. Nonetheless, this brief treatment is sufficient to alert you to these useful guides to interface design. They can help you even if, as in the example, you do not know the empirical coefficients a and b. (For more detail, see Card, Moran, and Newell 1983, pp. 72–74.)

FIVE

Unification

It is immensely ingenious, immensely complicated, and extremely effective, but somehow at the same time crude, wasteful, and inelegant, and one feels that there must be a better way of doing things.

—C. Strachey (speaking not of Windows
but of the IBM Stretch computer in 1962)

In trying to create a general-purpose interface that takes into account the requirements that we have delineated in the previous four chapters, we find that basic changes from present practice are necessary. Many directions are possible; one tack is to see what we can do within the limitations of the Internet and with the hundreds of millions of computers and information appliances that exist and that are being manufactured today.

The most common personal computer hardware configuration is nearly universal at present. By taking a point of view that emphasizes the commonality of physical actions across almost all applications, using the common hardware elements, rather than looking at the vast disparity of tasks, we can develop a general yet simple interface.

The list of actions a user can take to influence content—be that content textual, graphical, or multimedia—can be arranged into a simple taxonomy, which allows us to describe any application's interface in a uniform way. This organization can help guide us in simplifying interface designs. Implementing a universal undo/redo facility also helps to develop a unified interface, eliminating much of the need for individual programs to handle error recovery.

Different applications have different commands, and a user cannot in general use the commands from application A while working in application B and vice versa. By liberating commands from applications, we eliminate the inherent modality of applications. The total number of commands a user must master drops dramatically with this kind of unification, primarily because unification rids us of the immense duplication of commands. For example, on the Canon Cat, a total of 20 commands handled word processing: spreadsheet operations; database setup, retrieval, and sorting; calculations; and more. Contemporaneous systems of comparable power required more than 100 commands to accommodate the same set of tasks. In today's environment, the thousands of commands now provided would be reduced to the hundreds. Because not all commands apply to all data types, we would need to apply data-type transformers to objects to create new objects that, whenever possible, can be acted on by the chosen command.

Another division that can be erased is between facilities provided, at present, by commercial software and by the user. For example, menus are, at present, operating system objects that are set up by each application. However, they are just text. Is there any reason that a user cannot type up a list of regularly used commands, lock them so that they do not get changed accidentally, stick them up at the top of the display, and treat them like a system-provided menu? To make such menu creation easy, an interface could allow the user to lock and unlock text and to make the text either flow with other content or stay fixed with respect to the display. These are various states of text.

Eudora and Microsoft Word are programs that allow you to change the content menus, but you must use a facility that the program provides specifically for that purpose. Here we are discussing the ability to create menus with the same mechanisms you use for creating and editing any text. Menus become content in this view.

The next step in the simplification of the interface is to eliminate difficult-to-remember and annoying-to-create file names and system-provided file structures. If given suitable search mechanisms, a user will find both the file names and the provided file structures unnecessary.

5-1 Uniformity and Elementary Actions

Entities should not be multiplied unnecessarily.

—William of Occam

The hardware that makes up a computer interface has become formulaic: one or more text input devices (keyboard, handwriting tablet, speech recognizer), a GID, and a two-dimensional color display. The formula, not a bad one, has a few variations; for example, a touch screen can be the text input device, the GID, and the display. Microphones for sound, video inputs, and other electronic interfaces are devices that are not, except experimentally, part of the usual human-machine interface. Indeed, we use the interface to control the functioning of these devices.

If you were to watch a person who is operating today's standard hardware, without your seeing what is being displayed and without any idea of what the operator is trying to accomplish, you would generally not be able to guess what he is doing. There are exceptions: A user's fixated stare at the display, accompanied by manic gyrations of a joystick to the beat of a persistent and repetitive sound track, are strong hints that a game is being played. But in general, user actions in one application, such as word processing, look much like user actions in others, such as a data entry task or a spreadsheet manipulation.

This uniformity of user actions across applications is a clue that interfaces for various applications are not as different as they might seem when you are involved in using the computer yourself. Applications seem more different than they are because you are attending to the content of what you are doing—that is, to the widely varying semantics of each action. In particular, you are not paying attention to the physical manipulations you are performing.

Another way in which applications are similar is that nearly all of them require text entry. (Even games have you type your name when you do well.) It is thus worth ensuring that text handling—whether in the small, as when the user is entering the string on which to execute a Find command, or in the large, as when the user is writing a novel, is accomplished with a smooth and efficient set of operations.

We and our software are not perfect; not all text-entry keystrokes, pen motions, or acts of speech will cause the desired characters to be displayed. Therefore, an essential provision of an interface is that keystrokes can be erased with an immediate tap of the Backspace (or Delete) key, with analogous methods for other forms of input. Larger changes, such as adding a paragraph, require that the user be able to select regions and to delete them. Another fundamental requirement, except for brief inputs, is that the user be able to move the cursor to any point in the text and to insert additional characters. In short, whenever text is to be entered, the user expects to have available many of the capabilities of a word processor.

Whenever you are entering text, you are placing it into a document or a field, such as an area provided for you to enter your name on a form. With present systems, the rules about what editing functions are available change from field to field and from one document type, such as a word processor document, to another, such as a spreadsheet. The editing rules can change within a single document in systems that allow the document to include portions generated by separate applications (in Section 5-7, we look at a solution to this problem).

Two different but similar pieces of software on a system form a prime breeding ground for user confusion and frustration. Yet that is precisely what we do have on nearly every personal computer system. My computer has 11 text editors, each with its own set of behaviors, and there may be a few editors that I missed. The situation is unnecessarily confusing.

One important step in creating a humane interface for computers and or for computerlike systems, such as a Palm Pilot, is to ensure that the same rules apply whenever text is being entered and when editable text is selected. For example, on the Macintosh or in Windows, you cannot spell-check a file name in situ, so if you are not sure of the spelling of *rendezvous* and you want to use that word as a file name,[1] you will have to guess at the spelling or open a word processor and retype or drag *rendezvous* into that word processor to check it. I suspect that, if I suggested to software developers that users should be able to check file name spellings, they might well add a new feature. Such an ad hoc addition—which would probably take the form of a new menu item in one of the desktop menus, probably the Edit menu, would only increase the already absurd complexity of the software. It is better to simplify by means of the idea presented here, that one command for spell-checking should suffice for any text, whatever role that text might be playing at the moment.

Interface design should be such that *any objects that look the same are the same.* Insisting on this principle results in a boon of simplicity for user and programmer alike and is a concept that extends far beyond text. Every object for which this can be done is an affordance. If a user cannot tell what he may and may not do with an on-screen object by looking at it, your interface fails

---

1. Of course, if your operating system doesn't allow long names, you have another problem.

to meet the criterion of visibility as discussed in Section 3-4. You put the user in the position of having to guess what operations are possible and to guess what will happen when a given operation is performed. Requiring the user to guess at what a piece of software will do is an interface technique more suited to games than to tools.

The ideal of having appearance invariably indicate function is not, in general, achievable. For example, one object can mimic or spoof another. A bitmap of text looks exactly like text, but in current systems, text-editing operations fail on bitmaps. This kind of problem can be partially surmounted if the system always attempts to transform the object into a type to which the operation applies, a notion we discuss in Section 5-8.

5-2 Elementary Actions Cataloged

As you design an interface, you should have the palette of possibilities arrayed in your mind, much as a painter has his colors organized. The spectrum of **elementary actions** that a user can perform is remarkably limited. From this set of elementary actions, all user interaction is built. With a keyboard, you can tap keys or press and hold them while you perform other actions. With a GID, you can move a cursor within the bounds of the display (or displays) on your system, and you can signal using the computer, using the speed, direction, and acceleration of the GID, although you usually use GID speed and acceleration only as an aid to pointing. With a GID button, you can signal display locations to which you are pointing with the cursor. These elementary actions have widely varying semantics, depending on the application being run.

Pressure-sensitive graphic tablets can detect the angle at which the pen is held, which results in one or two additional numerical values being associated with each location to which the user points. Except when the user is doing freehand drawing, these parameters are rarely used. Musical keyboards may provide, as inputs to the computer, both the velocity with which the key is pressed and the pressure with which the key is being held down after being pressed. There are also joysticks and three-dimensional input devices. Nonetheless, most interaction is accomplished with a keyboard and a standard, two-dimensional GID. This section will address primarily the standard input and output devices. In many cases, it will be clear how the principles extend to more exotic physical or, eventually, mental interfaces. Having an explicit taxonomy and vocabulary of elementary actions and the elementary operations built from them is, I find, a great aid in discussing and designing interfaces.

The user performs the elementary actions in various combinations to a set of **elementary operations**. The elementary operations are performed on content and are used in nearly every interface. We first note that content can be

- **Indicated**: pointed at
- **Selected**: distinguished from other content
- **Activated**: clicked on
- **Modified** or used (by means of commands) by being

  - **Generated:** modified from empty to nonempty
  - **Deleted**: modified from nonempty to empty
  - **Moved**: inserted in one place and simultaneously deleted from another
  - **Transformed**: changed to another data type
  - **Copied**: sent to or received from an external device or duplicated at a different internal location—for example, printed, e-mailed, stored on a hard disk, copied into another document.

These elementary operations can and should be fundamental to the computer or appliance itself; that is, they should be part of the internal hardware or software rather than being reimplemented in multiple software packages, and each of them should always be invoked in the same way, regardless of on what objects they are operated. For the most part, *the cognitive differences among applications lie in how selections are presented and how the user can operate on them.* In a spreadsheet, values are presented in tabular form, and an operation might consist of changing a column without a sum underneath into a column with its sum underneath. In a word processor, text and illustrations are presented in page-layout form, and a typical operation is to change text from a roman typeface to an italic typeface. In a web page program, a word processor page might be changed into HTML. In a photo-processing program, an image with low contrast might be modified into one of higher contrast.

Most operations performed on content can be described in terms of these elementary operations. For example, in many systems, an object can be queried about its properties. (In systems equipped with two-button GIDs, the user usually performs this function by a click of the right button when the cursor is on the object and the system is in an appropriate state.) To **query** is to bring up further information or options on the item, but it also can be thought of as an operation on one object that brings into view another, related object. From the user's point of view, there should not be, and there is no need for there to be, any distinction between operating-system operations and applications operations.

That the interfaces of all applications arise from a small set of elementary operations confirms that the applications themselves, as rich and varied as they are from a task-oriented point of view, are not all that different from one another from an interface-oriented point of view. This fundamental similarity can be exploited to create powerful computer systems of unprecedented simplicity and productivity.

First, we need to define several methods for choosing and marking content on which we want to operate. Those methods are discussed in Section 5-2-1.

5-2-1 Highlighting, Indication, and Selection

Highlighting is adding, by any means, a recognizable distinction to a displayed object. The function of the highlight is to allow the user to determine, by passive observation, that the system has recognized a particular object as having a special status. The semantics of that status are dependent on the nature of the object and on the commands that the user can apply to it. For sighted users, the highlight is usually visual. Examples of visual highlighting mechanisms include brightness reversal, color change, change of contrast, underlining, blinking or other periodic change, and applying a stationary or animated border to an object. Nonvisual highlighting can be shown, for example, by different choice of voices or spoken inflection.

As the user moves the cursor over objects, the object to which the cursor is pointing should be highlighted. In text, the object typically would be an individual character. Highlighting the single object pointed to as a cursor is moved, without any other user action such as clicking, is **indication**. With indication, the user knows at all times to what object the system thinks she is pointing. In too many present systems, the user must guess at what will be selected or activated when she clicks the GID button; if her guess is incorrect, she will have to try again, wasting time and energy. Indication can be especially valuable when the objects that the user would like to select are small and close together, when they overlap, or when their limits are unclear. Indication is necessary if an interface is designed in accord with the principle of visibility.

The highlighting used for indication must not exhibit too much contrast or be overly dramatic, lest the flickering of objects become annoying as the cursor moves over them; in some situations, it may be helpful not to indicate objects when the cursor is moving faster than a threshold velocity. Note that a smaller object, as measured by the visual angle the indicated object subtends, requires higher visual contrast of the indication, but this is an ergonomic issue.

Indication is underused in present systems. If you use indication aggressively in your interface design, you can eliminate a good deal of clicking inherent in present designs. In fact, indication can often replace clicking, and clicking can be used, as when you follow a link in a browser by means of a single click, in place of double clicking. For example, say that a user wants to remove inactive windows from a display. Each window has a Close button. Both the Windows and the Macintosh operating systems require that the user first click on a window to make it active and only then click on the Close button to banish the window. This extra click—the one that activates a window just so that the user can close it—is especially annoying. If, however, merely moving the cursor over a window made it active, a single click on the Close button would close it. Of course, if you design a system that exhibits activation in only certain places and under only certain conditions, you will create a modal inconsistency that will bedevil users. Activation should be systemic. As it becomes more familiar, consumer demand will force its adoption.

Selecting is a process by which a user identifies a set of one or more objects as having a special status that can be recognized by the system, thereby creating a **selection**. Usually, a user creates a selection with the intention of applying a command to it in the near future. Unlike indication's more transient highlight, the highlight that signals selection persists even after the user has moved the cursor away from the selection. The user creates a single-object selection by clicking the GID button while the object is indicated. A user can also create a selection by dragging a rectangle or other shape across a set of contiguous objects: All objects that intersect the area of the shape become selected. Another convenient method of selection is to create a polygon or free-form shape; all objects completely inside the shape are selected when the user closes the boundary of the shape. When a selection is made, the previous selection should become the **old selection**. (In most present systems, the old selection is simply deselected.) This process can be iterated so that a user can create, in addition to the first old selection, a second old selection, a third old selection, and so on up to an nth old selection. A mathematician would be tempted to call the current selection the zeroth old selection. The highlighting that signals selection should be distinct from and more readily apparent than that used for indication; highlighting for older selections should also make them clearly distinguishable from one another and probably of lower visual contrast than newer ones. An alphanumeric designation may have to accompany old selections so that they can be readily identified.

Selection can be of discrete objects or of geometrical regions of the display, or they can be **composite**, consisting of the union of selections. In much of today's software, the user creates composite—possibly discontiguous—selections from a set of smaller selections by first making an initial selection. Then, with one common method, she presses and holds Shift and, while in this quasimode, clicks on additional objects to toggle them into or out of the selection.

But this method has three drawbacks. First, the command for creating composite selections is invisible. Second, it is easy to make errors when setting up a large composite selection; for example, if the user accidentally releases the Shift key in the middle of the process and clicks on another object, the work in making the complex selection up to that point is lost. Third, the mechanism is a toggle: The same gesture deselects an object if that object was selected and selects an object if that object was not selected.

The first problem—lack of visibility—is easily corrected, by use of an on-screen hint, for example. The second drawback is the high risk the user runs of making a mistake during the composition process. A more comfortable method for making complex selections includes a command that redefines the current selection to be the union of the old selection and the current selection. Given such a command, the user can concentrate on making a selection without any concern for what she has done previously; only after she confirms that the current selection is correct does she add it to the composite selection. Making old selections available and, of course, marked by a special highlight so that they are visible also allows multiargument commands, such as the two arguments to a command that interchanges a pair of selections. Compare your present method of interchanging two pieces of text with the following technique: Make two selections, then apply the interchange command.

Most present systems do not apply their Undo and Redo commands to the process of making selections. This omission is unfortunate because errors in making selections are frequent. An essential feature of any humane interface is a universally applicable pair of Undo and Redo commands. Only the amount of available storage should limit the number or levels of undos permitted. Undo and Redo should be pervasive, applying to any operation where undoing and redoing is logically possible. They should also be—again, as far as is logically possible—inverse operations. Undo followed by

Redo and Redo followed by Undo should cause no change to the content. Obviously, the commands should not apply to themselves. *The undo and redo operators are fundamental and are of sufficient importance to deserve their own dedicated key in future systems.* Redo should be *Shift↓ Undo↓↑↑*, with the key cap clearly marked with the words *Undo* and *Redo* (Figure 5.1). This key would be a good replacement for the problematic Caps Lock key.

Regarding the third drawback, I described the trouble with toggles in Section 3-2, in which I suggested that toggle should not appear in a humane interface. A simple solution is to use one command or quasimode to add an object to a selection and a different command or quasimode to remove an object from a selection. Trying to add an object already selected will not change the selection, and trying to remove an object not in the selection also will not change the selection.

An interface usually has one point at which its designers have interaction take place: the **focus**. For example, if you are a touch typist and your typing appears on the display, the place where the typing appears is the focus and, often, is colocated with your locus of attention. If you are not a touch typist, your locus of attention will alternate between the keyboard and the display. In interfaces that have a cursor, there is, at any moment, typically only one cursor. Its position is controlled by a GID, cursor-control keys, or commands, such as Find.

Figure 5.1. An Undo/Redo key.

Just as the locus of attention is always an object—physical, mental, or displayed—the same can be said for the system's focus. For example, in current word processors, it might seem that the cursor, when it has been clicked into a document—a click that should be unnecessary—is positioned between two letters, and thus, there is no object to be the focus. In fact, the focus is a pair of characters: the one to the left, which will be deleted if the next command is Delete, and the one to the right, where the next character inserted will appear.

When the human is leading the interaction, the focus will usually be the current selection. When the system is responding to a human or external action, the focus will usually be the result of the action.

5-2-2 Commands

Me, I have a science fiction writer's conviction that the damn robot is supposed to speak human, not the other way around.

—*Spider Robinson*

Some commands, such as Undo, are keyboard commands that are not necessarily related to selections. Other commands act only with respect to the current selection, such as the command that deletes the current selection. Certain of these commands are invoked by keystrokes; however, the number of keys on a keyboard or keypad is small relative to the number of possible commands. Each additional modifier key, such as Shift, Alt, Command, Control, or Option, doubles the number of possible key combinations. A full-chord keyboard, of which the computer can recognize any combination of keys, allows an astronomical number of key combinations; for example, software that uses any three-key double-quasimode combination on a 110-key keyboard can signal any one of more than one million commands with a single gesture. However, extensive use of modifier keys, especially in combination, quickly reaches finger-twisting, mind-numbing complexity. In addition, the combinations are rarely memorable or meaningful. (Do you know what *Control-Shift-Option-* tells your computer to do?) Learning arbitrary keyboard combinations is difficult; requiring such learning places an unacceptable burden on the user's memory. In addition, such commands violate the criterion of visibility unless the system displays what their effect will be whenever they can be invoked. Of course, if there are times when one of these gestures cannot be invoked or if the gesture has different meanings at different times, the system is modal with respect to that gesture, giving rise to problems discussed in Chapter 3.

If you divide the system into applications such that a particular command can be reused but is given different meanings in different applications, you increase the number of commands that a user can invoke for a given number of key combinations, but reuse of commands by applications that assign those commands different meanings causes the user to make mode errors. Varying the meanings of a gesture can also place an unnecessarily heavy burden on a user's memory. This burden is partially relieved by menus, although she still has to remember in which menu the command she seeks is hidden. (She may have to first recall which application contained the desired command, especially if several applications have similar capabilities.) This process of looking through menus is sometimes trivial, but it can be frustrating, especially if the command the user seeks is a few submenus deep and if what was to the designer the obvious way to organize the menus is not obvious to the user.

What is needed for invoking commands is a method that is as fast and physically simple to use as typing a few keystrokes and that also makes the commands easier and faster to find than does a menu system. We do not want to duplicate the dual method used in most popular GUIs, which includes both a slow menu-based system and an inscrutable set of keyboard shortcuts. For example, there is nothing memorable about using

Command ↓ *v*↓ ↑↑

for insert, aside from the *v* key's being adjacent to the slightly mnemonic *c* key used in

Command ↓ *c*↓ ↑↑

for "cut" or "copy."

An alternative approach solves many of these problems. Assume, for the moment, that the keyboard has a key labeled Calculate. When this Calculate key is tapped, the current selection is treated as an arithmetic expression and evaluated. In the following discussion, I will use underlining to indicate selection. Suppose that your text was

        I want to buy <u>3 + 4</u> shirts

A tap of the Calculate key would yield

        I want to buy <u>7</u> shirts

Before using the Calculate key, the *3 + 4* was ordinary text. Except that it was selected, there was still nothing special about it; the five characters, including spaces, of which the selection was composed could have been deleted or moved, or another typical word-processing command could have been applied to it. But in this case, the operation *calculate* was applied. The user did not need to open a calculator window or to invoke a calculator application.

Now consider that there was no dedicated Calculate key on the keyboard. (Although evaluation of mathematical expressions is certainly a candidate for a dedicated key, such a key would certainly be more valuable than many of the keys we do have, such as F9.) What we need is a more general mechanism for commands.

Before discussing such a mechanism, consider the requirements for an improved method of invoking commands. They might include that

- It not be modal

- It accommodate any number of commands—in particular, that it not be limited by the size of the keyboard

- You be able to invoke a command without taking your hands from the keyboard

- You be able to invoke a command with the graphical input device

- It not require a plethora of special keys

- The system not end up with too many quasimodes

One quite general method can best be introduced by means of an example. (This somewhat trivial arithmetic example is chosen to demonstrate the method; more efficient means of applying the method will be discussed later.) Assume that the text was

```
I want to buy 3 + 4 shirts calculate
```

Select the sum 3 + 4, and then select the word *calculate,* which makes the sum the old selection.

In an alternative method, one that gives the power of a command line interface to the user, a tap of the Command key can be used to invoke the selected command. If the command requires an argument, the old selection is used. In this method, the command itself is deleted, and the result of the evaluation is left selected.

```
I want to buy 7 shirts
```

The idea is that commands need not be restricted to supplied menus but can be part of your text, or, where appropriate, the command can be a graphical object instead of a word or a set of words. It is also important that commands can be provided by the user in the simplest possible way, by merely typing or drawing them anywhere. This use does not conflict with the method in which the command is selected from preexisting text.

Menus offer the advantage of making a list of commands visible. However, instead of selecting a command from a menu, the user could as easily select the command from a small document listing commands. It would not matter whether the document was provided for the user or whether she had typed it herself. Further, the document need not be limited to a bald list of commands. For example, each command could be accompanied by a description or even the user's own notes. A document that is used as a menu is an ordinary text document, not something that can be changed only by programmers or by using a special customization facility.

This approach has a number of advantages. For example, an online manual automatically contains functioning examples of the commands it is describing. In present systems, a menu command might or might not have a keyboard method. But in this approach, every command described by a sequence of characters in a menu has a keyboard equivalent. This is guaranteed not by the diligence of the designers but by the very nature of the system. If you find a command in a menu, that same spelling is the keyboard equivalent. It is the keyboard equivalent to which most users will habituate. Another advantage is that you can make up a menu comprising only those commands you use, by merely typing a list of the commands in your word processor. Of course, if you continually adjust the arrangement of a list as opposed to, for instance, adding to it, you lose the advantages of habituating to their location.

Just as web links in a text are often distinguished by being visually distinct—for example, they are often shown in color, typically blue, and are sometimes underlined—commands could be shown with some other special marking—red, with reverse italics, for instance. With such a distinction, the user would point to a command name so that a letter in the command is indicated, whereupon a tap of the Command key would invoke the command. This eliminates the step of having to select the command name in invoking a command.

If there were no special font or color for commands, it would be necessary to have another convention to show that a word or sequence of words was to be considered as a single command. It is wise to avoid some of the present-day conventions that are used to group separate words into a single entity delimited by spaces or other characters. For example, if there were a command that we wanted to call *change to JPEG bitmap,* present conventions would have us notate it as change.to.JPEG.bitmap, <change to JPEG bitmap>, or change_to_JPEG_bitmap. These notations are "computery," ugly, and discouraging, especially to newcomers to computers. *The syntax we choose for commands should not keep us from putting spaces or returns in them.* Any restriction in the character set we can use to name a command is likely to bite at a future time; moreover, any such restrictions have to be remembered when naming a command. Another principle to keep in mind is that *use of conventions not in accord with our natural-language conventions helps make computers feel unfriendly. We must bend the machine to work the way we do rather than change our language conventions to suit what is easiest to program.*

Another interaction of typing and selection causes problems in current interfaces. In a humane interface, typing does not replace selected text or cause the current selection to become unselected. This is the opposite of the common convention that typing replaces the current selection, a practice that occasionally causes users considerable grief when the new material unexpectedly overlays text they did not want to delete. The idea that typing should replace a selection was introduced to save a single keystroke: In most editors, when you wish to replace a block of text, you simply select some text and then type. Without this convention, you would select some text, tap Backspace or Delete, and then enter some text. The only keystroke the current convention saves is the backspace. With the usual convention, the text vanishes at your first keystroke, and your typing is inserted. This happens whether the text to be replaced was on screen or not and (usually) whether it was a few characters or three quarters of the novel you were writing; you may be deleting text that is 40 pages away from your locus of attention. To be sure, if you notice the problem in time, you can possibly undo it. However, if you do not notice the deletion—and there is nothing that lets you know that text has been deleted—you may be out of luck. A humane interface never puts your work at risk; the one saved keystroke in this case is bought at too great a price; if you lose even one character inadvertently, that character might be part of a phone number or part of an e-mail address that is unguessable from the remaining text. *The interface should require you to explicitly delete text if you want to delete text and not delete it as a side effect of another action.*

The concept of locus of attention is useful in defining what, exactly, we mean by a side effect: A **side effect** is an effect of a command that alters contents or events that are not your locus of attention. In the case just discussed, your locus of attention is the text being inserted, and the side effect is a deletion. *The elimination of side effects should be one of the goals of any designer of humane interfaces.*

Another word processor feature often considered helpful is the ability to drag a selection from one place to another in text. However, this prevents you from being able to create a new selection overlapping the current selection or to create a selection that is a subselection of the current selection. If you try to create either of those selections, the system assumes that you are trying to move the selection. This means that you have to click somewhere outside the selection to deselect the selected text before you can proceed. The dragging gesture has thus been given two different meanings, namely, selection and moving a selection. This can interfere with habit formation. Errors arise because, though the characters in the selection are your locus of attention, the current state of the selection is not your locus of attention, even though it is visually indicated. I have observed users inadvertently dragging a selection when they intended to create a new selection.

Another problem arises from dragging in text and also occurs in graphics applications: You will sometimes start to drag a selection only to discover that the destination is not visible on the display, in which case you have to put the selection back or into another place and change to the cut-and-paste method. The principle of monotony suggests that having only one method is preferable. Some systems begin to scroll when you bring the dragged selection to the top or the bottom of the display, but scrolling is much too slow if the destination is more than a few pages away. Scrolling can also be too fast, making it impossible to stop at, or even see, the desired destination.

If marketing could be kept from screaming too loudly, I would not design an interface with drag-and-drop in text, at least as it is presently implemented on personal computers. Users accustomed to having drag-and-drop in text would, I think, find sufficient compensation for this "loss" in having a system that causes less frustration and fewer errors. It would be better still to provide separate quasimodes for selection and dragging, because you could then have both selection and drag-and-drop without cognitive interference. For example, if the GID had a button that you pressed to make selections and if it also had a facility, such as a side-mounted button, that allowed you to squeeze the GID—with tactile feedback, such as a click, to let you know that the squeeze has been registered—to indicate that you've grabbed a selection, there would be little or no confusion between the two functions. After a few seconds of instruction and one or two trials, you would know how to use it ever thereafter. More pedestrian methods for separating the selection and drag gestures would be to use a different mouse button for dragging or to use a quasimode, such as holding down a special duly marked key while using the main mouse button. (See Appendix A for a more detailed rationale.)

Another use for a grab feature on a GID is as a replacement for scrolling. You can grab anywhere in the document and start it moving up and down: exclusively up and down for narrow documents; in any direction for wider documents. When the grab cursor—cleverly indicated by the image of a hand in some present systems—reaches a border of the display, scrolling continues in the present direction until the grab function is released or the cursor is moved back into the window. The customary method of scrolling via scroll bars is confusing. For example, pressing on the down-pointing scroll arrow makes the content of the screen scroll up; designing the arrows the other way around is only slightly more confusing. In addition, scroll-bar arrows are small features and therefore time consuming to use; being able to grab anywhere on the document is much faster, as a Fitts' law analysis readily shows.

The example of the need for a grab function on a mouse incidentally demonstrates that working on software interface design often generates ideas for improved hardware, just as hardware considerations can inspire improvements in the software design. It is always better to design hardware and software together, although opportunities to do so are rare. Trying to shoehorn a pure software interface into hardware designed for another interface is seldom completely satisfactory. Nonetheless, for most projects, that is what we must do.

5-2-3 Display States of Objects

A humane-interface feature must be both accessible to the naive and efficient for the expert, and the transition from one to the other should not demand retraining; a good interface should provide the user with one mental model that works for both classes of user—recalling, of course, that we are beginners or experts for different parts of a system independently. In the previous section, it was proposed that a key that executes text as commands can be used with selected text, whatever its source, to cause a command to be executed, assuming that the selected text is the name of a command; otherwise, there is no effect on the content. It is convenient to also allow the Command key to be held to create a quasimode during which a command can be typed. The convenience is highly dependent on the ergonomics of the Command keys. This last feature is an improvement on command line systems, which are much loved for their speed and convenience of operation and much hated for the difficulty with which they are learned. The improvements are two: You can issue the commands anywhere and at any time, and the commands are identical to those appearing on menus, so that the transition from menu to direct command is trivial.

Because it would be a waste of time and display space to designate a special location for typing commands, a command should be typed wherever the cursor happens to be at the moment the need for the command becomes apparent. The typed command name should be deleted after being executed, so that command names are not left scattered among your content. On the other hand, when you execute a command from a list of commands, you do not want the command to disappear; in effect, the list is a menu. To create such a menu, nothing more is needed than to type a list of commands, select the list, and then use a command, perhaps called Make Menu, that can change them to a distinctive style typically used only for commands and, at the same time, lock the list of items so that it cannot be inadvertently changed.

Here are some other commands that change the state of text. One convenience is to be able to simply lock text or other content, with a **Lock** command. Locked content can be seen, selected, and copied but cannot be changed or moved. The inverse, **Unlock**, can be applied to selected content and will unlock the selection if the selection was locked. (Otherwise, it has no effect; it must not toggle.) Another command, **Lock with Password**, locks the old selection, using the current selection as the password. It, too, has an inverse (**Unlock with Password**). Locked content has a wide range of utility; for example, it can be used to create forms to be filled out. The fixed parts of the form are locked or password locked. Simple locking prevents accidental changes; password locking prevents unauthorized changes. If the online instruction manual to a computer system were included as part of the text that the computer initially came with—which is not a bad idea—the online manual would probably be password locked at the factory.

Screen Lock and **Screen Unlock** lock and unlock the position of selected objects with respect to the display. With this facility, you can create menus that stay in place on the display as other objects move underneath them: You could simulate today's fixed-position menus. (Whether this is a good use of this facility is a different question.) To use this command, you would place the object as desired with respect to the screen, select it, and use the Screen Lock command. There could be a password-protected version of this as well, for occasions when it is undesirable for the user to redesign the menus.

Another useful command is one that controls the transparency of a selection. In some situations, such as when displaying error messages, it is useful to render the selection transparent enough so that underlying material can be seen and operated through (Figure 5.2). Similarly, another command

beyond building the most primitive of mechanical engines if

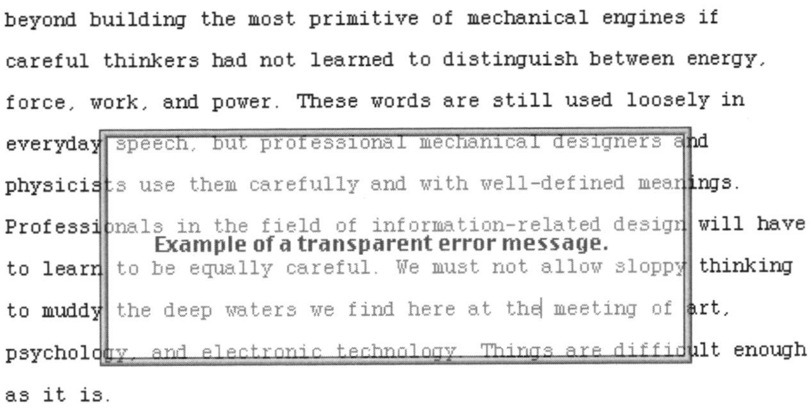

careful thinkers had not learned to distinguish between energy,

force, work, and power. These words are still used loosely in

everyday speech, but professional mechanical designers and

physicists use them carefully and with well-defined meanings.

Professionals in the field of information-related design will have

Example of a transparent error message.

to learn to be equally careful. We must not allow sloppy thinking

to muddy the deep waters we find here at the meeting of art,

psychology, and electronic technology. Things are difficult enough

as it is.

Figure 5.2. A transparent error message over background text has an efficiency of 1.

could specify whether an object hides or is hidden by or is viewed through another object. A transparent message box can fade gradually instead of abruptly, giving you time to notice it. A document that stores all messages for later review is essential.

Because you can click through a transparent dialog box, removing it requires no keystrokes; it is modeless and highly efficient, with an efficiency of 1. As with any method, this idea has its limitations and can be overused; a deluge of unnecessary messages is still distracting, even if they disappear when the user proceeds. In accord with the principle of visibility, a visible distinction should be provided to allow a user to determine whether text is locked, screen locked, locked with a password, and so forth.

A humane-interface principle is that the system itself should be built out of the same kind of pieces with which you are familiar from your everyday use of the system. This makes your product less forbidding.

5-3 File Names and Structures

Mankind are more disposed to suffer, while evils are sufferable, than to right themselves by abolishing the forms to which they are accustomed.

—*Thomas Jefferson, Declaration of Independence of the United States of America*

Because the restriction of file name length to 8 characters in earlier systems was truly dreadful, the 31-character maximum length offered by the Macintosh looked like heaven to many users. But this modification was just a different-size straitjacket. Aside from the real limits of the hardware, an interface should have few, if any, fixed-length limits. An interface should use dynamic memory allocation, linked lists, hashing, or whatever techniques seem best but should never present a user with software implementation limitations, such as "you can have up to 255 categories" or "paragraphs can be up to 32,000 characters."[2]

What is a file name? From the user's perspective, it is a handle with which to grab a file. As we know from long experience, file names do not work as one would expect; they are an impediment when you want to save, futile when you want to find. Let me be more specific: File names are bothersome when you are about to save work, because you have to stop in the middle of your activity, which is trying to store your work away, and invent a file name.[3] Creating names is an onerous task: You are required to invent, on the spot and in a few moments, a name that is unique, memorable, and within the naming conventions of the system you are using. Furthermore, at that moment, the question of a file name is not your locus of attention; preserving your work is. File names are also a nuisance when you have to retrieve a file. The name you thought up was probably not particularly memorable, and you probably forgot it after a few weeks (or less). I, for one, can rarely remember a file name unless it is quite recent; even looking through lists of file names is frustrating. Just what is in that file that is labeled "notes ybn 32"? The name seemed so clever and memorable when I created it. Then, too, many files are nearly the same. How many different, creative, readily remembered names can you think up for letters to your accountant about last year's taxes? Filing them by date may be useful, but how many of us remember that the letter about the deduction for the company truck was written on August 14?

Having to name files increases the mental burden on the user. Giving a file a name does nothing more than add a few characters to the file, and you are required to remember the file by that one tiny portion and by nothing else. I count this as one of the major horrors visited upon us by conventional computer systems. Many information appliances have also adopted this inhumane methodology.

There should be no distinction between a file name and a file. A human mind can more effectively use a fast, whole-text search engine, so

---

2. A word processor I once used quite a while ago had this paragraph size limit. I exceeded it as soon as I inserted a photograph into a paragraph; when I spoke to the designers, they admitted they had never thought of that. The moral: Never put in a fixed limit because it makes the software easier to write; it will always be too small.

3. This is in the context of present systems. You should never have to explicitly perform a save in future, humane systems.

that any word or phrase from the file can serve as a key to it. (Eventually, we'd want more: A request for "a letter about dragonflies" would cause a search that looked for something that had the form of a letter and looked not only for the word *dragonfly* but also for related terms or expressions, such as *Odonata*—in case dragonflies had been referred to by their scientific name—and if no instances of such letters were found, the search would look for nonletter documents with that content, and so forth, extending out to networked computers and to the Internet.) You do not remember the content of "Letter 12/21/92 to Jim" when you see that title, but you do remember that you once wrote to Jim about the blue Edsel that ran across your eyeglasses. A search on *Edsel* is likely to find only one or two entries on your whole system—unless you are an Edsel fancier, in which case you would probably choose another pattern on which to search. An unlimited-length file name is a file. *The content of a text file is its own best name.*

Graphics and sound files often require names; Section 6-2 discusses an approach that avoids the memory burden that traditional file structures impose for nontext files. Aside from nontext files, given a fast whole-text search, file names—one whole species of unnecessary entities—can be eliminated. With the removal of file names go all the mechanisms for dealing with file names, such as directories of file names, rules for editing file names, and syntactic restrictions on file names. When file names are eliminated, a significant mental burden and much internal machinery—machinery that is currently part of what you have to learn and what programmers have to implement—vanishes.

The best interface to a whole-text search is interactive, where you see each found instance in context as it is found. In this interface, as soon as you see what you want, you are there. Some systems present copies of the found instances in the line that contains them (Drori 1998). However, this method is not as efficient as the first kind of search, because you must then perform a second operation to reach the instance itself; for example, you must click on the copy of the desired instance.

For users who insist on a system that looks like conventional file structures, there can be a command that creates an "information document" or an extra page at the end of each document when the document is selected and the command applied. The information document or page would contain such information as the date and time the document was created or modified, a revision history, the length of the first document, or whatever information seems of value. The software to implement such a command would have to acquire and store the necessary information invisibly to the user. Various vendors might provide different facilities, depending on user needs. For users who wish to hold on to their old ways, a vendor could even go so far as to create utilities that create documents that look and act just like the annoying directories we now have.

Another source of organization, one that is easier to learn and to use than traditional file systems, comes from the inherent hierarchical structure of many natural languages: Words are separated by spaces. Sentences, or sequences of words, are separated by one of a small number of delimiters, followed by a space. (In English, these delimiters include periods, question marks, and exclamation points.) Paragraphs, or sequences of sentences, are separated by at least one explicit Return. Explicit page characters, or page breaks, separate chapters or whatever you wish to call the next level of organization.

In a consistent system, page breaks should be characters and, unlike most present systems, they should behave—in terms of insertion, deletion, and searching—just as any other characters do. As with Return, there may be implicit page breaks to accommodate the fixed length of physical pages, but these are not part of the content.[4]

There is good reason not to stop here in the hierarchy as many present systems do. Documents are sequences of pages separated by document characters, each typable, searchable, and deletable, just as is any other character. There can be higher delimiters, such as folder and volume characters, even section and library delimiters, but the number of levels depends on the size of the data. A set of two consecutive document characters makes a fine delimiter for sets of documents. If more levels of organization are needed, three or four consecutive document characters could be used as delimiters. It can be easier to repeatedly tap the Document key, even four times, than to type such rarely used keys as Folder, Volume, and Library. This convention also prevents an explosion of new keys on the keyboard. It is important for all delimiter characters to have dedicated keys, for otherwise, they would not behave as do all other typable characters. That is, we should not use a keystroke for, say, Return, and then use an Insert Page Break command; we must have a page character.

Because the various separator characters would behave exactly as did all other characters, there would be no need to teach users how to do searches for them. An individual who insists on having explicit document names can adopt the personal convention of placing the desired names

---

4. Dr. James Winter, at Information Appliance, further unified the structure by pointing out that English already has the same kind of hierarchical, character-delimited structure proposed for the higher levels of organization.

immediately following document characters. To find a document with the name "Dogs of Asia," you would search for a string that began with a document character followed by *Dogs of Asia*. Such a search would ignore all instances of *Dogs of Asia* except those used as document names. If you wanted a directory, there could be a command that would assemble a document comprising all instances of strings consisting of a document character, followed by any other characters, up to and including the first Return or higher delimiter.

Eliminating hierarchical file structures does not mean that you have to give up structuring your stored information. Nothing prevents you from creating tables of contents and indexes or putting all of your letters to Uncle Albert and Aunt Agatha on consecutive pages. Nothing prevents you from even putting a heading page (just another document) labeled "Letters to Uncle Albert and Aunt Agatha" in front of them. If that is done, you have created, in effect, a file name but without having added a special mechanism in the software. You can create, if you wish, a hierarchical file structure of your own so that, if you really love file names and hierarchies, you can have them. Structure, as you choose to create it, is part of your *content,* not part of the *interface.*[5] Instead of a file-finding facility, you simply use the general search mechanism to find the file names you have squirreled away. You can place a folder name as a document in front of a number of collected files; you can place a volume name in front of a bunch of collected folders. (Your pattern would be a volume character, followed by the name of the volume; such a pattern would eliminate matches to other occurrences of the name that happen not to be labels of volumes.) The absence of a built-in file organization does not prevent you from creating a file that fits your needs and one that, because *you* created it, you understand. But also, because the system has not been changed in any way, a guest can find things in your structure and, in fact, can ignore your structure and treat it as a flat, unstructured, file.

One advantage of filing information as you wish is that the structures were not dictated by the system designers, who may have ideas different from yours. Therefore, you do not have to develop a mental model of what the designers were trying to do. Many users do develop inaccurate models of how systems work; these mental models persist and cause continuing difficulties for those users (Norman 1988).

This discussion is not theoretical: On the SwyftWare and Canon Cat products, the elimination of file names, directories, and the various mechanisms usually provided for manipulating them proved one of their most

---

5. The same is true of file names and menus proposed in this book.

successful features. Users experienced at conventional computer systems sometimes found it difficult to make the transition to content-based organization, but once they had made the transition, the conventional methods soon began to seem cumbersome. Users who started on the Cat were not amused at having to learn the more complex and difficult methods of conventional file systems when they moved to a PC or a Macintosh.

To users accustomed to standard GUI practices, the methods outlined here may seem complex by comparison. But the apparent complexity is due to the new paradigm's lack of familiarity and to our having become habituated to the many steps we must take and to the problems we have with the current system. The learning curve has been long surmounted. But when you compare the progress of beginners with the two systems or compare the performance of experienced users, the advantages of the simpler system become apparent.

Consider that you have *n* documents that you want to copy to an external medium, such as a hard drive. With, for example, the Macintosh operating system (OS), you drag the icon of each document to the icon of the drive, and it is copied. In the new paradigm, it seems at first more complicated: You have to find the beginning and the end of each document, select the document, move the cursor to a place on the drive, and then move each document.

Recall that in the GUI, you start in the generating application. Your first step is to get to the desktop. You must also know which icons correspond to the desired documents, and you or someone else had to have gone through the steps of naming those documents. You also will have to know in which folder they are stored. So the apparent simplicity is arrived at only after considerable work has been done and the user has shouldered a number of mental burdens. A more efficient method involves an interface invention called LEAP. Assume, as we did for the GUI, that the cursor is in one of the documents you wish to move. With LEAP, the user can select the document with six keystrokes, and without having to look at the screen or recall the document's name. To type six keystrokes takes less time than to drag an icon.

LEAP works like this: There are two LEAP keys which lie under the thumbs. LEAP-Up searches forward and LEAP-Down searches backwards from the cursor position. Pressing and holding a LEAP key puts you into a quasimode during which whatever you type is used as a search pattern. To select the document you'd LEAP-Up to a document character (LEAP-Up↓ Doc↓↑↑). This puts the cursor at the beginning of the document. Then you'd LEAP-Down to a document character (the search will find the document character at the end of the document). A tap of both LEAP keys together selects the text. (This is probably most easily done when the LEAP keys are operated by the thumbs, which are otherwise underutilized in typing. See Figure 2.1 for a typical keyboard designed for this use of LEAP. A dedicated Select key is another alternative.) In order that the function be visible, a legend adjacent to the LEAP keys is needed. The legend could, for example, read "Press both LEAP keys together to make a selection." Note that you do not have to watch the display while you select the document. Once a document is selected, the cursor is LEAPed to wherever you want to place the document. When the drive was plugged into the computer, its contents became part of the contents of the system, so no special mechanism is required to find it. A Copy command completes the operation. When selected this way, the document includes its separators. Thus, if the document is moved, it retains its character as a document because the document separators move with it.

The same technique used to copy a document—or a selection of any length from a character to a set of documents or the entire contents of the system!—from here to there is used to move a selection; the only difference is that a Move command rather than a Copy command is given. The process is functionally no more complex than that needed in the GUI. It is often faster, and the number of methods, concepts, and structures that an individual must understand is lower.

Consider how you would use the LEAP-based paradigm to put a few selections from different documents together onto a drive, and then consider how you would perform the same task using a GUI. With LEAP, the method is the same as that just described for moving documents to the drive: The selections are *found*—and once found, do not have to be opened, because the concept of opening a document is superfluous—*selected,* as described previously, except using the text rather than document characters at the beginning and end of the selection; and *copied* into place. In a GUI, the user must first *open* a new destination document, possibly by using the New command in the File menu of the application; *find* a document that contains a selection the user needs; *open* the document; *find* the selection within the document; *select* it; *use* the Copy command; *activate* the destination document; *paste* the selection in; *activate* the desktop; *find* the next document that has a desired selection; and *repeat* until all of the selections have been pasted into the destination document. Then you must *save* the result to the drive by using a dialog box.

Even if the complexity of doing any task was the same in either paradigm, the conceptual simplicity of the methods outlined here would be preferable. In most cases, the work required is also far less.

5-4 String Searches and Find Mechanisms

One giant leap for mankind.

—*Neil Armstrong (1969)*

Before going further into LEAP, it is useful to treat the subject of the interface to searches with somewhat more precision. A **string** is a sequence[6] of characters; ordinary English words and sentences are examples of strings. **String searches** look through a (usually lengthy) string, called the **text**, for an instance of a (usually brief) string that the user specifies, called the **pattern**. Each occurrence of a substring of the text that matches the pattern is called a **target**. For example, if you were trying to find where you had written of a cat called "little Tatsu" in a long letter, *little Tatsu* is a good choice of target, and you might choose the briefer string *Tatsu* as the pattern to use in the search. The match may be exact, may be case-independent, or may represent another relationship between the pattern and the target; they might rhyme, for example. A commonly used matching criterion, one that tests well, is that lower-case letters in the pattern match *either* uppercase or lowercase letters in the text

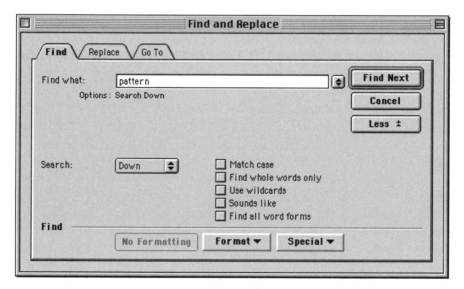

Figure 5.3. A modal-search dialog box with modal-search types and direction settings.

---

6. I use the term **sequence** as mathematicians do, to mean a set of objects having a first object, a second, and so forth.

but that uppercase characters in the pattern match only uppercase characters in the text. Searches usually start from the current cursor location and continue forward through the text. In most systems, a modal user preference setting can direct the search to proceed backward through the text (Figure 5.3).

Interfaces to searches are typically based on either of two search interface strategies. The most common strategy is the **delimited search**, found in most word processors. In a typical delimited search, the user enters a mode in which typing or other method of text input is regarded not as text but as a pattern. This is usually accomplished by using a dialog box containing a field into which the user can enter characters. After summoning the dialog box, the user types the pattern, followed by a delimiter, which is usually a character, such as Return, that is not permitted to occur in the pattern. In most dialog boxes, the user may also limit the pattern by using the GID to click a button with a label such as OK, Search, Find, or Find Next. When it is found in the text, a target is selected, and the cursor is placed immediately at the end of the selection.

This traditional method is rather punishing to the user, although most computer aficionados have become so accustomed to it that they no longer feel the pain. For example, an individual can type in a search string, make a typo—unnoticed until too late, of course, because he pressed Return by habit—and sit there, waiting for a search that he knows will fail. Most searches are not interruptible: a serious design error. Because the computer waits until the user has finished the pattern before beginning its search, delimited searches often keep him waiting unnecessarily.

The less common strategy is the **incremental search**, a popular example of which is found in EMACS, an editor used with the UNIX operating system (Stallman 1993). In most implementations of incremental searches, as with the delimited search, the user first summons a dialog box that contains a field in which the user can enter the pattern. When he types the first character of the pattern, however, the system uses this character alone as a complete pattern and immediately begins to search for the first instance of that character in the chosen search direction. If an instance of that first character is found before the next character of the pattern is typed, the instance is selected and the cursor placed immediately after the end of the selection. If the next character of the pattern is typed before an instance is found, that character is added to the pattern and the search continues, now looking for an instance of the now extended pattern. This method is repeated as each character is added to the pattern.

Using the Backspace or Delete key to delete a character from an incremental search pattern should return the search to the previously found instance that matched the pattern, as it was before the deleted character had been added to the pattern. The user can then add to the pattern, and the search continues without his losing the search already accomplished on the partial pattern. Many implementations do not have this desirable characteristic.

Incremental searching has a number of other advantages over delimited searching. Incremental searching wastes less of a user's time: The search begins when the first character of the pattern is typed; the system does not wait until the pattern is complete. With a delimited search, the computer waits for the user to type the pattern and delimit it, after which it is the user who waits while the computer does the search. When using a delimited search, the user must guess, beforehand, at how much of a pattern the computer needs to distinguish the desired target from other, similar targets; with an incremental search, he can tell when he has typed enough to disambiguate the desired instance, because the target has appeared on the display. Thus, as soon as he sees that he has reached the point desired, he can stop entering the pattern. If he types too many letters of the pattern—if the hand is quicker than the search—the pattern will still match, and the cursor will stay approximately where he wanted it. If he mistypes a pattern in a delimited search, he must wait until the search for the incorrect pattern is complete—or, at best, he can operate a mechanism for stopping the search—before he can correct his error. In a large text, the search can take a considerable period of time. In a well-implemented incremental search, the user can backspace at any time and be returned to the last match found. Because backspacing after an error is habitual, the process of correcting an error is very fast, and the search stops immediately. He can also resume the search by typing the correct character.

Another advantage of incremental search is that, as the user enters the pattern, it provides constant feedback as to the results of the search. With a delimited search, he does not find out whether his pattern is suitable or even if it was typed correctly until it is fully entered and a search attempt has been made. From the point of view of interface engineering, the advantages of incremental searching are so numerous and the advantages of delimited searches so few that I can see almost no occasions when a delimited search would be preferred.[7] In spite of near universal agreement about the desirability of incremental searches on the part of both designers and users, almost all interface-building tools make it easy to implement delimited searches and difficult or impossible to implement incremental searches. JavaScript and Visual BASIC are two examples of such.

Building a pattern incrementally allows the user to adjust the pattern interactively during the search, which leads the user to improve his search

---

7. A search is either incremental or excremental.

strategies through the feedback received. Even building a Boolean search pattern is made more effective when the early results of the pattern appear as the user adds to the pattern's specificity. The found instance should appear in the middle of a display area, not at the top or the bottom. Thus, material both before and after the instance is visible; that is, the found instance is displayed in context. The instance of the pattern found should always appear in the same place relative to the display or window so that the user soon learns where to look for the result of the search. In the Canon Cat, it always appeared at the vertical center of the display. It should not appear adjacent to any edge of the display area, so that material on all sides of the found instance is shown.

If an instance of the pattern does not occur in the text, the search fails. Many systems cease operating in this event and remain unusable until a particular key—typically Enter or Return—is pressed or a particular on-screen button is clicked. A modal message is placed on the display to let you know that you must make the required obeisance before you will be allowed to continue using the computer. In multidisplay systems or if the screen is visually busy, this message may be nowhere near your locus of attention. You may not notice it at all. It then seems to you that the computer will not respond to the keyboard; it seems to have crashed. In an incremental search, it is clear, without any special indication, that a search has failed; the cursor returns to its original location, and additional keystrokes do not have any effect. A short beep or a screen flash can also be helpful, especially if the search exceeded the duration of short-term memory, say, 10 seconds, so that the user has forgotten the appearance of the display prior to the search. The beep is also a useful cue for visually impaired users.

5-4-1 Search-Pattern Delimiters

Another major deficiency of delimited searches is that the delimiter used to end the pattern cannot be typed into the pattern. Often, other delimiters are excluded as well. I looked at four popular word processors, one did not allow a Return in a search pattern at all. In the second word processor, the user types ^r to insert a return into the search pattern. In the third, \ \ is used; and in the fourth, a Return is put into a search pattern by the use of a special dialog box with a pull-down menu of delimiters (Figure 5.4). It is easier to simply press the Return key when creating a pattern. After all, that's how you enter it into text; why should it be different in entering a pattern? The general principle is that *the same sequence of characters should always be typed the same way; you should not have to use one method here and*

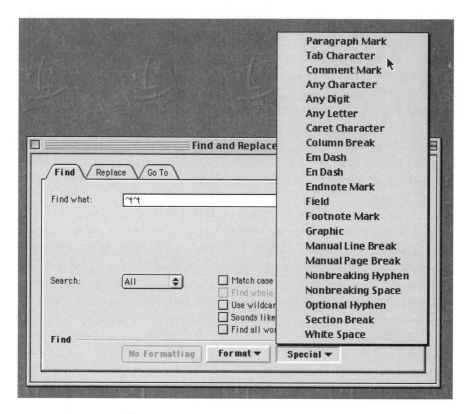

Figure 5.4. The Word search box opened to show the list of characters that can be inserted. With a better search design, the user could put, say, a tab in a search string just by tapping the Tab key. Note the two codes for tab characters inserted into the pattern (the Find What box).

another method there. Another way of saying this is that there should be nothing special about special characters.[8]

Although incremental searches are better than delimited searches, further interface improvement over the EMACS style of incremental search is possible. For example, the search should leave the cursor on the first character of the target rather than on the last. In general, you have little control over what will be the last character in your pattern, because you type just enough pattern to find your target. Thus, you do not know exactly where the cursor will be when you are finished. If the cursor lands on the first character of the pattern, you can predict how the target will appear. This also

---

8. A parallel problem is the use of reserved words in programming languages.

means that the search mechanism can also be used to quickly position the cursor in text, because your locus of attention is the character on which you want the cursor to be placed. Trying to invent a pattern where this is the last character in the pattern is far more difficult than typing the desired character and whatever follows it on the display.

In conventional GUIs, both delimited and incremental searches are initiated modally, by means of a dialog box. LEAP is modeless. The concept of using a quasimode for searches can be extended to a button on a microphone (or GID) that is held to create a quasimode during which words, sketches, or handwritten letters are used to create a search pattern. Other input techniques have analogous means for creating a search quasimode (Raskin and Winter 1991).

The speed of incremental searches is increased when a few implementation tricks are used; for example, when you type the first character of the search string, the computer instantly proceeds to find the first instance of that character in the text, which is highlighted and, if it is not there already, moved with its context into the display window. This is usually a fast process because there are a lot of potential matches, and one is likely to be close in text. While waiting for the user to type the next character, a search can be started for the next instance of the first letter, followed by each of the next possible characters, working in decreasing frequency-of-use order to maximize the probability of an early hit. The program can save pointers to each as they are found. When the second character is typed, the computer will often be ready to display the found target, seemingly instantly.

String searches can also be speeded by such methods as the Boyer-Moore algorithm for fast string search (Moore and Boyer 1977), whereby search time decreases as search-string length increases. In case the user backspaces through the pattern, keeping a pointer to the last-found location—one for each character in the search string—can make going back blindingly fast. Indexing all local mass-storage devices can make searching over a local system or network take only milliseconds. Interaction at high speeds, with wide area networks or the web, also depends on indexing methods. Incremental searching, in various versions, has been available in such commercial products as Borland's IDE, Global Village's fax program, the Canon Cat, and SwyftWare.

5-4-2 Units of Interaction

Incremental searches are just one example of a broader humane-interface design principle: *A program should interact with you on the basis of the smallest meaningful unit of input.* Interaction with input from a keyboard should be on a character-by-character basis, not on a line-by-line basis. Voice input should interact on a word-by-word basis; for some applications, interaction could be on a morpheme-by-morpheme basis, and so on.

Interaction by means of entering an entire line of text, that is, text delimited by a Return, at a time is a holdover from the days of the Teletype and should be relegated to a museum alongside the hardware of that time.[9] Today, we can and should have interfaces able to react to each character as you enter it, whenever such a reaction could improve the quality of the interaction. As always, designers must be considerate: Character-at-a-time interaction should not be used to deliver spelling-error messages in the middle of typing a word, correctly judged a nuisance by touch typists.

In the small texts for which string searches were originally designed, searching usually proceeded from the current cursor position to the end of the text. In larger texts, it is generally a good idea to continue the search, if it has not found a target by the time it has reached the end, circularly from the beginning back to the cursor location, in case the user has forgotten that the desired target is farther back in the text. Unpublished testing at Information Appliance demonstrated that, if the search is fast, the circular search is especially favored by users. Fast means here that there is not enough time for a user action between the time the search is launched and the time it succeeds or fails: as usual, about 250 msec. In many systems, the user can also choose to have the search stop at the end of the file or search circularly. This causes a typical mode problem: If the search is set to noncircular and the user is not aware of the setting, a "string not found" message can give the misimpression that there is no instance of the pattern in the text. Or, what I have seen happen on many occasions, the user repeats the search a number of times because he distinctly recalls that there was an instance of the pattern in the text, and he is puzzled and frustrated by the search's repeated failure. It can be many seconds or even minutes before he either figures out the problem or gives up in frustration. If it is necessary to have different kinds of searches, this can be accomplished modelessly by using a different command or on-screen button to launch each kind of search.

In many circumstances, modality can be avoided by having a set of launch buttons, one for each variety of an operation, instead of having means for setting up the desired variety and providing only one launch but-

---

9. There is an ever increasing need for a museum of interaction (MOI), as we have museums for hardware and software. The Internet might be an appropriate home.

ton to initiate the operation under conditions you have established. This improvement not only eliminates a mode but also saves keystrokes. Also, the user's locus of attention is the task that he wants done, not the setting up for the task. Figure 5.5, a typical set-up-then-launch dialog box found in Microsoft Word, exhibits a second interface problem: Should the radio buttons be always in the state shown when the user opens the box? Should they be in the state that he last left them, or should there be a preference setting as to which is the default?

All three interface options are wrong. If the user is always updating the entire table, the first option forces two clicks—or a click and a Return—every time. If the box is left in the last-used position, the user cannot use the box habitually, because he has to stop and check on its state each time. If there is a user preference (see Section 3-2-2), then a mode has been set up.

The dialog box of Figure 5.6 solves all of these problems at once, and the larger buttons have a Fitts' law advantage over the radio buttons. The Cancel button could be eliminated if this box were transparent, as discussed in Section 5-2-3. The two buttons would not be transparent, showing that they are active.

Figure 5.5. Dialog box with check boxes for different kinds of searches, and one launch button.

Figure 5.6. More efficient dialog box with different launch buttons.

Delimited-search dialog boxes usually provide a facility that allows you to reuse the current pattern in a search that begins just after the last instance was found. This can be thought of as a "look again" or "find next" facility; in some implementations, it is invoked by operating the same button used to launch the initial search. With an incremental search facility, a command dedicated to searching again for the same target is required, because no command was necessary to launch the original search. It is dangerous to use a tap of the Search quasimode key to repeat the search, as a user might intend to do a search, press the key, and then change his mind and release it. Under such circumstances, an unwanted search would be started, and he could lose his place as a result. Although a complete undo facility can ameliorate the danger, it is better not to create the problem. A specific method for repeated searches is discussed in Section 5-6.

In larger texts, a search can proceed circularly not only through the local document but also afterward in automatically expanding domains, up to and including the entire Internet.[10] After the local document has been completely searched, the search then proceeds through the following documents until the end of the folder is reached, when the search continues from the beginning of the first document in the folder until the current, already searched document is reached. After cycling through the folder, the next larger domain is treated similarly, and so forth. When, during an incremental search, a user sees that his search has gone too far afield, he can stop searching, confident that any nearer instance of the pattern does not exist. It is usually easy to tell in what domain you are searching, because you see the results in context; what you see is not just a list of file names, as with many present search systems.

Generally, people will use more efficient strategies than simply relying on this expanding sweep of the hierarchy. For example, if you are looking for a particular document in the current folder, you would be likely to do a repeated search for document characters and would thus quickly be able to review the beginning of, and any heading on, each document. When the desired document is found, an incremental search for the target is initiated. This guarantees that the chosen document is searched first; the advantage of this is that you can typically use a shorter pattern if the area to be searched is smaller. If you did not know in what document the target resided or if you did not want to look for the document, you could perform a specific search from the beginning, which would find the target anyway.

---

10. It is entirely possible, by such techniques as lookahead and indexing, to maintain the 250 msec response time.

5-5 Cursor Design and a Strategy for Making Selections

The traditional intent of both delimited- and incremental-string searches is to find and to select a target string in the text. Patterns that people use in searches tend to be short because long patterns are tedious to type and, in most systems, must be accurate to the character if they are to match the target. Therefore, string searches typically are not used to select even moderately large targets—say, those greater than 10 or 15 characters in length—much less truly large blocks of text. One application of string searches is to help you find the location of a desired selection, after which you use another technique, such as using a GID to drag from one end of the selection to the other, to establish the selection. However, if the ends of the selection are not visible simultaneously, you must use another strategy. The strategy consists of (1) marking one end of the selection, with the method of marking depending on the system being used; (2) using such facilities as scroll bars to make the other end of the selection visible; and (3) marking the other end of the selection. In most systems, marking the second end of the selection establishes the desired selection.

A more efficient approach is to design the search mechanism such that it positions the cursor on a particular character. Two such positionings can be used to define the first and last characters of a selection. The multiplicity of mechanisms conventionally needed to find the ends of a selection—cursor motion, scrolling, various page and pattern find facilities, and so on—and to mark them are replaced with one mechanism used twice, making learning, operation, and habituation easier and simplifying the implementation.

It is now useful to examine the graphical design of cursors. Currently, the most common form of text cursor is one that appears between characters, as shown in Figure 5.7. One problem with the standard text cursor is that users try to place it precisely between pairs of characters, aiming at a smaller horizontal target than is necessary and thus incurring a Fitts' law time penalty. During testing at Information Appliance, we were surprised to discover that this popular form of cursor caused an interesting cognitive

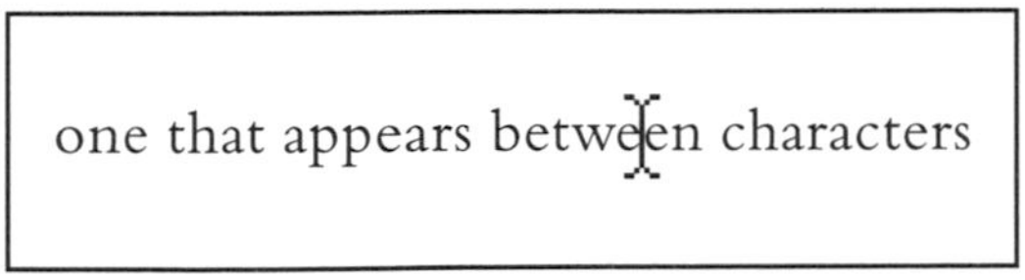

one that appears betwe‸en characters

Figure 5.7. The standard between-character cursor.

problem as well: You must place the cursor differently, depending on what you plan to do next. In particular, if you wish to delete an existing character with the usual Backspace key, you place the cursor to the right of the character in English and other left-to-right languages; to insert a character in the location of an existing character—the existing character will be shifted to the right when you do so—you place the cursor to the left of the existing character. We were surprised because the standard cursor's operation is so familiar that we had not given any thought to its possibly being the cause of problems.[11] As anybody who has tried to use one knows, the standard cursor is not difficult to understand. Nonetheless, a small amount of confusion and a few errors can be observed when newcomers to computers first use it. Their confusion is exacerbated by the invisibility of the loci of action of the commands.

It is no solution to provide a mode in which deletion occurs in a direction opposite to the usual one. This method, called forward erase, does allow you to always place the cursor to the left of the character to be acted on, but you will sometimes unexpectedly delete in the wrong direction because the current deletion direction is not your locus of attention. If two-way deletion is desired, it is better to use separate buttons or to use a quasi-mode for opposite-direction deletion.

A useful improvement to text-related interfaces is to use a cursor that visually indicates both (1) the insertion location and (2) the character or characters that will be deleted if backspace is used. The second form of highlighting can be identical to that used for highlighting a selection. One way to do this is shown in Figure 5.8.

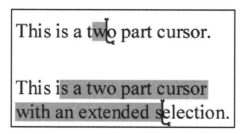

Figure 5.8. A two-part cursor, both with a single character and with an extended selection. The insertion portion of the cursor is blinking to make it easier to find on a cluttered screen.

---

11. This example is another demonstration of the importance of testing an interface on the intended audience.

Moving a cursor to a target with a GID is an iterative process; the user visually acquires the target first and then moves the cursor toward the target. If she does not remember where the cursor is, she may have to search visually to find it as well. She then reacquires the target, and so on, until both target and cursor are in the same, approximately 5 degree, foveal field of vision. This amounts to several time-consuming processes the human must undertake in cursor moves using a GID. Nonetheless, a GID is required for pointing to graphical objects or when working in a totally graphic environment.

The sloth of the GID in text pointing is exacerbated in the case of having to point to off-page locations. In these cases, exclusive use of a GID forces you to use scroll bars, page number selectors, or other mechanisms to view the content to which you wish to point. Each of these methods has to be learned, and many of them are slow.

LEAP offers the user the cognitive advantage of not having to choose, depending on the remoteness of the target, between different strategies (Alzofon et al. 1987). Having both LEAP and a GID does mean that there are two basic cursor-moving methods; however, instead of choosing your method depending on the distance between the cursor and your target, you choose your method depending on the content of the target. As is usually the case, the content is your locus of attention, which makes a LEAP/GID split cognitively simpler.

LEAP is useful in voice-controlled systems and for users with motor impairments or repetitive stress injuries, for whom the minimization of keystrokes is of especial value. A button, perhaps placed on the microphone, establishes the LEAP quasimode. The target of a LEAP is always a particular character in the text, and that character—whether the user is seeing it or thinking about it—is usually the locus of attention during the LEAP. Unlike using a GID, the user does not have to visually find the target before being able to move the cursor to it. This property is so strong that LEAP can be effectively used by the blind. This was tested at the Veteran's Administration Hospital in Palo Alto (unpublished).

What is most important, however, is that LEAP is used so widely in systems designed around it that its use soon becomes automatic, and there is nothing in the design of LEAP that prevents beneficial habit formation or that causes problems after habitual use is established. For LEAP to work properly, it must be fast, always finding the next instance of the current pattern within human reaction time, thus not giving the user any motivation or time to act during the search. The necessary speed can be achieved by the methods discussed in Section 5-4.

A GOMS keystroke-level analysis can be used to compare GID and LEAP timings. Where the user's hands start on the keyboard, using a GID to point to a letter in text requires operations HPK. By the rules for placing the M operator, we obtain $HMPK$, or $0.4 + 1.35 + 1.1 + 0.2 = 3.05$ seconds. The time to perform a LEAP depends on the number of characters you have to type to reach your target. Testing showed that the average number of characters used in LEAPing was about 3.5 for operators tested during their first week of use of the Canon Cat. The operations required to move the cursor to a particular target are pressing the LEAP key and then typing 3.5 characters. An average LEAP thus consists of typing 4.5 characters. Adding the M operator gives, according to the rules, a time of $1.35 + (4.5 \star 0.2) = 2.25$ seconds.

A timed experiment, with experienced users as subjects, compared the mouse with LEAP. The cursor had to be moved between two randomly chosen characters on a display 25 lines by 80 characters and where the timing did not start until the mouse began to move or the LEAP key was pressed. The measured average times were about 3.5 seconds for the mouse and 1.5 seconds for LEAP. The longer-than-calculated times for the mouse are probably due to the small size of the targets, which were individual characters: a Fitts' law effect. The unexpectedly short times for LEAP are probably due to the small size of the text, which allowed an average pattern length of about 2 characters. The subjects were given unlimited time for planning their actions before using the mouse or LEAP. *Very often, you can complete a cursor move with LEAP faster than you can move your hands from keyboard to mouse.*

5-6 Cursor Position and LEAP

The target of a LEAP is a single character. Should the cursor land to the right or to the left of this character? Placing the cursor to the left of the character is correct only if you intend to insert at that character location. Placing the cursor to the right of the character is correct only if you intend to delete that character. The computer, it would seem, has to know your intentions before it can position the cursor properly.

For insertion, consider instead the old-fashioned cursor that forms a rectangle about or an underline beneath the letter. When you LEAP to a letter, the cursor should land *on* the letter itself. (The cursor does not interfere with the readability of the letter; see Figure 5.9.) Now you can insert or delete at that location without ambiguity. The block cursor allows you to more accurately indicate where insertion and deletion will occur than does the standard, between-character cursor.

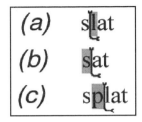

*Figure 5.9. (a) The cursor has been placed by a **GID** move or a **LEAP** to the letter* l *in* **slat**. *(b) If you backspace, you get* **sat**. *(c) But if you had typed a* **p**, *you'd get* **splat**. *Note that in (a), the insert and delete portions of the cursor are both on the* l, *indicating that you can either insert or delete there. After deleting (b) or inserting (c), the insert and delete portions of the cursor have separated, still indicating where insertion and deletion will take place. Using a cursor-moving (arrow) key also causes the cursor to separate.*

This solution engenders another problem: Suppose you had the word *tongs*, with the cursor on the *o*, and you type the letter *h*. You get *thongs*. But where should the cursor go? Again, you seem to need to know the intent of the user: If the cursor is on the *h,* does it indicate whether that letter will be the insertion point or the deletion point? Deletion should be the inverse of insertion, so that a tap of the Backspace key should delete the *h*, returning the word to *tongs,* but if you type another letter, say *r,* it should displace the *o* to the right of the *h* to make the word *throngs.* It would seem that an on-character cursor also has to have precognition to be in the right place.

The solution to the problem is this: When you move the cursor, it lands on a single character. As soon as you type or delete, the cursor splits into two parts that are associated with two consecutive characters, as shown in Figure 5.9: The first character has the delete cursor on it, the second has the insertion pointer wrapped partially under it. One part of the trick is to have a two-part cursor designed so that when the parts coalesce—as they must, after a LEAP or other cursor movement—it is graphically clear that they both reside on the same character independently. This may all seem complicated when written out in detail, but the LEAP cursor is easier for a newcomer to learn than is the conventional cursor of Figure 5.7. All that you have to tell a learner is what the selection and insertion markers look like, that the Delete key deletes the selection, and that what you type appears at the insertion marker.

The characters are consecutive rather than adjacent, for although two consecutive characters are usually adjacent, they are not when the first of the two is at the end of a line. For left-to-right languages, the delete cursor is typically to the right of the insert character; for right-to-left languages, it is the other way around. For vertically oriented languages, the insert cursor would be below the delete cursor, and they would alternate directions on each line for boustrophedonic scripts.

Target acquisition is easier when using a GID with the two-part cursor, because the targets, or characters, are larger than the spaces between them, and the hot region is easier to visualize. (The hot region for the PARC cursor extends about halfway into each character, on both sides of the space between them, but nothing visually delineates the boundary, making the target seem smaller. In practice, many users try to place the cursor between characters, incurring the Fitts' law penalty that goes along with small targets.)

As we have discussed, naive users sometimes have trouble understanding how the standard, between-character, cursor works: a transient phenomenon involving an interface detail that is so familiar that it is rarely, if ever, questioned. With the two-part cursor that condenses on a single character after a cursor move, the initial confusion about which character a cursor points to disappeared, solving the original problem.

At times, it may be advantageous to limit the range of a LEAP. A limited search can be made by (1) selecting the region to be searched; (2) selecting a command or current selection, as discussed in Section 5-2-1, that limits the next LEAP to that region, which becomes the old selection; (3) and then using a LEAP. What must not be done is to create a mode that restricts LEAP. When the user is not aware of that mode, using LEAP will be very frustrating, and he will not be able to find things he has always otherwise been able to find. Canon introduced a concept called "Local Leap" on the Canon Cat, and it caused precisely the problems that a student of this book would predict.

Another function needed when LEAP is implemented is LEAP AGAIN, which simply performs a LEAP in the same direction as the most recent LEAP, to the next instance of the same pattern. In SwyftWare and the Canon Cat, searches usually took the form of LEAPing to a pattern and then using LEAP AGAIN repeatedly until the desired instance was found.

LEAP unifies searching and cursor motion in text, recalling that text includes spreadsheets, labels in graphics, and any other use of alphanumeric characters. After a short while using LEAP, the user becomes unaware of LEAPing, just as a touch typist concentrating on creating content is unaware of the mechanical motions of typing. When you want to put a target on your display, you LEAP to it; you do not stop to ask where in the system's universe of content the target is. You do not track down any hierarchies or open folders; you LEAP directly to what you want. But when people accustomed to standard file structures first encounter a system with LEAP, they often try to think in terms of where the desired item is hierarchically, searching for it by trying to find the general location and then working their way in to the specific instance they seek. If the universe over which you are searching has been properly indexed, it makes no difference to the user whether the item searched for is in memory, on local or networked mass storage, or on a local or global network.

When considering searching methods, the observations of Landauer and his colleagues are pertinent. They have shown that the most common forms of advanced text search, where the Search key is specified in terms of Boolean combinations of strings or by means of regular expressions, are inferior to a full-text search mechanism. The latter is both faster and easier, and users find a higher proportion of the relevant items for which they are searching (Landauer 1995). LEAP, on the basis of both GOMS and efficiency measures, is superior to the search-launching methods used by Landauer and should therefore show an even greater advantage.

5-7 Applications Abolished

The time it takes your favorite application to complete a given task doubles with each new revision.

—Lincoln Spector

The present structure of computer software, consisting of an operating system under which application programs execute, is inherently modal. This implies that for an interface to be nonmodal, an approach that does not include applications in their present form is required.

Because gestures, such as those that invoke commands, in one application may not be available in another, you must be conscious of which application is currently active. But you cannot reliably do this when your locus of attention is the task you are trying to accomplish. You will sometimes use a gesture with either no result or the incorrect result. A separate difficulty caused by application programs is the unavailability of the facilities of one application when you are in another; you wish to do a task that you could have done in application *A*, but you are in application *B*, which has no comparable command. Computer scientist Dan Swinehart called this the dilemma of preemption (Tesler 1981, p. 90).

Three approaches at solving the preemption dilemma are well known. The most common method is to provide, in each application, all those facilities the user is likely to need. This was discussed in Section 5-1, where it was pointed out that every personal computer has many different text editors, each part of an application or other facility. Most personal computer word processors have multiple and different text editors; for example, a typical word processor has a weaker editor for typing a pattern into the Find dialog box than for working in the main body of the text. This approach forces applications to become gargantuan, as each of them must solve a host of user needs that are peripheral to the primary thrust of the software. For example, my word processor has an embedded drawing program so that I can create simple illustrations without having to leave the text editor. At the same time, my drawing program has an embedded text editor so that I can include formatted blocks of text in my drawings without having to leave the drawing program. The drawing facilities in the editor and the text-editing facilities in the drawing program are inferior to the software dedicated primarily to those tasks. Ideally, all of the commands and abilities of both the drawing and the editing programs should be available at all times.

Similarly, every program has facilities for saving and retrieving named files. However, these facilities operate differently and have different features in different programs. This is confusing, difficult to operate, and requires immense amounts of largely redundant software, all of which you must pay for, learn to use, keep the documentation for, and provide adequate main memory and mass storage. The same is true of a host of other features, such as printing, that are duplicated or nearly duplicated among programs.

There has been some industry recognition of these difficulties; a number of companies designed software that permits a single **compound document** to have parts created by different applications. When you click at any point in a compound document, the application that created that portion of the document becomes active. Once the compound document has been created, this technique allows you to avoid having to open the individual applications explicitly. Of course, to create such a document, you must still manually invoke the applications, create the parts of the compound document, and then assemble them, usually by cutting and pasting or by dragging.

Although providing a modicum of convenience, the dilemma of preemption is not solved by this method, which is exemplified by Apple's OpenDoc, HP's NextWave, and Microsoft's OLE software and their descendants. When you are working in one part of a compound document, you do not have the facilities of the applications used to create the other parts of the document. Worse, you now have a document that seems to have no boundaries but whose behavior changes from place to place without warning. A table and a spreadsheet may look identical, but one operates according to the rules of the word processing program, and the other operates according to the rules of the spreadsheet program. This is modality with a vengeance. The only warning you get as you click here and there is that the menus, which are usually positioned far from the locus of attention, change. As we have seen, this is an ineffective means of alerting a user as to system state; there is, of course, no completely effective means.

The original approach to eliminating the modes inherent in applications was to create the windowing paradigm. At Xerox PARC, Alan Kay proposed overlapping windows, in part to eliminate the modality of applications. He also wanted to eliminate the distinction between operating system and applications but succeeded primarily in making the functioning of the operating system visible in the form of the desktop. This was a true advance, but as PARC's Larry Tesler put it, "windows are, in a sense, modes in sheep's clothing" (Tesler 1981, p. 94). That is, windows do not eliminate the modality of applications but instead make multiple applications simultaneously visible and accessible. Kay's insight, and the other ideas developed around windowing, formed an important step forward that has benefited users for more than a decade, but the problem of modes and the preemption dilemma posed by the existence of applications had not been solved. Since that time, the sheep disguise has worn thin, and the wolf bites us all too often. Section 5-8 presents one way of dispatching the wolf completely.

Calculator or Computer?

It's true. Many of us keep a calculator beside our computers. Why do you need this simple-minded device when you have a whole computer in front of you? You need it because you have to go through contortions worthy of a circus sideshow in order to do simple arithmetic with the computer. There you are, tapping away at your word processor, when you want to do a division: 375 packages of Phumuxx cost $248.93; what is the price for one package? On my computer, I have to open up a calculator window. To do this, I move my hand from the keyboard to the mouse, which I use to do a click-and-drag to open the calculator. Transferring my hands back to the keyboard, I type in the numbers I need or tediously cut and paste them from my document. Then I have to press a few more keys and finally copy the results from the calculator window into my document. Sometimes, the calculator window opens right on top of the very numbers I need, just to add insult to injury. In that case, I must use the mouse to move the calculator window out of the way before proceeding. It is much faster to grab the pocket calculator.

A better solution is a Calculate button or omnipresent menu command that allows you to take an arithmetic expression, such as 248.93 / 375, select it, and do the calculation whether you are in the word processor, communications package, drawing or presentation application, or just at the desktop level. In other words, it is an example of a universal function that can be used anywhere.

Using an experienced computer and calculator operator as my test subject, with his word processing program open before him, I measured the total time it took for him to pick up a calculator, turn it on, do a simple addition, and return his hands to the keyboard to resume typing. It took about 7 seconds. I then measured the time it took for him to use the built-in calculator. He had to move the cursor to the menu bar at the top of the screen, find the calculator program, open the calculator, enter the sum, and then click back in the word processor so that he could resume typing. This took about 16 seconds.

The same subject was asked to do the calculation from the middle of a document on a Canon Cat, which has a built-in Calculate key and can do arithmetic in text. The time was 6 seconds, using the top-line numeral keys for data entry. There is no time advantage to using an external calculator in this case. On the Cat, the result was left in the document, in the likely case you needed the result inserted. But the result was also left selected, so that a tap of the Delete key made it vanish if you did not want it in your text.

Here's another facility that should be generally available: Anywhere a number can be entered, you should be able to enter an arithmetic expression that evaluates to the number. Commands such as

• Check the spelling of the current selection
• Treat the current selection as an arithmetic expression and evaluate it
• Transmit the current selection as an e-mail
• Transmit the current selection as a fax
• Let's see what's at this URL on the web
• Execute the current selection as a Java (or whatever) program
should be available at all times. It is eminently doable.

5-8 Commands and Transformers

A good design is better than you think.

—Rex Heftman

We are justifiably annoyed when a product, a piece of software, or a computer system imposes complexity beyond our needs and presents difficulties we do not understand. We want to do some simple word processing, but we are forced to take in hand hundreds or, as in the case of Microsoft Office, thousands of commands and methods that we do not need. If, on the other hand, we brought in each of those commands as we understood our need for them, then the feeling of imposition and the immense cognitive burden would be lifted, even if the eventual system turned out as complex as the original application.

By applying the concept that a system should not be more complex than your present needs and by allowing the system to increase its power incrementally, the dream of providing products that are initially truly simple can be achieved without their being made to merely look simple and without impairing their flexibility. To understand one means of doing this, recall from Section 5-1 that almost all that a computer does involves the content that you provide or obtain and a set of operations you wish to perform on this content. Also recall that the interface to every such operation consists of two parts: choosing the content and invoking the operation. For example, in a game, you might shoot a monster, or, in our more prosaic terms, perform the operation of changing the image of a monster into an image of an explosion. The content is chosen by moving the cursor to the monster, and the operation is invoked by pressing the GID button—a lovely interface, by the way: fast and satisfying.

Invoking a command on a selection results in three possibilities:

1. The operation can be performed on the selection.

2. It makes no sense to apply that operation to the selection.

3. The selection can be modified to make the operation possible.

In the first case, the operation is performed and the content modified. In the second case, the content is left unchanged. In the third case, another process must be invoked by the computer to modify the selection before the command can be performed.

Suppose that you select a part of a photograph of a city street scene and try to apply the command that checks spelling. The command expects a sequence of characters (text), but what it finds is a photograph (a bitmap). Among the computer's capabilities is the ability to transform content from one data type to another.[12] In this case, the data type is bitmap and the command expects text, so the computer sees whether any transformer has bitmaps as inputs and text as output. Such transformers exist; they are called optical character recognition (OCR) programs. OCR programs are usually employed to convert input from scanners into editable text. (Some of the quotes in this book were obtained by scanning the article that contained the quote and then using an OCR program to convert the resultant bitmap into text.) Assume that the computer has an OCR program available. The OCR program is automatically invoked and inspects the bitmap. If it finds some characters it recognizes—say, a stop sign and a partly obscured sign with the characters *North First Stree,* then these texts are presented to the spelling checker, which reports finding one unknown word *(stree)* and suggests that perhaps tree, strew, or street was meant.

Instead of a computer's software being viewed as an operating system and a set of applications, the humane interface views the software as a set of commands, some of which are transformers that can be invoked automatically when the data type expected by the command does not match the data type of the object selected. More than one transformer may have to be invoked. For example, suppose that a computer with one transformer converts *A* to *B* and another that converts *B* to *C;* if the command expects data type *C* but the data type of the selection is *A,* both transformers will have to be applied before the command can be carried out. If no transformers are available to do the job, no change is made to the selection; the user is informed, if necessary, and the selection is left unmodified.

Instead of providing application programs, software vendors will provide command sets that offer a collection of related operations. For example, instead of a program for doing photographic manipulation, a vendor would provide a number of independent commands that, collectively, provide exactly the same range of operations. The user would install as many or as few as she finds useful rather than having to install a huge application, of which only a fraction would be used. By means of Internet sales of software, a forward-thinking vendor could sell software on a command-by-command basis, perhaps with significant discounts for buying certain sets or certain numbers of commands.

---

12. This class of abilities is sometimes called *filters,* but the term *filter* implies selectivity rather than a general transformational ability. Thus, I prefer the term *transformer,* which is seldom used in computer science, outside of circuit descriptions, whereas *filter* has many uses, such as a *digital filter program.*

When users complain about the absurd complexity of applications and ask for simpler programs without what are perceived to be unnecessary bells and whistles, industry observers respond that "lite" versions of software packages tend not to succeed in the marketplace. There is good reason for the failure of lite packages. Because the user never knows which of the facilities offered by the complete package he might some day need, he purchases the whole package because that is the only way he can obtain these facilities. If he buys a limited, lower-cost version, the only way he can upgrade is by buying the complete package, even if it is only one small feature from the larger program that he would need to add to the lite version. Therefore, it is safer to purchase the full version from the beginning and to put up with the complexity. No wonder we feel trapped. Commands that could be purchased as needed are a more humane option.

Various surveys report a range for the amount of typical software application features that are never used. The numbers have tended to rise over the last decade and have increased over that time from about 15 percent to the latest surveys nearing 50 percent. That is a lot of clutter. By providing command sets, each command of which can be installed independently, instead of applications, individual users can drive that statistic to nearly 0. Other advantages for vendors in this methodology are the ability to refine their products incrementally and to more easily and frequently provide (and sell!) new features, because they do not have to rerelease the whole package in order to do so. The web is an ideal medium for such repeated, piecemeal sales.

Vendors, not necessarily the vendors of application command sets, will supply transformers. These, too, can be sold individually. If a majority of users regularly employ most of the word processing commands from vendor *A,* and vendor *B* thinks of a useful command that *A* does not provide, then *B* can sell that command to *A*'s customers. However, *B* might use a different data structure. In that case, *B* would be wise to provide a pair of inverse transformers that go from *A*'s data structure to *B*'s data structure, and back again. If *A*'s product has a very large customer base, then *B* might be wise to create a version of the command that works directly with *A*'s data structure. Besides, another vendor, *C,* might be a specialist at providing transformers. It may become common practice for users to purchase transformers from such vendors and for command vendors to license the transformers they need. This commercial structure exists, in part, at present: Companies such as DataViz specialize in providing transformers.

The pieces needed for a commands-plus-transformers computer environment also exist. It will not be difficult to put them together into a working system. Users will find such systems both easier to use and more flexible than today's application-bound designs. It is a solution that can decrease excessive feature bloat and complexity, incompatibility among applications, and the need to learn multiple solutions to the same problem. In the process, the operating system can disappear from the user's view entirely. If this program is carried out properly, not even the present, wool-coated version of the operating system—the desktop—will remain.

Of course, not all programs require all this mechanism. A game, for example, would simply be launched and would run independently: This is done in the usual way by clicking on, or selecting, the desired game's name, probably from a text consisting of a list of names of games, and then using the Execute command. Section 6-2 discusses an alternative method.

Considerate Programming: Applications as Visitors

Consider that you have been invited to stay at the house of your good friends, the Grimbles. You even like their dog. The only problem is their beloved portrait of Aunt Ashtabula that hangs over the bed. It gives you and your wife the willies, and you can't possibly sleep in a room with Aunt Ashtabula looking on. You dare not tell the Grimbles how you feel, so how do you handle this situation when you visit?

1. Take down the picture and burn it.

2. Hide the picture in the wine cellar, where it will take the Grimbles a month to find it.

3. Put the picture in the closet, where they will find it sooner.

4. Put the picture in the closet and restore it to its original position just before you leave.

Any considerate guest knows that option 4 is the best of those presented. The ethical principle is: Make a change in someone else's environment if you must, so long as you leave things just as they were before the host returns.

Today's computers have many environmental parameters that can be set: speaker loudness, screen resolution and depth, menu behavior, and default system font. A Macintosh computer has hundreds of settings. In an IBM-compatible computer running Windows and Microsoft Office, the number is over 1,000. The parallel with the visit to the Grimbles? If you go and use somebody else's machine and change any settings, it would be considerate of you to change them back when you leave.

Many programs demand a particular screen resolution, a certain number of bits per pixel, or another specific parameter setting to run properly. Their behavior, when the system does not have the correct parameter settings, ranges from genteel to uncouth to vandalism. Here is what various programs I tested do when they encounter incorrect display parameters:

1. Crash the computer, forcing a manual reboot.

2. Crash the computer, giving an indecipherable numeric message; you must press the Restart button to reboot the computer.

3. Give an error message saying that the screen settings must be adjusted, and when you click on the OK button, it crashes the computer.

4. Give an error message saying that the screen settings must be adjusted. When you click on the OK button, you can then open the appropriate control panel and adjust the settings.

5. Ask whether it should change the screen settings, and if you click on the OK button, the settings are changed. If you click Cancel, the program is not launched, and the screen settings are not touched.

6. Change the screen settings and run the program without comment.

7. Announce that it will change the settings in a dialog box. When you click on the OK button, it changes the settings and runs the program; when you quit the program, it changes the settings back to the way they were.

A reader from the future may think that crashing the computer is a bit extreme. None of these methods goes all the way to being a good guest, although item 7 is close.

The safest behavior is a combination of item 5's message and item 7's exit behavior. In the unlikely event that changing the screen settings will interfere with some other parallel or background process, you might decide not to run the program and might welcome the warning and a chance to opt out.

8. Change the screen settings and run the program without comment and reset the settings when exiting.

In other words, you'd launch the program, and it would simply run: doing just what you expected and wanted, and no other program would be affected. That is my definition of a well-behaved computer system. But what if two programs requiring different screen settings are displaying pictures at the same time? That is a horse of a different color or a fish of a different resolution, perhaps.

Item 7, which might seem acceptable and is in common use, fails us by giving us a "dialog" box that is no dialog. This is user abuse: The information imparted cannot be acted on, and it only wastes your time. (The transparent-message method of Section 5-2-3 solves this problem.)

Application programs per se are an imposition, as this book argues, but so long as we are still saddled with them, let us make sure that they are well behaved (also see Raskin 1993). To summarize, a program or, in the future, a command should automatically reset whatever it needs in order to run; it should execute properly; and when the user dismisses it or when it is done, it should restore all parameters to the state they had when it was launched. If resetting is irreversible or could have an undesirable side effect, a warning explaining what damage might be caused can be given, so long as that message gives the user a choice as to proceed or not.

Right now, you cannot run different resolutions on the same screen at the same time. But that's another kind of problem. In the meanwhile, I think that users would be happier if every user interface guideline added item 8.

SIX

Navigation and Other Aspects of Humane Interfaces

The average man suffers very severely from the pain of a new idea.

—*Admiral William S. Sims*

One of the most laudatory terms used to describe an interface is to say that it is "intuitive." When examined closely, this concept turns out to vanish like the pea in a shell game and be replaced with the more ordinary but more accurate term "familiar."

Our present systems of navigation, never satisfactory in the first place, are completely inadequate in the face of the terabytes of information we have to scan. But people and animals have been navigating through complex environments for millennia and have some useful techniques for doing so. These abilities, which have evolved over the eons, can be co-opted to our purposes with what can be termed a "zooming interface paradigm."

6-1 Intuitive and Natural Interfaces

In every respect the burden is hard on those who attack an almost universal opinion. They must be very fortunate as well as unusually capable if they obtain a hearing at all.

—John Stuart Mill, from "The Subjection of Women"

Many interface requirements specify that the resulting product be intuitive, or natural. However, there is no human faculty of intuition, as the word is ordinarily meant; that is, knowledge acquired without prior exposure to the concept, without having to go through a learning process, and without having to use rational thought. When an expert uses what we commonly call his intuition to make a judgment, with a speed and accuracy that most people would find beyond them, we find that he has based his judgment on his experience and knowledge. Often, experts have learned to use methods and techniques that nonexperts do not know. Task experts often use cues of which others are not aware or that they do not understand. Expertise, unlike intuition, is real.

When users say that an interface is intuitive, they mean that it operates just like some other software or method with which they are familiar. Sometimes, the word is used to mean *habitual*, as in "The editing tools become increasingly intuitive over time." Or, it can mean *already learned,* as was said of a new aircraft navigation device: "Like anything, it can be learned, but it would take a lot of experience to do it intuitively" (Collins 1994).

Another word that I try to avoid in discussing interfaces is *natural*. Like *intuitive*, it is usually not defined. An interface feature is natural, in common parlance, if it operates in such a way that a human needs no instruction. This typically means that there is some common human activity that is similar to the way the feature works. However, it is difficult to pin down what is meant by *similar*. Similarities or analogies can occur in many ways. Certainly, that the cursor moves left when a mouse is pushed to the left and right when the mouse is pushed to the right is natural. Here, the term *natural* equates to *very easily learned*. Although it may be impossible to quantify naturalness, it is not too difficult to quantify learning time.

The use of the mouse itself is often claimed to be natural and intuitive. It is difficult to do the experiment now, when the use of this most famous of GIDs is so widespread, but when it was less well known, I asked people unfamiliar with the mouse to use a Macintosh. My protocol was to run a program called The Manhole, an entertaining and well-designed children's exploration game that required no input beyond clicking at various locations on the display. With the keyboard removed from the computer, I would point to the mouse and say, "This is the mouse that you use to operate the game. Go ahead, give it a try." If asked any questions, I'd say something nonspecific, such as "Try it." The reaction of an intelligent Finnish educator who had never seen a Macintosh but was otherwise computer literate was typical: She picked up the mouse.

Nowadays, this might seem absurd, but the same point was made in one of the Star Trek series of science fiction movies. The space ship's engineer has been brought back into our time, where (when) he walks up to a Macintosh. He picks up the mouse, bringing it to his mouth as if it were a microphone, and speaks to it, with a heavy Scots accent: "Computer, . . ." The audience laughs at his mistake. I admired the creators of the film for recognizing that the use of the mouse was not something you could expect everyone to immediately guess. In the case of my Finnish subject, her next move was to turn the mouse over and to try rolling the ball. Nothing happened. She shook the mouse, and then she held the mouse in one hand and clicked the button with the other. No effect. Eventually, she succeeded in operating the game by holding the mouse in her right hand, rolling the ball on the bottom with her fingers, and clicking the button with her left hand.

These experiments make the point that an interface's ease of use and speed of learning are not connected with the imagined properties of intuitiveness and naturalness. The mouse is very easy to learn: All I had to do, with any of the test subjects, was to put the mouse on the desk, move it, and click on something. In five to ten seconds, they learned how to use the mouse. That's fast and easy, but it is neither intuitive nor natural. No artifact is.

The belief that interfaces can be intuitive and natural is often detrimental to improved interface design. As a consultant, I am frequently asked to design a "better" interface to a product. Usually, an interface can be designed such that, in terms of learning time, eventual speed of operation (productivity), decreased error rates, and ease of implementation, it is superior to both the client's existing products and competing products. Nonetheless, even when my proposals are seen as significant improvements, they are often rejected on the grounds that they are not intuitive. It is a classic Catch-22: The client wants something that is significantly superior to the competition. But if it is to be superior, it must be different. (Typically, the greater the improvement, the greater the difference.) Therefore, it cannot be intuitive, that is, familiar. What the client wants is an interface with at most marginal differences from current practice—which almost inevitably is Microsoft Windows—that, somehow, makes a major improvement. This can be achieved only on the rare occasions when the original interface has some major flaw that is remedied by a minor fix. (Parts of this section are based on Raskin 1994.)

6-2 Better Navigation: ZoomWorld

If you wanted to design a navigation scheme intended to confuse, you might begin by making the interface mazelike. The maze would put you in a little room with a number of doors leading this way and that. The doors' labels are usually short, cryptic, or iconic, and they may change or disappear,[1] depending on where you've been. You cannot see what is on the other side of a door except by going through it, and when you have gone through, you may or may not be able to see the room you've just left. There may not be a way to get directly back at all. Some rooms may contain maps to part or all of the system of rooms, but you have to keep track of the relationship between the map representation and the rooms you are presented with; furthermore, maps are not well suited to situations best represented by three-dimensional networks. The rooms in this description correspond to computer interface windows and web sites, and the doors are the tabs, menus, or links that are provided to bring you to other windows or sites.

As legends and stories from ancient times inform us, humans always have been notoriously bad at mazes. If we could handle them easily, they wouldn't be used as puzzles and traps. When using a complex program, I often find, deep in a submenu, a command or a check box that solves a problem I am having. When I run into the same problem a few weeks later, I cannot remember how I got to the box with the solution. We are not good at remembering long sequences of turnings, which is why mazes make good puzzles and why our present navigational schemes, used both within computers and on the web, often flummox the user. Many complaints about present systems are complaints about trying to navigate. Partial solutions, such as "favorite locations" in browsers, have been created.[2] But what we are truly better at is remembering landmarks and positional cues, traits that evolution has bred into us and traits we can take advantage of in interface design.

The antithesis of a maze is a situation in which you can see your goal and the path to get there, one that preserves your sense of location

---

1. Adaptive menus have this annoying trait.

2. This works until you have so many that you cannot remember what they all are; then you need a "favorites of favorites" or another scheme to keep track of them.

while under way, making it equally easy to get back. An elegant solution is the zooming interface paradigm (ZIP), which in many situations solves the navigation problem and also provides a way around the problem of the limited screen real estate that any real display system must confront. Imagine, if you will, how readily mazes could be solved if only you could fly above them, see their layout, and go directly to your destination. A zooming interface paradigm offers that kind of fluidity and facility for many tasks you perform with computers. Although a ZIP is not optimal for all situations, I will concentrate on its positive aspects, with the aim of demonstrating that there are alternatives superior to desktop-oriented graphical user interfaces.

The ZIP described here is called ZoomWorld and is based on the idea that you have access to an infinite plane of information having infinite resolution. The plane is ZoomWorld. Everything you can access is displayed somewhere on ZoomWorld, whether it is on your computer, on a local network to which your computer is attached, or on a network of networks, such as the Internet.

To see more of ZoomWorld, you think of yourself as flying higher and higher above it. To look at a particular item, you dive down to it. Zoom-World also has a content searching mechanism. The overall metaphor is one of flying, climbing to zoom out and diving to zoom in. You navigate both by flying above ZoomWorld and by doing content searches.

ZoomWorld is conceptually similar to the walls of a project planning room. After a while, the walls become covered with annotations, tacked-up sheets of paper, sticky notes, photos, or whatever else helps us to remember and to explain our ideas. When you come into the room, you may stand in the center and glance around, spot a place, walk over, and look at the material in detail. At other times, you walk directly to the place where the information you want to review or modify has been posted.

We can find things in such a planning room because we tend to remember landmarks and relative position, a fact sometimes called the psi effect and long known to psychological researchers. "The stuff about marketing is on the right wall, sort of lower down near the far corner," someone might tell you. On another occasion, you go right to a particular document because you remember that it is just to the left of the orange piece of paper that Aviva put up. As you work in the room, you sometimes step back to get your bearings. You don't have to step back far before you can no longer read the small print, but you can see headings and larger diagrams. From still farther away, you can make out only a few of the largest headings, colors of whole sheets, layouts of areas, and tell whether there are illustrations, diagrams, or cartoons on them, even if you can't make out just what is being illustrated or diagrammed.

The ZIP readily permits labels to be attached to images and to collections of images yet does not impose any structure, hierarchical or otherwise, beyond association due to proximity. I suspect that most users will tend to organize collections of images into clusters and that some will create informal hierarchies. For example, a large heading Personal Photos might, when zoomed in on, reveal smaller headings on groups of pictures labeled Baby Pictures, Vacations, Pets, Hobbies, Friends, Relatives, and so forth. Zooming in to the writing under the heading Baby Pictures might reveal the children's names, Agatha, Gideon, and Hermione. A professional photographer is likely to have a very carefully constructed and organized collection. Note that you are not required to remember the names; you find them as you zoom and glide about and decide whether the image you want is likely to be in the named category. The same can be done with films and collections of sound, although you may have to activate a film or a sound to make sure that it is the one you want.

The totally disorganized have hope: If you are one such, you can just lay out the images any old way and zoom around until you find the one you want. You may remember its approximate position due to your spatial memory, which will speed the search.

If you want larger characters, say, in a document you are reading, it is clear that zooming in makes the characters larger, but you may not be able to fit entire lines into the width of the display, making reading from the screen difficult. The solution in this case is to use a command to enlarge the font, making the line length, in terms of number of characters, shorter.

Our inherent tendency to remember position and landmarks can be put to work in ZoomWorld. The method of getting around will not be via scroll bars, which are slow. (Just consider, in Fitts' law terms (Section 4-4), the size of the arrow boxes you must click on.) Nor will it be by clicking on zoom-in and zoom-out icons or menu items, which are also slow, but rather by emulating what a person does in a planning room: stepping back to view large areas, then walking up to just the one that is desired, and finally leaning forward to read the fine print or using a magnifying glass to see a detail in a photo.

Zooming in, so that you can see portions of the space in detail, is probably best implemented as a quasimode (see Section 3-2-3). In this quasimode, the graphical input device button causes a real-time zoom-in to wherever the cursor is located: The center of zooming follows the cursor. The secondary graphical input device button can be used for this function.

For compatibility with the application-free systems described in Sections 5-7 and 5-8, the zoom quasimodes can be positioned elsewhere, such as on a second graphical input device, on the keyboard, or as dedicated, labeled extra buttons on the graphical input device (see Appendix A).

Wherever the zooming controls are located, the point you are zooming in on is the cursor location, which can be adjusted during the zoom by the graphical input device, being used in its role as a positional pointing device. That is, during zooming, the system moves the ZoomWorld plane so that the cursor position is at or near the center of the display. If zooming is quick—at least a factor of 2 in linear dimensions per second—and has the appearance of being continuous, zooming to and from the cursor position will suffice as a graphical navigational tool.

In the planning room, you might put up larger signs over the main areas, signs you can read from anywhere in the room. Zooming operates similarly; the sizes of headings and text determine how far in you have to zoom before you can see details. This technique substitutes for, and improves on, hierarchical directories. A fast text search, such as LEAP, is an important adjunct, used when you need to find a textual detail quickly. A few distinctive geometric landmarks can also be used; see the rules for effective use of icons in Section 6-3 for what is meant by "few." A large red cross, for example, might signal an area containing emergency medical data—in both the planning room and in a ZIP.

Without having the phenomenon pointed out to them, users quickly become familiar with the textures of the kinds of work they do. Spreadsheets, tables, text, bitmapped images, drawings, and other products of computer use each have their own visual characteristics even when seen from afar. The products of various coworkers, groups, vendors, and other creators of material will often be immediately recognizable.

A zooming space gives you a great deal of flexibility in layout. If a document grows in length or width, it can simply decrease its scale uniformly to make the entire document fit within the same region it did before its content increased. Similar space-making tactics can be used when a table or a spreadsheet is enlarged. Because you can zoom in, the text can always be made large enough to read. The opposite occurs when a document or drawing gets smaller. Blank space is unlimited, if the system is implemented properly; a command allows a new document to be started anywhere—by copying a blank document, the ZIP analog of the GUI New command—and documents can be allowed to overlap adjacent documents or be restricted in their growth by them. Internal links and pointers to web sites (URLs) can bring you immediately to other documents at a place and size determined at the creation of the link. Buttons can have as much information on them as you wish, including a complete manual, with examples, without affecting their simplicity when viewed from afar. Every feature can have an explanation built into it.

Zooming can also be nonlinear in time, starting more slowly and accelerating to full zoom speed, allowing for fine control of small changes without impeding large changes in scale. It can also slow down and briefly stop at certain predefined zoom ratios, making it easy to get characters to standard sizes.

Working effectively in a ZIP often permits, and sometimes requires, strategies that are unlike those used in desktop-based GUIs. For example, you can have a number of views of the same data kept on hand because real estate poses no limitations. As with the efficient temperature converter solution in Section 4-3-2, we let the machine do extra work or preparation that may never be used, in the interest of easing human workload. Comparisons can be effected by a split screen, which requires controls for splitting but that allows for independent zooming, and by a typical ZIP trick: moving copies of the two documents or two copies of the same document so that the parts to be compared are adjacent. The ability to move and to scale any object certainly applies to text objects, which is how you can make a document bigger and thus visible at a higher hierarchical (and graphical) level.

A footnote can be more than just a reference. You can zoom in to the entire referenced work. Zooming here is functioning like a link, except that to get back to the main discussion, you zoom out; you do not have to keep a trail of where you have been. To make it easy to find a set of documents, the documents themselves can be arranged in a distinctive pattern that is visible when zoomed out. A page with very large lettering can be seen while zoomed out and used as a title. Zooming out can serve in the role of a Back button in a browser.

Small-scale collaborative endeavors are easily modeled by having collaborators all zoom on the same document, with appropriate rules to prevent interference. A network can be represented as a space in which everyone's work is placed in his or her own region. In a ZIP collaborative space, you can choose to keep as much of your work visible or invisible to others as you wish. Invisible documents are also a way to implement varying levels of access permission.[3]

---

3. An interesting zooming user interface (ZUI), called PAD++ (it is now called *Jazz*), has been developed independently, originally at the University of New Mexico. See http://www.cs.umd.edu/hcil/pad++/. I am grateful to Dr. Donald Norman, then at Apple, for pointing out this work to me.

Figure 3.4. Fluke scopemeter: powerful and rugged, zillions of functions, a paucity of keys, but difficult to learn and sometimes slow to get to the function you need. On the other hand, its color-coded leads eliminate a traditional source of confusion about which lead does what.

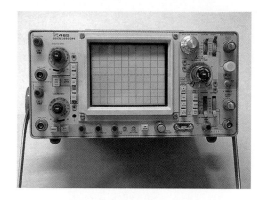

Figure 3.5. The Tektronix oscilloscope has a myriad settings, but although initially intimidating, it is quick and easy to operate. All knobs that can uncalibrate the unit are in red.

Figure 3.7. The Sony 2010 multi-band radio achieves ease of use by providing thirty-two dedicated buttons for presets. When a preset is tapped, it simultaneously sets all parameters to the state they were when the user stored the station. Unlike many radio preset systems, which assign presets only with one particular band (for example, AM or FM), any button may access any station on the Sony 2010.

Storing stations is also easy: A dedicated and labeled SET button establishes a quasimode during which a press of a preset button stores the current station and all other pertinent operating parameters. It is nearly impossible to accidentally store a station when you intend to listen to one, and the label makes the SET function visible.

It is rare when a product combines both superior electronic technology and interface technology. Perhaps this explains why the Sony 2010 has been in continuous production for over a decade in an industry where most models fade in months.

Figure 3.9. Canon Cat's Use Front key and some of the command keys. The words USE FRONT are light blue, as are the legends on the fronts of the keys that are enabled by the Use Front key.

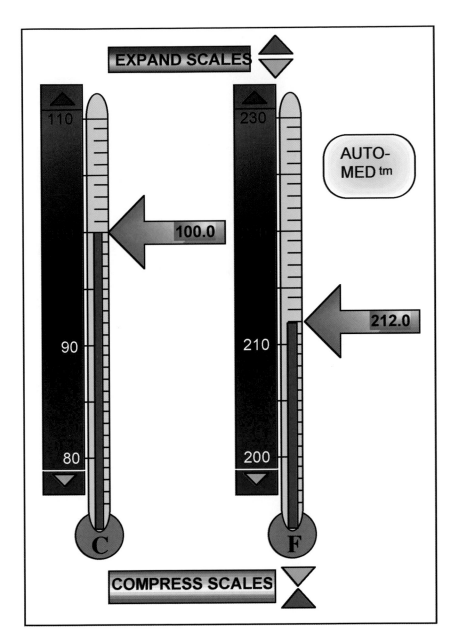

Figure 4.3. A GUI for Hal's interface.

Figure 4.7. The Macintosh menu, at the top edge of the screen, effectively increases its size compared to a menu that floats away from the edge.

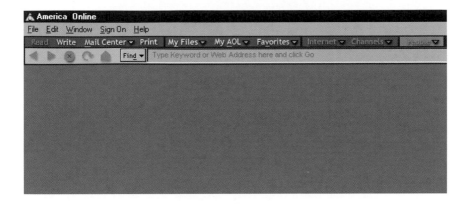

Figure 4.8. The Windows menu is below the top edge of the screen; you have to place the cursor more carefully to pull down a submenu.

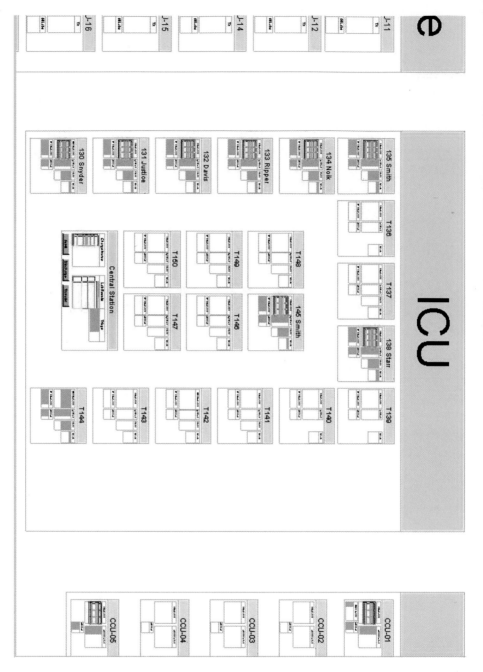

Figure 6.1. A ZIP view of an ICU. The numbered rectangles are rooms, and the names are those of the patients in them (no real data shown).

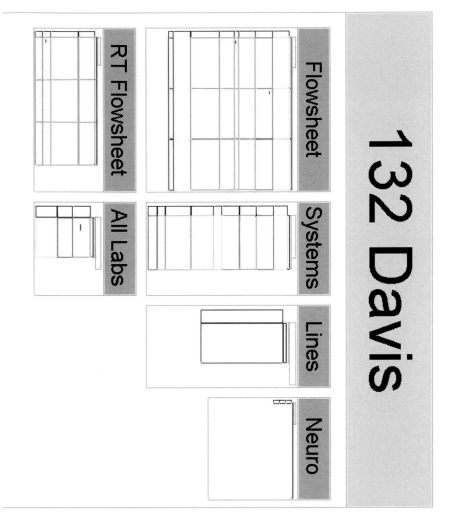

Figure 6.2. The charts for a particular patient can be seen when zoomed in this far.

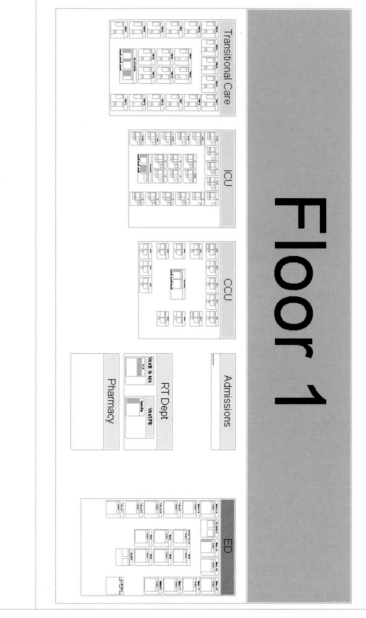

Figure 6.4. Zoomed out beyond the view shown in Figure 6.1, the entire first floor is visible.

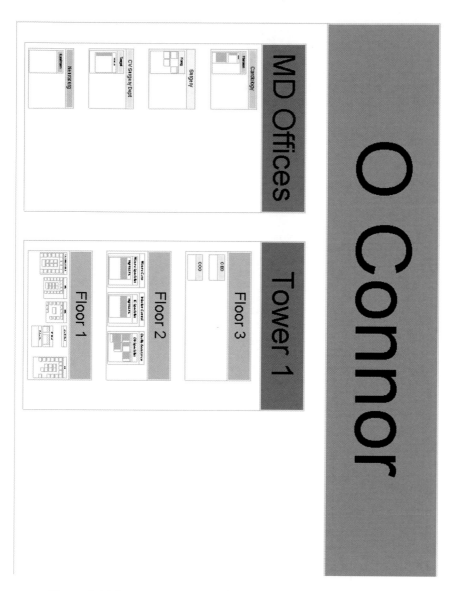

Figure 6.5. The entire O'Connor hospital can be seen.

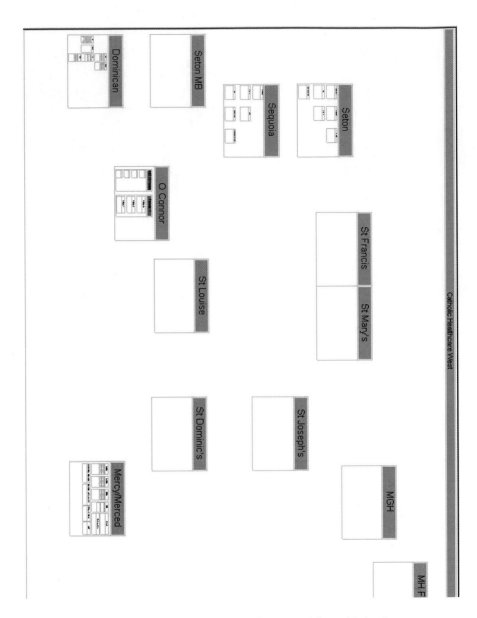

Figure 6.6. The entire enterprise can be accessed from this level.

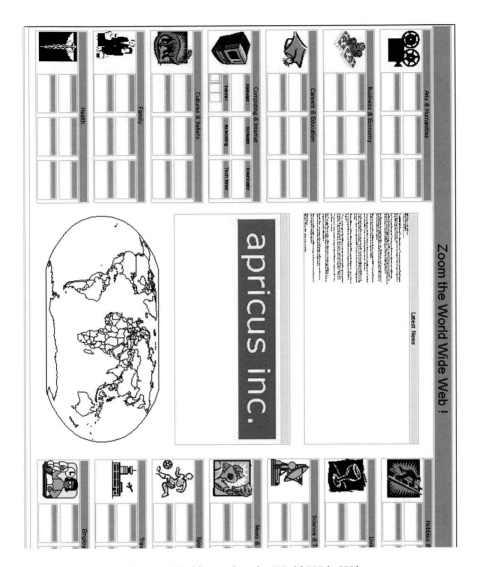

Figure 6.7. A ZoomWorld portal to the World Wide Web.

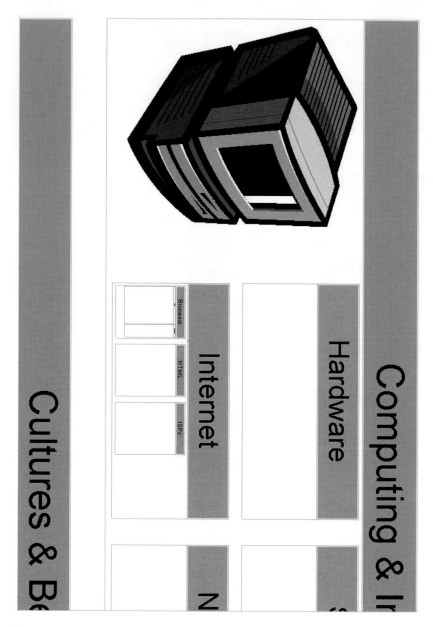

Figure 6.8. Zoomed in to one area of the World Wide Web.

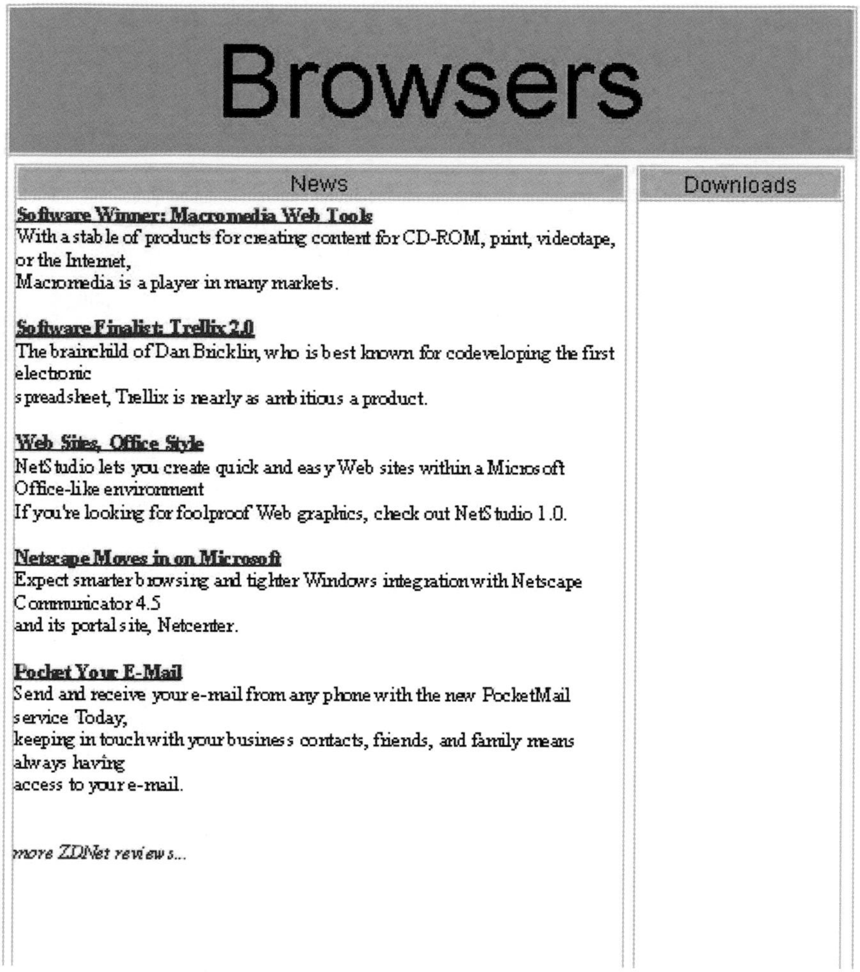

Browsers

News	Downloads

Software Winner: Macromedia Web Tools
With a stable of products for creating content for CD-ROM, print, videotape, or the Internet,
Macromedia is a player in many markets.

Software Finalist: Trellix 2.0
The brainchild of Dan Bricklin, who is best known for codeveloping the first electronic
spreadsheet, Trellix is nearly as ambitious a product.

Web Sites, Office Style
NetStudio lets you create quick and easy Web sites within a Microsoft Office-like environment
If you're looking for foolproof Web graphics, check out NetStudio 1.0.

Netscape Moves in on Microsoft
Expect smarter browsing and tighter Windows integration with Netscape Communicator 4.5
and its portal site, Netcenter.

Pocket Your E-Mail
Send and receive your e-mail from any phone with the new PocketMail service Today,
keeping in touch with your business contacts, friends, and family means always having
access to your e-mail.

more ZDNet reviews...

Figure 6.9. Zoomed in on a list of browsers. Of course, ZoomWorld is a fine browser in its own right.

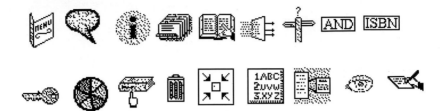

Figure 6.11. Bibliographic icons (from: http://www.scran.ac.uk/ iconstd/). Many are inscrutable, as you can ascertain by looking at each and deciding what bibliographic category or operation it is supposed to represent.

A typical application for ZoomWorld arose in a design created for Apricus, which was trying to find a way to computerize a large (about a square meter) medical chart of the kind used in an intensive care unit (ICU). All of the methods tried proved slower than accessing the chart manually and also required excessive training; multiple displays could not be used to show the entire chart at once. Not only could ZoomWorld accommodate the chart, but also the same interface could serve as an enterprisewide database without significant extra development effort, allowing the company to extend its sights beyond automating the ICU database. The better interface allowed an expansion of the business model and the range of applications without requiring a more complex interface or any additional interface implementation, although a larger database was, of course, necessary. Figures 6.1–6.8 show versions of ZoomWorld that were developed at Apricus.[4] In testing, it was found that nurses could use the system after less than one minute of training.

In Figure 6.1, the ZIP shows an ICU unit, surrounded by other units. You can zoom in to see the kinds of data available for any of the rooms, some of which are unoccupied. In Figure 6.2, you have zoomed in to room 132, and the major charts can be seen.

You can continue to zoom in to a particular chart. When the text becomes large enough to be readable, it also becomes editable. In Figure 6.3, a horizontal time scale and a vertical set of legends have automatically appeared. These "float" over the background image so that as you move around in the chart, the scales stay in place relative to the screen. They automatically disappear if you zoom out to or beyond the point where the text is unreadable or if you zoom inside an entry in the chart.

For example, you might zoom in to a particular value and find useful data, such as normal ranges for the measurement or even a lengthy quote from a medical text. Note that such detail does not get in the way or take up any apparent display space, yet it is there, where it is needed.

The zooming can take place in the other direction. Climbing high above Figure 6.1, our first view of the hospital, you can see that the ICU unit is on Floor 1, and you can tell what other units are on the same floor. In addition, the physical layout of the floor is apparent (Figure 6.4).

---

4. My thanks to Apricus for permission to describe its version of ZoomWorld and for the use of some of the screens as illustrations. Many details and the implementation were provided by Drs. David Moshal and Emanuel Noik and their crew. The customization to the hospital setting is due primarily to Betti Newburn, R.N.

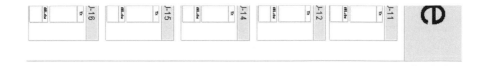

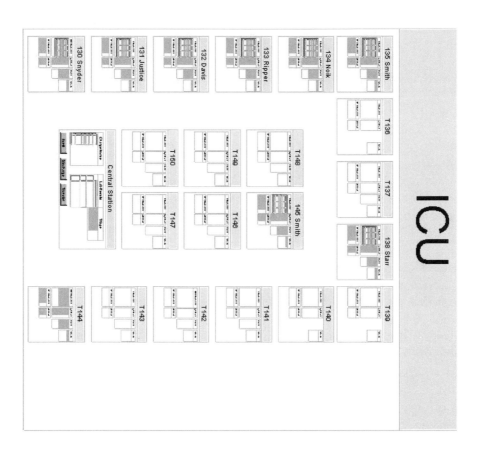

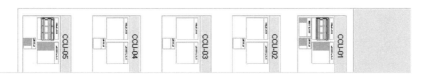

Figure 6.1. A ZIP view of an ICU. The numbered rectangles are rooms, and the names are those of the patients in them (no real data shown). (See color insert.)

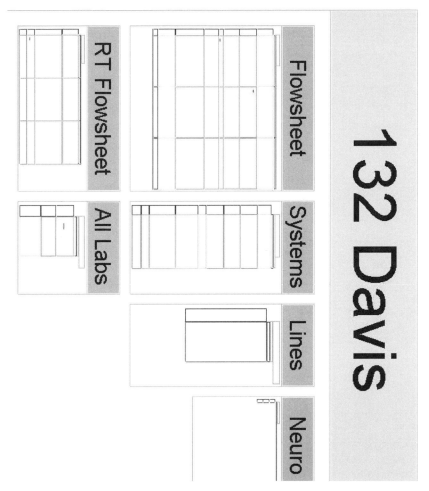

Figure 6.2. The charts for a particular patient can be seen when zoomed in this far. (See color insert.)

Fly still higher above the first-floor view, and the entire hospital becomes visible, with a one-story set of doctor's offices and a hospital tower of three floors (Figure 6.5).

Gradually climbing still higher, the entire chain of hospitals can be viewed (Figure 6.6), roughly in their geographic alignment. It is a matter of

Patient: Davis, Shawn
DOB: 8/7/1942
Sex: Male
Admitted: 2/21/1999
Med Record: 44444444
Dx: Sepsis
Physician: Demo, Doctor
2/21/1999

			8:00 AM	9:00 AM	10:00 AM	11:00 AM	12:00 PM	1:00 PM	2:00 PM	3:00 PM
Neuro										
Glasgow Scale	Eye Opening		3	4	3	3	3			
	Verbal Response		3	4	4	4	2			
	Motor Response		4	4	5	5	4			
	GCS Total		10	12	12	12	9			
Pupils: Size	R		2mm	2mm	1mm	1mm	1mm			
	L		2mm	3mm	2mm	2mm	2mm			
Pulses	R		Strong	Weak	Norm	Norm	Strong			
	L		Norm	Weak	Norm	Weak	Norm			
Pain Assessment	Score		0	1	unable to eval.	0	unable to eval.			
	Location		Neck	Neck	Head	Neck	Head			
	Observation		Grimacing	Grimacing	Verbalizes	Intermittent Crying	Calm			
Note 1										
Circulatory/Hemodynamics										
Pulse										
Arterial BP		S	200	190	189	160	139			
		D	120	100	90	90	80			
		Mean	146	130	123	113	99			
IABP		S								
		D								
		Mean								
PAP		S								
		D								
		Mean								
PCW										
RAP/CVP										
CO										
CI										
SvO2										
PVR										
SVR										

Figure 6.3. The chart's entries are now visible and can be operated on. Floating headings have appeared so that the columns and rows can be identified.

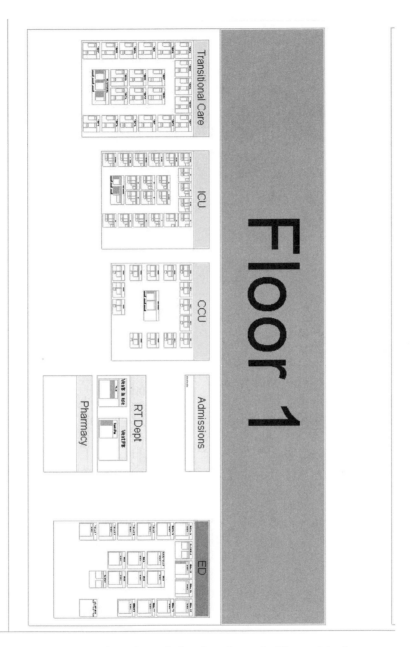

Figure 6.4. Zoomed out beyond the view shown in Figure 6.1, the entire first floor is visible. (See color insert.)

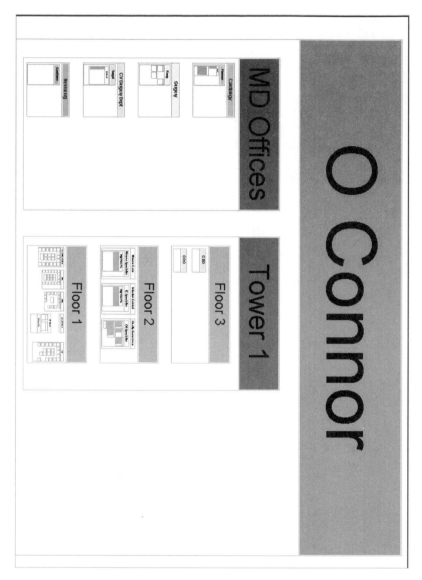

Figure 6.5. The entire O'Connor hospital can be seen. (See color insert.)

seconds to get to any patient's chart in any hospital, and the means to do it are evident with only a few seconds of instruction. You could operate this interface from what you've read here, and you would do it correctly.

It is not only patient charts that can be found from the ZoomWorld image of the hospital system. Assuming that you had logged on at the appro-

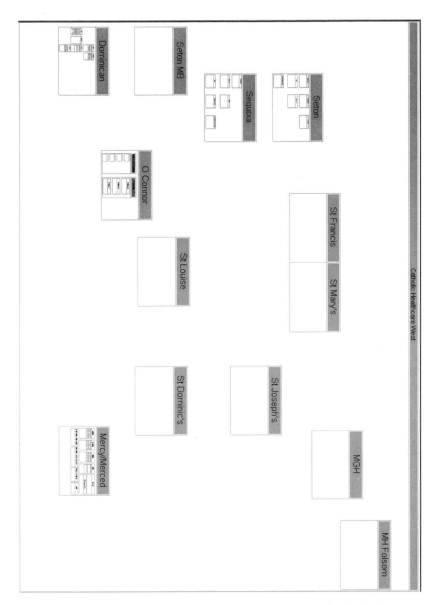

Figure 6.6. The entire enterprise can be accessed from this level. (See color insert.)

priate level of security, you could also zoom in on the comptroller's office, check on budgets, inventory records of medicines and supplies, and check human resources records or any other facet of the enterprise.

It is clear that ZoomWorld can serve as a database search interface for an enterprise or for a set of enterprises, governmental agencies, schools, and scientific data sets, to name a few examples. Three-dimensional objects are represented by a two-dimensional projection or other transformation on displays, although a three-dimensional ZoomWorld can be created.

Although moves within ZoomWorld are usually accomplished by zooming out and in to the new location, a short move that preserves readability and context is sometimes needed. Therefore, interface designer Emanuel Noik's implementation of this system included a convention that delayed the beginning of zooming. If the graphical input device was moved during the brief delay—a few hundred milliseconds—instead of moving the zooming point, the graphical input device dragged the image. In testing, it worked well, although in general, the use of such delays can cause problems (see Section 6-4-5); in this case, an occasional zoom when a drag was intended and vice versa was observed. Faster and more certain is to drag the image while both GID buttons are held. Either mechanism is superior to conventional scroll bars, which, aside from the difficulties already discussed, may require the user to decide whether to move horizontally or vertically first and then to decide whether to use the arrows, to move the scroll box, or to click above or below the scroll box. Such decisions cause Hick's law delays (see Section 4-4). Scrolling itself is inherently slow. The user is limited by the system's speed of scrolling, which cannot be made too fast because the user will not be able to see what is flitting by the window; zooming can be fast because the visual images don't change but only scale, and you do not lose your sense of where you are. Note also that when you zoom in, that area is active to the extent that you can operate within an area. You do not have to click or otherwise signal the system that you want to use whatever facility you have zoomed in on. The conventional concepts of "opening" and "closing" documents or applications do not apply, either in ZoomWorld or in the complementary methods discussed in this book.

If we zoom out from Figure 6.6, the image of the hospital enterprise gets smaller and is surrounded by empty space, like an island. As this happens, other islands come into view, and when we zoom in one of them, we find that it is a portal to the World Wide Web (Figure 6.7). From that portal, we can zoom in to a specific area of the World Wide Web (Figure 6.8).

It is clear how the World Wide Web is surfed in ZoomWorld (see Figure 6.9). Another island is your local system, its mass storage, and any other information that can be reached without going over a network. When a volume, such as a DVD, is mounted, it appears adjacent to your local system island.

The consequence of this discussion should now be obvious: *The zooming interface paradigm can replace the browser, the desktop metaphor, and the tra-*

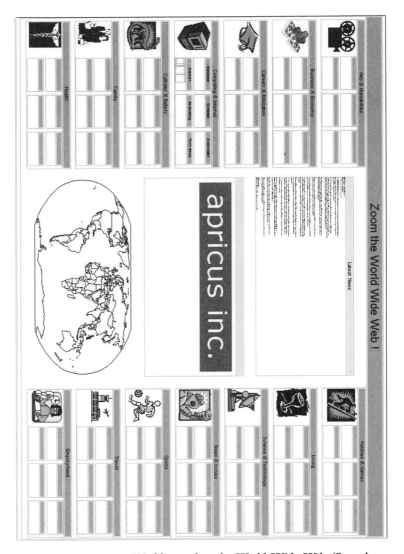

Figure 6.7. A ZoomWorld portal to the World Wide Web. (See color insert.)

ditional operating system. Applications per se disappear. Combined with the methods described earlier in this book, ZoomWorld can simplify the use of computer systems in general. With care and understanding of cognetic principles, it can be built so as to completely conform to the requirements of human cognitive abilities and would be easier to implement, learn, and use than present software methods.

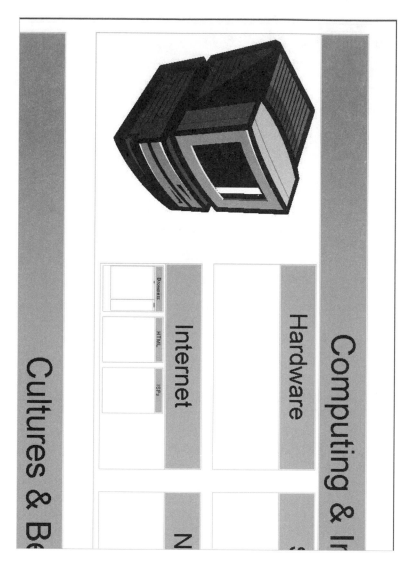

Figure 6.8. Zoomed in to one area of the World Wide Web. (See color insert.)

ZIPs may help alleviate another seldom-recognized interface design problem. We have acquired a fashionable verbal terseness in our interfaces trying to find the ideal one word that will make the menu item meaningful and have been forced into being cryptic in order to cram more labels on our displays. Sometimes, a few words or a sentence would better serve the purpose; in communicating, one should always use as few words as possible, but

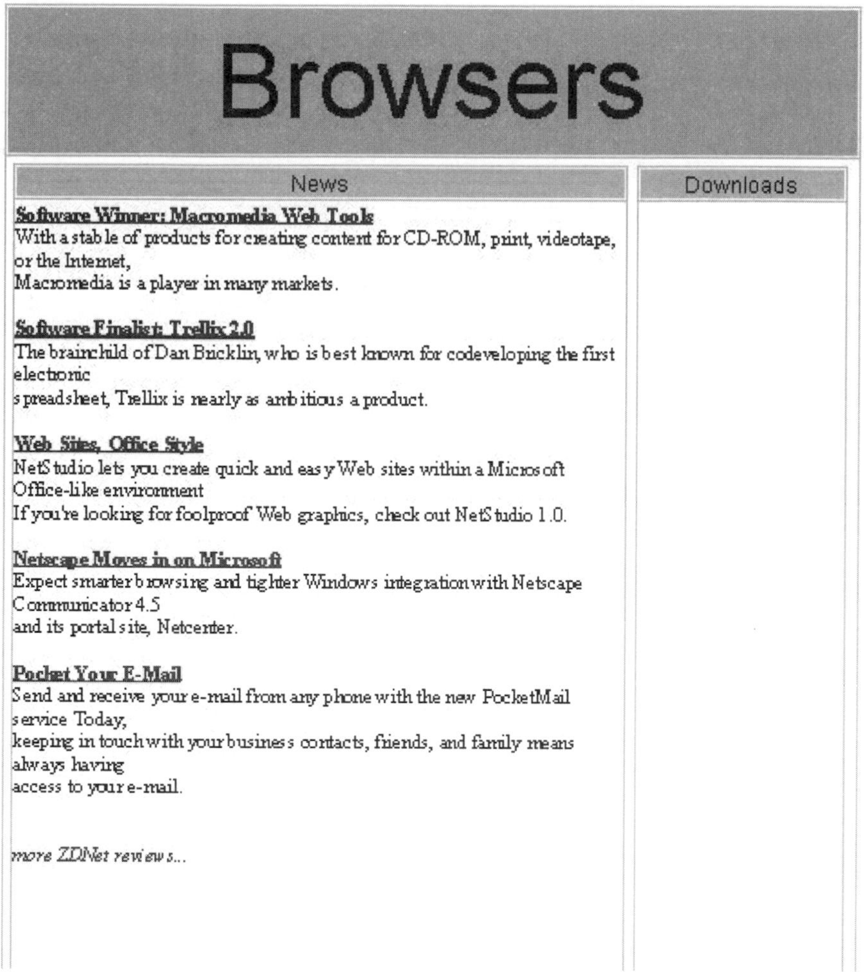

Browsers

News	Downloads

Software Winner: Macromedia Web Tools
With a stable of products for creating content for CD-ROM, print, videotape, or the Internet,
Macromedia is a player in many markets.

Software Finalist: Trellix 2.0
The brainchild of Dan Bricklin, who is best known for codeveloping the first electronic
spreadsheet, Trellix is nearly as ambitious a product.

Web Sites, Office Style
NetStudio lets you create quick and easy Web sites within a Microsoft Office-like environment
If you're looking for foolproof Web graphics, check out NetStudio 1.0.

Netscape Moves in on Microsoft
Expect smarter browsing and tighter Windows integration with Netscape Communicator 4.5
and its portal site, Netcenter.

Pocket Your E-Mail
Send and receive your e-mail from any phone with the new PocketMail service Today,
keeping in touch with your business contacts, friends, and family means always having
access to your e-mail.

more ZDNet reviews...

Figure 6.9. Zoomed in on a list of browsers. Of course, ZoomWorld is a fine browser in its own right. (See color insert.)

computer interfaces sometimes go beyond possible to the point of incomprehensibility. With a ZIP, screen real estate becomes more available, and we can more easily afford to maximize clarity rather than to minimize the use of pixels. Of course, even without a ZIP, *we should always prefer clarity over brevity in our labels*.

The current crop of interface-building tools cannot be used to build ZoomWorld. It must be programmed in a language such as Perl, C, C++, or Smalltalk; a reasonable mockup can be done with Macromedia Flash. If the programmers have not studied the rationale for the change in paradigm, when ZoomWorld or LEAP is implemented, the programmers and designers working on the project tend to slip in details that work the old ways. Many times I've come in to review a client's progress only to discover that someone had built in a toggle or another modal feature or had used dialog boxes. This is one of the difficulties in maintaining the quality of these interfaces, namely, our old design habits. *The only solution to keeping an interface design on track is careful study of and attention to the fundamentals of interface design so as to take cognitive issues into account. That often means retraining the whole team,* from management to designers to testers, so that they understand the parts of cognetic technology pertinent to their roles. The training needs to include a study of design heuristics not discussed in this book but well known to the human factors community.

On the hardware side, a mouse for working with a ZIP might have three buttons: two marked Select and Activate on top and one marked Grab on the side, and which might zoom in when you twist it clockwise and zoom out when you twist it counterclockwise, as with standard screw thread direction, on the side.

6-3 Icons

Icons, those familiar little pictures used to identify buttons and other objects, are a shibboleth of modern interface design. Apple Computer, which is well known for its leadership in this field, advised us that "icons can contribute greatly to the clarity and attractiveness of an application. The use of icons also makes it much easier to translate programs into other languages. Wherever an explanation or label is needed, consider using an icon instead of text" (Apple Computer 1985, p. I-32). Later versions of the manual were not so dogmatic about using icons, but the damage had already been done.

Icons contribute to visual attractiveness of an interface and, under the appropriate circumstances, can contribute to clarity; however, the failings of icons have become clearer with time. For example, both the Mac and Windows 95 operating systems now provide aids to explain icons: When you point at the icon, a small text box appears that tells you what the icon stands for. The obvious reaction, which I have observed repeatedly when users first see this facility, is Why not just use the words in the first place? Why not indeed? *Instead of icons explaining, we have found that icons often require explanation.* If you wanted to obscure or to encode an idea to keep it from prying eyes, substituting icons for the words might not be a bad start. The problem with icons can be considered an issue of diminished visibility: The interface presents an icon, but the meaning of the icon is not visible, or it may give the wrong message to someone for whom the graphic is unfamiliar or has a different interpretation. For example, an icon that shows the palm of an upraised hand indicates "halt" in the United States but signifies "here's excrement in your face" in Greece (Horton 1994, p. 245).

You do not have to be an interface expert to be bothered by icons. A car reviewer's complaint is typical, "You had to get out the manual to understand the [radio's] controls—there were no words on the buttons (you know, like 'volume'), only symbols" (Hotchkiss 1997, p. 14A).

Sometimes, the use of icons is rationalized on the grounds that they are language-independent, which is a useful property for software to have in an increasingly international marketplace, although, as noted, icons are not culturally independent. But even if an icon does not require translation, the linguistic aids and help screens used to explain it must be translated, nullifying any supposed advantage. With either icons or words, careful translation by an acculturated expert native speaker and writer of the language used by the target audience is required, as well as review by editors who have grown up and lived in the culture. Although words can be understood in at least one language, an icon is an equal-opportunity puzzle, potentially lacking comprehensibility across the entire spectrum of Earth's tongues.

In this example, the meaning of an icon was understood by only a minor subculture, to the detriment of nearly everybody else: On the Apple IIe, each connector on the back was identified by a distinctive icon. One especially enigmatic icon consisted of a horizontal line under which was a dashed three-segment line of the same total length (Figure 6.10). Of the thousand or so people I have asked, primarily at conferences, fewer than a dozen have known unequivocally its meaning and fewer still its derivation.

The icon represents an oscilloscope trace: An oscilloscope (Figure 3.5) is a device used by electronics technicians to render electrical parameters, such as voltage, visible. The dashed line in Figure 6.10 is the zero volt position, and the solid line is what you would see on the display of the oscilloscope if you put the DC voltage from the power supply across its inputs.

In the preface to *The Icon Book,* author William Horton says, "I've used systems with graphical user interfaces for a decade and would prefer to

Figure 6.10. A particularly obscure icon.

click on an understandable image than to enter technojargon commands—even if I could remember how to spell them" (Horton 1994). Of the two poor choices he presents, icons may be preferable, especially for the newcomer or the occasional user. However, he omits another choice: clicking on a button identified by a well-chosen word or two. To be fair to Mr. Horton, he states that in certain places, both words and icons are needed, and he correctly emphasizes the importance of testing, whether words or icons or both are used in an interface. Bob Horn (Jacobson 1999) has developed a style of combining the attributes of words and icons into combined symbols, which reinforces the dictum that *text is often the best visual cue*. We are expert at visually differentiating one word from another, and words can convey quite specific content. Ergonomic factors, such as case, font size, color, and other attributes of the text, are also important.

Mayhew (1992) cites a number of research studies on the use of icons. Unfortunately, most of the studies did not compare labels to icons. But from these and other studies, we can conclude that icons are most effective when there are at most a dozen of them and when at most a dozen are seen at one time. In addition, it is essential that they

- Are visually distinct

- Do a good job of representing the appropriate concept

- Are presented at a reasonably large size, typically larger than a text label would be

In every study that considered the question, icons were demonstrated to be more difficult to understand than were labels, especially at first viewing, which contradicts one of the most frequently cited reasons for using icons, namely, comprehensibility for beginners. GUIs often present us with windows full of identical icons, each with a label. The icons are small and numerous, and there are dozens of different icons. The limited conditions under which icons are effective do not obtain in present computer systems.

Although it is true that tiny icons can take less screen space than labels, you have to ask: At what cost? The smaller a button, the longer it takes to operate it, and the more difficult it is to find; also, it is difficult to make a small icon distinctive. Another small point: Icons take more time to create than do words.

A major problem with icons is that it is often difficult to figure what to call them, whether for communicating with others, when writing about them, or even if you want to think about them in a verbal way. How do you sort or classify them; where do they fit in an index? For example, one icon on Macintosh keyboards looks somewhat like a diagram of a freeway cloverleaf interchange. In print, it has been called a cloverleaf, the propeller, or the pretzel. In this case, the key does have a name: In Apple manuals, it is called the Command key. This leads to the natural question as to why, on a keyboard that has explicitly labeled Shift, Option, and Return keys, did Apple not put the word *Command* on this key? What advantage does this icon confer on the user? How can you tell, by looking at it, that it is the Command key? The key with the little window on it on current Windows-specific keyboard falls into the same category of marketing triumphant over usability.

If we are to be consistent, pressing a key with a funny shape on it should simply type that funny shape into our document; keys with words perform other functions. (Arrow keys are probably a useful exception.) I suspect that the increase in sales due to such shenanigans is nil, whereas the difficulties that they cause—for example, requiring a new character in the fonts used for writing the manuals of every product that will require mentioning that key—are unending.

Trying to describe icons with words can lead to extreme verbal calisthenics. Consider the elaborate vocabulary that describes the heraldic symbols of English nobility. A shield might be emblazoned "Per pale or and vert a lion argent rampant."★ Will we require such a language to describe icons when you phone up someone to get help in making a computer work properly?

There are, of course, many places where words fail. A color palette is such an example. One program on my computer offers the palette in words, presented in (mostly!) alphabetic order. Here is a portion of the list:

Cyan	Blue Violet
Blue	Brick Red
Magenda [sic]	Burnt Orange
Apricot	Burnt Sienna
Aquamarine	Cadet Blue
Bittersweet	Carnation Pink
Blue Green	Corn Flower
Blue Gray	Forest Green

★ I believe the translation is: a shield divided into left and right halves, with the left half gold and the right half green. In the center of the green half is a silver image of a lion in heraldic style, set at about a 45 degree angle to the horizontal, with its head to the right and above.

Gold	Indian Red
Goldenrod	Lemon Yellow
Gray	Maize
Green Blue	Maroon
Green Yellow	

What color is "Bittersweet"? What if you are botanically challenged and don't know a dandelion from a corn flower? The index for a collection of clip art is often effective when it has thumbnail representations of each image, but the list of categories of images, or any higher-level organization, should be text. An image of a number of a flowers does not convey the same information as the word "flowers." The image might represent "summer," "a listing of florists," or "hayfever sufferers chat room."

On the desktop of my Mac, I have exactly one often-used icon outlined in red; changing the border color of an icon is a system option. The color does make that particular icon easier to find among the dozen or so icons that clutter my desktop. I do not have the option, which I would prefer, of having one red word. Horton (1994) points out that "color coding can fail if you use too many colors or if there are too many icons in each color." He specifies that if the icons are close together, you should use no more than seven colors; if they are scattered about, you should use no more than four colors. He is right, and his suggested limits apply to the use of color with words, as well. But too many GUI designers seem not to be reading Horton.

Apple's early guidelines state that "To use the screen to its best advantage, Macintosh applications use graphics copiously, even in places where other applications use text. As much as possible, all commands, features, and parameters of an application, and all the user's data, appear as graphic objects on the screen" (Apple Computer, Inc. 1985, p. I-31). However, the best advantage for the user is to achieve clarity and ease of use. The tendency to overuse graphics has been an impediment to good interface design.

In creating a telecommunications interface, its designers had to indicate the following states: dialing, ringing, busy, no dial tone, excessive noise on line, attempting to connect, and connected. After some months of trying icons and testing them, they found it impossible to design a set of icons that would invariably convey the information to users. When consulted about this problem, I asked: How do you draw the sound of a busy signal? I suggested that they use the list of words they had provided instead of icons; they did, and testing confirmed the utility of the solution. That they did not see this for themselves is probably a result of the effective "brainwashing" of interface guidelines such as those quoted.

Using icons sometimes prevents designers from seeing the possibility of direct manipulation. To discard a document in most GUIs, you drag its icon to the wastebasket or trash can. If the document is visible at the time, why not drag the document itself? In a case like this, the icon is an unnecessary proxy and a level of abstraction you must learn and understand. We can do even better and avoid having a trash icon altogether: Why not simply select the document to be erased and use the Delete key? That would make deleting a document monotonous with other forms of deletion.

Icons seduce designers into looking for a representation, model, or analog for the task and then implementing an operation on the representation instead of the thing itself. On occasions such as the one just mentioned, this is a design error. Sometimes, icons seduce designers into creating yet more icons. A bibliographic database application designer asked me to comment on the quality of his team's choice of icons. I responded that most people who use bibliographies can read and that therefore words might be preferred. Figure 6.11 shows a few of the dozens of icons they had created. See whether you can decipher them (footnoted answers on next page).[5]

The clearest ones are probably Menu, AND, and, especially if you are professionally interested in books, ISBN. Having read the intended interpretation of each only two days before writing this paragraph, I find that I still cannot remember what they all mean, especially the one that looks to me like a beach ball.

To summarize: Surprisingly, icons violate the principle of visibility: It is their *meanings* that are not visible. Use icons only in the few situations

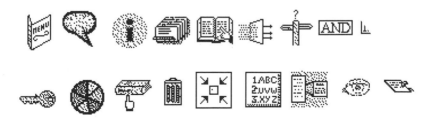

Figure 6.11. Bibliographic icons (from: http://www.scran.ac.uk/iconstd/). Many are inscrutable, as you can ascertain by looking at each and deciding what bibliographic category or operation it is supposed to represent.

where research has shown them to be advantageous. Otherwise, words are better.

6–4 Techniques and Help Facilities in Humane Interfaces

Be a driver, not a mechanic.

—Automobile advertisement

A desktop-based interface has a very low efficiency because you do not accomplish your tasks when you are in the desktop. A humane design that has neither desktop nor applications should leave the user involved with content at all times.

As we have seen, we can eliminate files and file names, leaving only one universe, or content space. You do not need to open or close documents; you zoom to them and just start working. You do not open applications; you duplicate a blank document (or whatever). You do not launch a game; you zoom in on it (a multiuser game may even be in progress). Separation of text into user-defined content areas uses the separators from the character set, user-chosen words or codes, or by making positional distinctions.

As the testing that led to SwyftWare and the Canon Cat demonstrated, neophytes find a system without a desktop or named files very easy to use. However, if experienced users of present systems are not given a few minutes of explanation, they can find these interface concepts so alien to their experience that they seem puzzling. An extreme example of this was when IBM reviewed the Canon Cat for possible interest in the interface. To avoid having to execute a nondisclosure agreement, IBM chose two ex-IBM employees who were experienced personal computer users to review the interface. Their self-chosen modus operandi was to see whether they could quickly learn the interface without manuals, online help screens, or tutoring.

At the end of the time, they reported failure. They had experimented with a range of command techniques, from the slashes of the IBM punch

---

5. *Answers:* display the main menu, change language, display information about this facility, browse, thesaurus, reduce the number of returned results, display information about the selected object's location (for example, the URL of a web page or a shelf location in a library), retrieve items in search for which both Boolean expressions are true, international standard book number, keyword, subject, title, clear current information, reduce view of current information, display a brief list of current search results, show all fields, show the results of the current search, author.

card–based Job Control Language—an ugly style of delimiter that, amazingly enough, persists to this day in web addresses—to IBM DOS commands, in their attempt to get the word processor started. They were, of course, typing and erasing text as they made these attempts. But they assumed that they were doing this at a "system level."

An interface, as far as is possible, should be self-teaching. This does not mean that an interface is, or can be, intuitive but that a user can readily find comprehensible explanations or instructions when she needs them.

To facilitate learning, a display of instructional text should be presented the first time the product is activated. A tutorial and the complete reference manual should be part of the interface, accessible at any time. Help displays are simply part of the content. No special mechanisms or techniques are required to use them. A LEAP to any keyword—and perhaps a few taps of a LEAP Again key—will suffice to find the desired information. Alternatively, you can zoom to a help area and then into the particular portion you need. Help systems in GUIs are an addition to the rest of the interface and have their own rules and implementation, which are an additional burden on the user and on the system's implementers. To where do you turn if you need help learning to use the help system in a conventional GUI: the help system's help system? As with lists of commands, which were removed from the realm of programmer-only creations and became a specie of ordinary text (in Section 5-4), the help feature of a humane interface can be operated without any special methods.

You're in Locked Text and Try to Type

You can move the cursor into locked text, say, by LEAPing there or just positioning the cursor directly. Now, if you try to type, what should the system do?

The more or less traditional computer method is to give you a beep and possibly flash the screen or the menu bar to indicate that you are doing something wrong and perhaps offer a dialog box with a message saying that you are doing an illegal operation. This is not a humane interface: It gives you an error message that you have to dismiss, and any characters you typed are lost, violating our parallel to Asimov's first law, that all user content is sacred.

It is also unacceptable for the system to move your input point to somewhere else in the document or universe. You have determined what you want to look at, and the machine shall not change it. A number of options do not violate the cognitive principles of humane-interface designing. For example, the screen could split, one part showing the cursor in the locked text, with the material you are typing in the other part, say, just after the locked text. Another solution might be to provide a transparent overlay with the message that you are trying to modify locked text, that same overlay accepting the text you do type, and selecting it so that you can readily move it to wherever you wish. As soon as you move the text to where you wish it to be, the overlay disappears.

Transmitting e-mail is a separate application in most systems. In the system being discussed here, sending e-mail consists of selecting the text, selecting the address, and executing a Send command. Because nearly every operation begins by making a selection and ends by executing a command, the standard sequence of operations becomes habitual, and the operation of sending e-mail does not feel like three distinct steps but only one.

Your e-mail directory is simply your address list or any list containing names and e-mail addresses. It is just ordinary text, not a special mechanism. Say that you want to send an e-mail to your Uncle Herman. You type the note and select it. You then LEAP to *Herman Jackson* or however you have him listed and then select his e-mail address. Lastly, you type or select from a menu the Send command and execute it as previously described, with the Command key. Instead of a single name, of course, you could have selected a list of names for an e-mail broadcast.

Another approach is to have an e-mail command use the first line of the selection as an address, the second line as the subject heading, and the remainder as the content of the message. A command would be used for making a selection an attachment to an e-mail. No doubt various vendors would supply different methods for sending e-mail. A wise user would buy only one.

Here is a seemingly peculiar method of receiving e-mail that, in practice, works much better than it sounds. When an e-mail arrives, two document characters, which sandwich the growing contents of the e-mail, are inserted immediately before your current cursor location. You can, of course, continue to work as the e-mail streams in. No special window or "You have mail" message is needed. You can ignore the e-mail or read it in progress. At any time, during transmission or afterward, you can select the e-mail and then move it to wherever you wish. An experienced user is likely to have a spot labeled "E-Mail Repository," "E-Mail Goes Here," or some such so that it can be LEAPed to and the e-mail (deposited there automatically as well as being presented at the focus as it arrived) can be read at leisure. The value is that the e-mail, with any attachments, comes in automatically and visibly and becomes part of your text; you already know how to move text to where you want it. Attachments download in the background so that your work is not interrupted and that, if there is fear of software viruses, can be placed into a nonexecutable software quarantine. A command that gathers recently received e-mail and puts it into a particular area in your universe is a feature that software vendors might supply.

Encryption is a matter of selecting some text and applying the encryption command. Encrypted text can be left in place, e-mailed, or otherwise used. Decryption is similar.

Any abilities now provided by applications also fit into the same mental model. Consider spreadsheets: If a selection has the syntax of an algebraic expression and if a Calc command is executed, the expression is stored, and the results of the expression are displayed in its place. Another command reverses the process and shows the stored expression, which, if necessary, can be edited and recalculated. If expressions are permitted to have variables, if values can be given names, if a syntax that allows position-relative references is provided, if there is some notation for ranges, and if the expressions are put into a table, a fully functional spreadsheet has been created. But it is more than just a spreadsheet, because references to the spreadsheet values can be incorporated anywhere in text, and any value in the text can be incorporated, by name, in the spreadsheet. That is, the results from a spreadsheet in a report can be used in the introduction to the report, and values in the text can be used in the spreadsheet—without having to set up any special mechanisms. There are no sharp demarcations among text, mail, and spreadsheets or, for that matter, any other content.

6-4-1 Cut and Paste

Another problem with conventional interfaces is the cut-and-paste paradigm. Most users of cut and paste have experienced the loss of some work when they inadvertently performed a second cut before pasting the first. When text is deleted, it should not disappear into limbo, especially not into an invisible cut buffer. One solution is to have the cut text appear as the last item in a document that collects deletions. The deletion document is just an ordinary document and can be treated as ordinary text. (It may be useful to have a special command that deletes in a more permanent way.) The essential point here is that nothing mysterious happens to deleted text, and no special command or knowledge is needed to find the document containing deleted text, beyond having to know that the plaintext words, such as "This document contains deleted text," are in it. The user could type in any phrase to use as a target for this document. Of course, any phrase in the recently deleted text can also serve to find it, just as if it hadn't been deleted.

Any humane design for deletion

- *Has deletion operating no differently from other commands*
- *Puts nothing at risk when text is deleted or moved*
- *Creates no special buffer or other "system-level" or hidden place to where text is moved*
- *Treats single-character deletions no differently from multiple-character deletions*
- *Can be undone and redone*

6–4–2 Messages to the User

Always do right. This will gratify some people, and astonish the rest.

—Mark Twain

Whenever you find yourself specifying an error message, please stop; then redesign the interface so that the condition that generated the error message does not arise. In other words, an error message signals an error, to be sure, but the error is usually in the design of the system or its interface, not on the part of the user. On occasion, the work my associates and I have done in trying to eliminate an error message has resulted in our realizing that fundamental design decisions were incorrect and that design revisions were in order. In this regard, and in this regard only, error messages are a great boon. For example, in designing a package to do arithmetic, there seemed, at first, to be no way to avoid giving an error message when the user tried to divide by 0, but a better solution was the creation of a value called *undefined*. The IEEE (Institute for Electrical and Electronic Engineers) 754 standard for arithmetic uses NaN, or "not a number," for this. Arithmetic on *undefined* is well defined (*undefined* + 3 = *undefined,* for example), and results involving it are more useful and diagnostic than simply stopping the calculation. Using *undefined* also solves the problem of what to do when the Calculate command is applied to an object that does not have the syntax of an arithmetic expression. The information that something has gone wrong appears as the user's locus of attention, namely, as the result desired. More informative is to replace the simple *undefined* by divide-by-0 and other messages as appropriate. Arithmetically, they all behave as does *undefined*.

Another example of where the desire to eliminate an error message affected a hardware decision arose in the design of the Macintosh; it is also an example of a "bet the farm" kind of decision that often arises when you are creating a new product. At the time, we were choosing the storage medium for the Macintosh. Hard drives were too expensive to be considered. The 5¼-inch floppy was in nearly universal use, and a number of technologies were competing to replace it. The Macintosh team decided on the 3½ inch floppy, which turned out to be the right decision, as the rest of the personal computing world went the same way. Had IBM, for example, chosen otherwise, users might have found it difficult to buy diskettes for the Mac.

But the choice of the Sony drive was, for us, sealed by a humane interface consideration: Most of the brands of drives we examined allowed you to eject a disk by pressing a button on the disk drive. Unfortunately, nothing prevented you from doing this before your current work had been saved on the disk. In that case, we would need a warning message to let users know that they had made an error: "You have removed the diskette that this document came from. To save your work back onto the diskette, please replace the diskette in the drive." Of course, if the user had already moved away from the computer, taking the disk, the next user would be stuck. Then I learned of a drive that did not have an Eject button but that ejected the disk only on a command from the computer. Now, when you wanted to eject the disk, you signaled the computer, and the computer had time to check that your command was appropriate before ejecting the disk. If your command would lose some data or would otherwise cause a problem, the system could correct the situation before ejecting the disk. We chose the self-ejecting disk drives, which, during the reign of the floppy, was one of the many factors that made the Mac easier to use than its competition.

If a message must be given and no user response is required, the message can usually be eliminated. If, for some reason, the message absolutely must appear, it can be presented as an overlaying transparency, as discussed in Section 5-2-3. With a transparent layer for messages, the underlying screen can be seen and used as if the transparency were not there. In other words, no special action need be taken to dismiss the message. You just work through the message, and the message disappears when you perform any operation on the underlying layer; moving the cursor is not an operation in this sense. Unlike a standard dialog box, no extra user actions are required to dismiss a message, and a message never totally obscures any information on the display, a problem common in today's interfaces.

The claim is sometimes made that responding to a message is necessary to meet a legal standard. This presumption could, I believe, be challenged in court by pointing out that a user closes such message boxes habitually and that closing the message box does not imply that the user has read, or even consciously seen, the message (see Section 2-3-2).

Messages: A Case Study

One of the more remarkable designs that came from eliminating a set of error messages was the set of methods developed by Dr. James Winter for storing and retrieving information from mass storage on Canon Cat. Users of GUIs are familiar with the many messages associated with storing and retrieving information; for example, you are warned if you try to close a file that has not been saved. Originally, I had proposed that we have a pair of commands, each activated by a dedicated button, for saving and retrieving the user's universe; there was, as I have discussed, no file structure.[6]

Dr. Winter showed that only one command was needed and that this interface would be more secure. My first reaction was that it could not possibly work, a common response to good, radical ideas. After all, what could be simpler than my two commands? Dr. Winter's method did all that he had claimed, and it was implemented in the commercial product, where it proved successful and popular. In particular, many errors made in saving and loading information, which can so often devastate a user's data, could not occur.

To follow his idea requires a bit of background. The Cat had already dispensed with the concept of files in the usual sense, so that all work was stored in a user's workspace. The removable storage—in those days, a floppy disk—contained the same amount of information as memory, so the entire workspace was kept whole whether in memory or on disk. One then had the mental model of swapping entire workspaces, a concept users found very comfortable. Once a workspace was swapped in, the computer kept track of whether it had been modified, and every disk was given a probably unique serial number derived from a checksum on its contents.

---

6. Ideally, there would be no commands for saving your work whatsoever. Your material, including all intermediate states of its development, should be automatically preserved, unless you deliberately permanently deleted any or all of it. Our hardware resources at the time did not allow such an implementation.

Winter's idea was this: Only one command, which he called DISK, was needed. It would consider the state of affairs and automatically do the right thing. To demonstrate that this would work, he created a simple chart that showed the action the system would take when the DISK command was activated under various conditions. Here is the central portion of that chart.

State of memory:	Unchanged	Changed	Empty
State of disk:			
Same	no action	save	no action
Different	load	warn	load
Blank	save (dup)	save	no action

If you have placed a workspace from disk into memory and not changed it, the memory state was "unchanged." If that same disk were in the machine and you pressed DISK, there is no need to do anything; it was suggested that this might trigger a verification of the memory contents against the disk. However, if the disk had been removed and replaced with another disk ("different"), because there was a copy of the workspace—on the disk from which it had been taken—so that the system knows that no information would be lost, it erased memory and loaded the workspace from the disk. In the third case, there might be a blank, unused diskette, in which case the user probably wants to make a copy of the workspace, and that's what the system does; diskettes did not have to be formatted, as this was done "on the fly," as necessary. If the system has guessed wrong in any of these cases, no harm has been done.

The rest of the chart is self-explanatory. The term "warn" means that a message was made available that told the user that because the workspace had been changed and the disk in the drive had also been changed, the system could not do anything without losing information. It recommended that if the user wanted to retain the changes, he or she return to the original disk or save the workspace to a blank disk. After that was done, the DISK command would load the new workspace. There was a way to force a load. The system also automatically performed a DISK command if the system were left unused with the workspace in the changed state for a few minutes, adding further safety to the system.

Winter had originally proposed an even easier method, based on making use of a disk drive that could detect when a disk was inserted and eject it under program control. Unfortunately, these drives were made by Sony, and we could not convince Canon, a competitor, to use them: an example of making users suffer in the name of corporate pride. Given the Sony hardware, we would have needed no disk-related commands at all, just an Eject button on the drive that would have been read by the system and the disk ejected or not, depending on the chart. At Apple, which did not make disk drives, we were able to specify the Sony drive; however, I did not have the benefit of Dr. Winter's insight at the time I was writing the specifications for the Macintosh project.

In classroom testing, the DISK command was often praised by educators. Aside from requiring almost no class time to learn, and no time was wasted formatting diskettes, it prevented one of the most frequent excuses for lost work: If a first student left without saving her or his work and a second student put a disk in and tapped the DISK command, the warning would appear. The second student would then either rush to find the first student or would save the material on a blank disk for the first student, because the second student's disk would not load until that had been done!

Winter's DISK command was easy to use. The instructions reduced to: Whenever you want to do something with the disk, tap this button. It also made every attempt to preserve the users' work. The one-disk-equals-one-workspace concept also vastly simplified the user's mental model; the CAT became a "window" that apparently looked at the information on the diskette.

It has been suggested that the DISK command created a modal situation. The objection, however, occurs only if the DISK command is thought of as Load and Save commands hidden behind the same key. But if you don't know about those commands, as on conventional systems, you may just think of the DISK button as the "do-what-needs-to-be-done-with-the disk" command. In the event, no mode errors were observed in testing.

If your computer still uses floppy disks, you are probably aware that you must either "format" a floppy before you can use it or purchase "preformatted" floppy disks. On the Canon Cat, disk formatting was done as data was stored, so that it seemed to take no time and the user did not have to be aware that the process existed. Because the user gets no utility from being able to control the formatting process, there is no reason for the user to know that it exists. This is another example of the general principle: *If a control must always (or never) be operated, don't provide it.*

6-4-3 Simplified Sign-Ons

Users are doing more work than necessary when signing on to most systems. You first state who you are—your "handle," "online name," or "system name"—and then you provide a password. The name presumably tells the system who you are, and the password prevents unauthorized persons from using your account.

In fact, you are telling the system who you are twice. All that is logically required is that you type in a password. There is no loss of system security: The probability of guessing someone's name and password depends on how the password was chosen, its length, and the like. Finding the user's online name is usually trivial; in fact, it is commonly made public so that she can be communicated with. A badly chosen password, such as your dog's name, is the most common reason for poor security.

The technical argument that typing two separate strings of characters gives more security is false. If the online name is j characters and the password is k characters, the user, to sign on, must type $j + k$ characters, of which only k characters are unknown to a potential interloper. If the password was chosen randomly—this is the best you can do—from a character set with q characters, the probability of breaking into the account on a single guess is $1 / q^k$.

Requiring a password of even one additional character and eliminating the requirement that a user supply a name increases the difficulty of guessing the password by a factor of q and saves the user from having to type $j - 1$ characters and from having to wait for, recognize, and respond to two prompts, or fill in two fields, instead of one. We get greater security, use less screen real estate, *and* gain greater ease of use by increasing the minimum password length by one character and eliminating the name field. We lose nothing by just dropping the name. Less bothersome security techniques, such as voiceprinting or using fingerprints or another unmodifiable physical characteristic of a user, would be better yet for some applications, although you could not tell a trusted associate how to sign on to your account unless there was also an alternative way to pass the security check.

The question arises: How can you ensure that everybody has a unique password in a password-only system? What if two or more users choose the same password? One option is to have the system assign them. Badly implemented, the passwords are unmemorable, such as *2534-788834-003PR7* or *ty6*>fj`d%d*.

There are many ways of creating memorable passwords, and in such quantity that you can give the user a choice of five or six. For example, you can have the computer choose two adjectives and a noun at random from a large dictionary, and present a list such as

- savory manlike oracle

- exclusive malformed seal

- old free papaya

- blooming small labyrinth

- rotten turnip sob story

from which the user can choose her favorite. In English, there are at least two trillion such combinations. With a million tries a day, it would take an average of over 25 years to guess such a password. That's reasonably secure.

When the idea of improving the interface to a web site or a computer system by simplifying the sign-on process to require only a password is suggested, it is usually rejected on one of two grounds. Either the programmers say that that's just not the way it's done, or they say that they have no control over the sign-on procedure. But someone, of course, does have that control.

6-4-4 Time Delays and Keyboard Tricks

We are likely to have conventional alphanumeric keyboards attached to our computers for a while. In spite of many attempts at reform, such as the Dvorak arrangement of keys, the inertia of the mass of millions of people trained to touch-type on the QWERTY keyboard has proved impossible to overcome. All we can do as interface designers is to peck at the edges and make small improvements that do not require tedious retraining. Here are some small improvements that we might get away with.

Initiating automatic repeat on most keyboards requires that you hold a key for 500 msec, after which the repetition begins. This is an example of a fixed delay; however, there are good reasons to avoid using fixed timed delays in interface design. Any choice of delay is likely to be both too long and too short, depending on the user and the circumstance. In this case 500 msec is too short when you linger while holding down a key, perhaps because you are thinking about what you want to type next. In this case, you may awake from your reverie to discover a few lines of sssssssssssssssssssss on your page. (My cat is adept at eliciting this behavior from my computer.) A slow typist or a person who suffers from any of a number of neurological or physiological problems may also find the 500 msec autorepeat delay too short.

Nevertheless, 500 msec is also too long. For one thing, delays are just that: delays. The user has to wait for an effect to take place. An example that users find particularly annoying occurs in the Macintosh interface: To change a file name after you open a volume or a folder, you click on the name and then wait for about half a second for a special border or color to appear, indicating that it is now editable. The reason for doing this was to allow you to select a file name with a simple click, without risking accidentally editing it. Once the file name changes to the preeditable state, you must click on the name again to put the system in the editing state. Evidence that the delay annoys users comes both from interviews and from the number of times that magazines mention tricks for getting around the delay. Users do not like to be forced to wait.

John Bumgarner, while working at Information Appliance, came up with an elegant solution to the autorepeat problem. He began with the observation that in most phonetic languages, the same character is almost never typed three times in a row. He also observed that autorepeat is rarely used unless more than five instances of the repeated character are required; otherwise, the user simply types the character the desired number of times. His autorepeat software started to autorepeat if a key was held down for more than 100 msec after the third consecutive instance of a key being typed. In other words, to get a line of equal signs, you would type

$$= = =\downarrow$$

You would then wait until the desired length of equal signs was produced before releasing the Equal-Sign key.

Pressing the same key repeatedly is faster than typing different letters, and a GOMS analysis shows that the expected time for starting autorepeat drops from the conventional method's 700 msec to 400 msec. Bumgarner's autorepeat proved easy to learn and, in our testing, was never activated accidentally. (It won't autorepeat even if your cat sits on the keyboard.) One negative that it shares with the standard autorepeat method: It is an invisible function, labeled nowhere on the computer.

Well-designed computers and information appliances have **chord keyboards**, so that the software can recognize multiple keys held down simultaneously. Older and more primitive computers had keyboards that could recognize only a few special keys, such as Shift, that could be recognized as being pressed at the same time as were other keys. Chord keyboards allow us to solve a number of otherwise difficult interface problems. For example, how to do an overstrike: A logical method of creating two symbols that appear in the same character location is needed. For example, if you wanted to create a dollar sign by overstriking an *s* with a vertical bar (|), you should be able to use a temporal "overstrike" on the keyboard to represent the physical overstrike:

This would not conflict with the overlapping keystrokes that occur in normal high-speed typing, whereby the key pressed first is released only after one or more other keys have been struck. The word *the* is often typed not as

t↓ t↑ h↓ h↑ e↓ e↑

but, to give one of many possible sequences, as

t↓ h↓ e↓ t↑ h↑ e↑

Modern keyboards and their enabling software can accommodate these overlapped keystrokes, a phenomenon called **rollover**. Most keyboards have ***n*-key rollover**, which means that the system will not get confused if as many as *n* keys are held down at once while typing continues. Given human anatomy, there is little need for *n* to be greater than 10, although there is no technical reason for *n* to be limited at all if the computer has a chord keyboard.

Given the convention of creating overstrikes by holding one key while tapping another, accents and diacritical marks could be treated as overstrikes and handled in a uniform way. For example, *é,* as in the name Dupré, is produced on the Macintosh with the unguessable key sequence

Option↓ e↓↑↑ e↓ e↑

Note that this is an example of a modal, verb-noun method, a violation of Apple's own guidelines. It also operates inconsistently. If you type the following sequence, you get a quote followed by a *t,* not a *t* with an acute accent, as you might expect:★

Option↓ t↓↑↑ t↓ t↑

Typing accents and diacritical marks becomes simpler and more logical if overstriking is accomplished with a quasimode:

e↓ '↓'↑ e↑

You hold down *e* and, while holding it down, tap the accent. You could also type *é* by overstriking in the reverse order:

'↓ e↓ e↑'↑

It makes no difference, logically, in which order you perform the operations.

Overstriking is also useful in creating mathematical and other special symbols and for some computer languages, such as APL. You might argue that rather than accommodate overstriking, we should just add whatever characters

---

★ If you guessed Option↓e↓↑↑ t↓ t↑ to get an accented t, you'd still be wrong.

we need to the character set; after all, we have fully bitmapped displays. True, but not all of us want to take time or have the skills to design and to install a new character and add it to every font in which we want the new character to appear. Also, it seems absurd that on a modern computer we cannot accomplish what we used to be able to do with the lowly mechanical typewriter!

Overstriking need not be limited to two characters; any number can be overlaid, such as

Shift↓ *s*↓ *Shift*↑ |↓ /↓ /↑ |↑ *s*↑

That sequence will produce a dollar sign with a slash through it. Considerations of esthetics and readability, rather than hardware or software concerns, should form the only limits to overstriking.

To give immediate feedback to the user as each key is typed, assuming that *n*-key rollover and this book's overstriking technique are both operating, the interface may have to temporarily display a pair of overstruck characters as adjacent characters. The reason is that it cannot tell the difference between overstriking and rollover until the keys are released, at which time overstruck characters would coalesce automatically. I will mention here an essential keyboard reform that I touched on earlier—the elimination of the Caps-Lock key. It introduces a mode.

6–5 Letter from a User

When I was working on a project for a large company, an experienced user of that company's software wrote a letter that illustrates a few of the points made in this book. The quoted statements are from the letter.

- "The software was represented to me as a more mature product." Interviewing the programmers revealed that schedule was put ahead of quality in the priorities. What had been offered to the customers was the dream of the original project leaders. What was delivered was a schedule-driven "minimal usable subset." Many desirable details had to be omitted because the tools, which had been chosen prior to the completion of the interface design, could not implement the desired interactions.

- "The user is required to press Enter or click the mouse button many more times than is necessary to enter information." When entering material into a field, it is *not* necessary to have the user press Return or Enter or do anything else at all. *When the user moves to the next field or screen or uses a menu or a button, the system should just accept the input as it stands.*

Using Tab instead of arrow keys to move between fields caused problems. Two of the fields on one screen had free-form text input. In those fields, a user could tab to indent paragraphs or make indented lists. Therefore, Tab would not get the user to the next field. It was painful to watch a user repeatedly tap the Tab key to try to get to the next field.[7]

These examples represent two common interface problems. The first is the use of Return to delimit a field, a custom that dates back to the limitations of the teletype machine as used in time-sharing and minicomputer applications many decades ago. The second is the overloading of Return and Tab, using them to mean one thing in free-form text fields and another in shorter fields.

• "When a search option is selected, the cursor should appear in the appropriate text box so the user can start entering information without having to click the box with the mouse or press the Tab button." This is a specific case of a general principle: *If the user can do only one thing next, have the computer do it.*

• "Useless dialog boxes are probably the major cause for wasted user input and frustration." The dialog boxes he showed were the kind that inform the user that something has happened and require a mouse click or a press of the Enter key to get rid of them. There is no choice; you must click the box to go on. This is another specific case of the general principle just mentioned: If the user can do only one thing next, do it for him. As the writer said elsewhere in his letter, "It is important that every time a user must interact with a dialog box that there is a productive outcome to the interaction." This can be generalized to: *Every time a user must interact with a computer, there must be a productive outcome to the interaction. Moving forward in the work flow in and of itself is not a productive outcome.*

The writer went on to complain that another dialog box merely "tells the user that the item is already listed" when the name or number of an existing item was entered on the screen that allowed you to enter a new item. You had to dismiss the dialog box before you could go on. He suggested instead that three buttons should appear, allowing you to leave the item as is, to delete the listed item, or to bring you to a screen where you could edit it. His design is better than what was provided, but we can do better still. Part of this problem is the idea that entering a new item is different from editing

---

7. A Next Field key would seem to be a useful addition to computer keyboards.

or deleting it. Here is a simpler method: The user summons the form and puts in the item descriptor; if it is new, the item is entered, and the user continues as she had expected to continue. If it is an item already on the list, that item's data is brought up so that the user can instantly see that it already exists. She can then edit it directly. Deletion, of course, is just one of the ways you can edit.

• The writer pointed out that a screen soon fills up with identical icons differentiated only by the names that appear underneath each of them. He suggested that a greater variety of icons be used because the "environment is a *visual* one." He's right in that the icons in a screen full of identical icons just wastes space. He suggested that four different icons be used. But with only four, there will still be lots of identical icons lying around. The solution is to realize that the icons are unnecessary. In making graphics-based interfaces, we must remember that *text is also a visual cue;* it is a very powerful one that is full of specific content and one that we all know very well (see Section 6-3).

• "If you have a purchase order open and you want to do an item inquiry, you receive the following dialog box:" The box says: "This application may not be used when 'Create / Update P.O.' is running." The correct user reaction is "Why not?" Here, the designers were not aware of the real work flow of the user's task.

The general principle is that almost any overly structured work flow approach to system design risks impeding a user whose task or inspiration demands a different approach. In this case, the interface moves from aiding the user to being a dictator. *A computer should be a servant, not a peer or a boss.*

• "There is a tendency in the computer industry to conform whether or not it has a productive outcome. . . . Conforming and having a standard design are very important . . . because it takes the user less time to get up to speed . . . , but if by conforming or standardizing, you are creating uselessness, then you have failed in your design." This is exactly one of the points made a few years back by Grudin's well-known article "The Case Against User Interface Consistency" (Grudin 1989). Obviously, Grudin's analysis has not permeated into the industry. *Abandon a standard when it is demonstrably harmful to productivity or user satisfaction.*

• "When the software was designed, it used the standard Windows menuing style." His example showed: "All the menus have uselessness built into them. One menu has the Exit command hidden below the File menu." He was trying to point out that Exit was the *only* item in that menu. "Exit should sit on the main menu line and the choice File should be removed." As he says, "one item does not make a list." *It is wasteful to have to open a menu when there is no further choice.*

- The writer often made specific suggestions to improve a detail when there was a deeper design flaw that needed correction. For example, in making up a purchase order, the user is first given a screen, called Purchase Order Direct Entry (Add), for a particular product. The user must then choose a quantity. The default quantity is 0, and as the writer points out, "The default value should be 1. I really doubt that anyone will order a quantity of 0." He's right. But the whole screen is a mistake. The user should be presented with a list of items that he can scroll through or access by means of a search. Then he would just change the quantity in the list. In this case, 0 would be an appropriate default. In some applications, the list should retain a particular user-chosen quantity—for example, the last quantity ordered—as the starting point. Depending on the demands of the task, it might be useful to have a Set All Quantities to 0 button. Clearly labeled and undoable, of course.

  There is also a Purchase Order Direct Entry (Remove) screen in the system. This screen is unnecessary: Setting the quantity to 0 in a Purchase Order Direct Entry should remove the item from the purchase order.

  The screens have another wasteful convention. There are buttons, marked *Save* and *Exit,* at the bottom. Most users are not sure what they do. Does *Save* both save and exit, in which case it should be labeled *Save and Exit,* or do you have to click them both in sequence to get out of the screen with the entry saved? If you exit without saving, do you get a warning, such as "Do you want to save your changes before exiting?" or does it just dump your work? In any case, having either button is unnecessary. Once you move the cursor outside the box and start to do anything else, the system should allow you to do it, saving the contents of the old dialog box.

- When a customer takes the time to carefully analyze and make constructive suggestions about your product, pay attention! It is not an attack or an embarrassment. This person is not an enemy attacking you; he or she is showing loyalty to and interest in your product.

SEVEN

Interface Issues Outside the User Interface

It is a profoundly erroneous truism, repeated by copybooks and by eminent people when they are making speeches, that we should cultivate the habit of thinking of what we are doing. The precise opposite is the case. Civilization advances by extending the number of important operations which we can perform without thinking about them.

—Alfred North Whitehead

This chapter presents a potpourri of other technology-related areas where some out-of-the-box thinking (or nonthinking) may be of value to designers. Section 7-1 addresses the fact that programming language environments contain some of the worst human interfaces in the industry. We look at two aspects that could be improved. One is that the initial hurdle in terms of system and development environment has become so large that the beginning programmer is not encouraged to experiment and to learn by doing. The second is that although the benefits of documentation are well known, not much of it is done. A small change to programming languages might make the process easier.

Section 7-2 looks at the profusion of cables growing like snakes on Medusa's head from our computers. We never seem to have the right adapter, extension, or proper kind of cable for what we need. This problem would be far more tractable if we didn't have special male and female ends to cables but if instead every cable for a given function could plug into any like cable or connector on the computer. It is possible to do this.

Section 7-3 discusses a question of ethics: Building interfaces puts the designer into intimate and extended contact with the mind and body of the user. This entails certain responsibilities. Much has been written about how to make sure that there are appropriate curricula and training for practitioners of the interfacial arts, to protect users of their work, but not much has been said of what safeguards and societal protections are needed to allow the competent designer to do good work.

7-1 More Humane Programming Language Environments

7-1-1 System and Development Environment

Programming environments have had even less benefit from research into cognetics than user interfaces have had. There is no question that modern systems are becoming increasingly complex and that programming tools need to accommodate this increasing complexity. Simple things have been made unnecessarily difficult, and we have failed to provide sufficient and sufficiently well-designed software tools needed to ease the difficulties of working in today's computer environment.

I will start with a simple example. To write a program that adds two numbers on the long-dead Apple II, you turn it on (boot time is undetectable!) and press *Control-B,* which gets you into BASIC. If you then type PRINT 3+4 and press Return, you get 7 instantly and painlessly. From launching BASIC to result: five seconds. As the industry is well aware, ease of use requires copious resources of memory and speed. Therefore, we know that the Apple II can operate with such dispatch and ease of use because it is a powerhouse of brute hardware: 2MHz 8-bit processor; 48K bytes of RAM (all that you could stuff in!), and a 400Kb disk. A 1999 400MHz 32-bit processor with 192MB of RAM (and there's room for more!) and gigabytes of disk storage takes more than three minutes. Considering bus width and processor speed, the new machine is about 1,500 times faster than the old. Considering the time it takes to get started on writing a program, the new machine is about 36 times slower.

I asked two professional programmers to write a Visual Basic (VB) program that adds 3 + 4 and prints the result. The first began by complaining that the machine was hobbled by having only 8MB of memory and was powered by an obsolescent 75MHz 32-bit processor. Not counting the two-minute boot time, BASIC was up in 54 seconds. Then an Insert Module had to be opened, a Get Options box was opened and manipulated, a button and a form were created, and the programmer then had to type the middle line of the following:

```
Private sub Command1_Click ()
MsgBox 3 + 4
End Sub
```

Before this program could be used, it had to be launched and then a button clicked to make it run. Only two or three errors were made during this process, which took 3:40 (again, not counting boot time).

Another programmer, with a 75MHz 32-bit Pentium processor and 40MB of RAM, launched Visual Basic and did the same task in 28 seconds (over five times slower than the Apple II). The program, created by a slightly different process, was

```
Private sub Form-Load ()
MsgBox Str (3 + 4)
End Sub
```

I asked the second programmer why he didn't use what the first programmer had:

```
MsgBox 3 + 4
```

He said he wasn't sure that it would work. In other words, he wasn't sure how VB worked in this case. There's nothing odd about this; like other modern computer languages, VB is huge and inconsistent in design. The rationale for its size is that it makes large projects easier, but that is no reason to make little things more difficult. To the extent that big things are made out of lots of little ones, making small tasks easier also makes the overall task easier. It is only bad language- and system design that explains why one experienced VB programmer made errors and another was not sure of the proper syntax for an elementary program. I got similar times and results with three Smalltalk programmers, thus demonstrating that it is not just VB that has these problems. Obviously, each of these languages also offers many advantages, but if they and, especially, their environments had been better designed from a human factors viewpoint, the advantages could have been had at less human cost.

Something wonderfully straightforward has been lost: in particular, the immediate feedback that humans need in order to quickly iterate their way to an effective program. I am not so naive as to think that we can keep the former simplicity in toto and achieve the level of program complexity that is now demanded, but I am certain that we can do a lot better than we have.

7-1-2 Importance of Documentation in Program Creation

Many sources explain that it is important for programmers to copiously document the code they write. Two reasons are usually given: to aid the reader of the program in understanding it (Knuth 1992, p. 99) and to make it easier to adapt the program to new circumstances (Weinberg 1971, p. 164). A typical program has an occasional line or two of comments and somewhat more frequent single-line comments attached to lines of code. Many programs are almost totally devoid of comments.

As Knuth also noted, writing the comments *before* or as one creates the code seems to make writing code easier, improves the design of the algorithms, lowers the number of errors and iterations required to complete a project, and also gives the advantages usually cited for providing comments. There seems to be a good cognitive reason why Knuth's impressions are correct.

When we develop algorithms and write code as experienced programmers, the process is accomplished, in part, by the cognitive unconscious. As has been noted, this mental facility can sustain contradictions. I suspect that the cause of some programming errors is that your cognitive unconscious is sustaining a contradiction between what you want to do and what the code is telling the computer to do.

However, to write out your intentions clearly in natural language forces you to make your reasoning process conscious, and it is in the cognitive conscious that contradictions most readily become apparent. Even if this hypothesis is incorrect, writing comments makes you think through the problem an extra time, in a different medium, and from another point of view.

Unfortunately, programming environments have been designed to make comments difficult to add. For example, comments in many computer languages are limited to one line; where multiple-line comments are allowed, there is often no word wrap or other features that the simplest word processors have to aid the typing process. (Two exceptions are UCSD Pascal and Oberon.) If you want to edit a paragraph-length comment in Visual

Basic, a language of the 1990s, you have to word-wrap it by hand. Programmers are, according to legend, not especially proficient in spelling, so you would think that a spell-checker would be part of every programming environment, but such a facility is almost never present in a programming environment. In the current iteration of Mathematica, a generally superb program for working with mathematics, comments have been stripped out of programs and put into separate windows, a move in exactly the wrong direction. A few systems, such as Knuth's WEB (1992), were created specifically to aid the documentation process. Another approach, less sophisticated but effective, was taken by the author (Lammers 1986, p. 226).

To keep a program working, any changes to a program must be preceded by changes to the explanation. There should be no separation between programming and any other activity you do with your computer, just as we have seen that there is no need to separate other forms of computer use into applications. Experience has shown that most computer users are reluctant to even try programming. Perhaps if it were integrated into the environment so that snippets of programming would be useful without having to learn a whole programming language or a programming environment, some of the benefits of programming could be more widely realized. It would also be advantageous to be able to take capabilities from various languages and blend them, not into a potpourri, such as PL/I, but in a way analogous to what has been proposed in this book for merging applications. It might be rewarding to be able to meld LISP's structures for list processing, APL (or its progeny, J) with arrays, SNOBOL's powerful string handling, Smalltalk's inheritance and objects, and so Forth.

Cognetics can improve computer interfaces, but the blend of state-of-the-art language design and what we know of human factors has yet to be exploited to any major degree; language designers and interface experts too seldom work together. This is true even though one of the earliest books in the human-computer interface field examined this very question: Weinberg's *Psychology of Computer Programming*, published in 1971, was very far ahead of its time. We haven't caught up yet.

7-2 Modes and Cables

Software runs on hardware. If you can't figure out how to connect the hardware, the software is just so many lost bits. Among the simplest piece of hardware is the cable, a few wires or fiber-optic strands bundled together with a connector at each end. Cables should be able to be plugged and unplugged without having to worry about whether the computer was on or not. (Cables that are not "hot-swappable" are modal!) You should not have to configure devices, as is required for SCSI connections. With the USB and FireWire standards, these desiderata are finally being addressed. But there are still interface issues that have not been addressed, even with the new standards. For example, it is frustrating to have a cable with the right kind of connector but of the wrong sex. Because there are male and female ends to cables and because some pieces of equipment have connectors that mate with the male ends of cables and others that mate with the female ends of cables, you end up owning a surprising number of variations of each kind of cable. Many computer owners find themselves also purchasing sex-changing adapters because adapters are smaller and less expensive than cables. For example, say you own only male-to-female cables but you need to connect two devices that both have female connectors. You might choose to purchase a male-to-male cable, or you might choose instead to buy a male-to-female adapter and attach it to the female end of the cable you already own. Attaching the adapter results in a cable that is, effectively, male to male.

This dilemma is avoidable, but the methods usually proposed do not work. One solution I have heard is that all connectors on equipment could be standardized to be, say, female, and therefore all connectors on cables would be male. Even so, you would still need female-to-female adapters to join two short cables into one longer one, and a manufacturer would be wise to supply male-to-female cables to act as extensions for existing cables. Following this logic, you can construct situations that require every possible combination of male and female ends on cables and adapters, even with the convention specifying that all connectors on equipment will be female.

A conventional connector pair is typically built as a male connector with pins and a mating female connector with sockets. This approach results in an inventory of eight kinds of parts that can be used as connectors on equipment or cables:

- Male connector for equipment
- Female connector for equipment
- Male connector for cables
- Female connector for cables
- Male-to-female adapters
- Female-to-male adapters
- Male-to-male adapters
- Female-to-female adapters

With hermaphroditic connectors, any two cables connect together, and any cable connects to any connector on a piece of equipment. The inventory is reduced to two items:

- Connector for equipment
- Connector for cables

Electronic requirements force us to have different cables for different kinds of signals, but within each class of cables, nothing in the nature of electronics or manufacturing keeps us from designing hermaphroditic connectors, which are neither male nor female. Any two hermaphroditic connectors of a given class will mate. Surprisingly, any kind of electronic signal connection or electrical power connection can be made via hermaphroditic connectors. This includes multiple-pin connectors, power connectors, and coaxial cables.[1]

If you have two hermaphroditic cables of a given class, you can use the cables either as two separate cables or joined together into one extended cable. In some cases, the hermaphroditic connector would be no more expensive or complex than a standard, sexed connector. This will not always be true; in many cases, a hermaphroditic connector will be somewhat more complex and more expensive to manufacture, but the added expense is counterbalanced by such factors as

- Increased user satisfaction
- Simpler manuals
- Fewer manufacturing setups are required
- Distributors and retailers needing to stock fewer different items

Figure 7.1 shows the schematic of a four-conductor linear hermaphroditic connector. For n conductors in a linear arrangement, you need a minimum of $2n - 1$ contacts. You can trace the conductors in Figure 7.2 to see how it works. Figure 7.3 shows the conductors for a hermaphroditic coaxial connector. The idea can be extended to multiple coaxial conductors. To make better human-computer interfaces possible, we are willing to pay for more complex computers. The same reasoning should be applied to the maddening tangle of wires and cables in which computer and electronics

---

1. Some cables used in setting up widely spaced components, such as a photographer's remote strobe lights, have hermaphroditic connectors. The now obsolete GR coaxial power radio frequency connectors are another example.

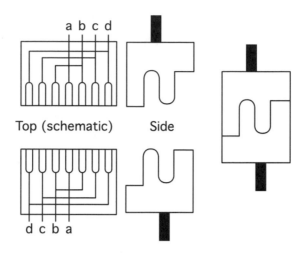

Figure 7.1. *A hermaphroditic four-conductor connector. The four conductors are labeled a, b, c, and d.*

users are perpetually enmeshed. It may seem that some linear scheme with fewer than $2n - 1$ contacts is required, but keep in mind that connecting cables have also to work as extension cables.

7-3 Ethics and Management of Interface Design

The reasonable man adapts himself to the world; the unreasonable one persists in trying to adapt the world to himself. Therefore all progress depends on the unreasonable.

—George Bernard Shaw

It is difficult to create a good interface when management does not think that interface design is important. In the short-term view, careful interface design may appear to add to the expense of creating a product and to lengthen the development time. In my experience, the short-term view is wrong even in the short term; improving the user interface often simplifies the design. Careful design and detailed specifications do not hinder but rather speed implementation. A superior interface is also an exceptional long-term investment that returns

- Higher productivity for the customer
- Increased customer satisfaction

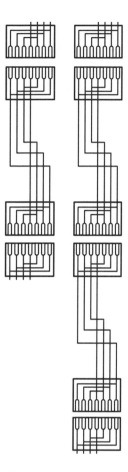

Figure 7.2. Hermaphroditic connector-equipped cables can be used to connect to units (at top and bottom of each column) or as an extension cable (right column).

- A greater perceived value
- A lowered cost of customer support
- Faster and simpler implementation
- A competitive marketing advantage
- Brand loyalty
- Simpler manuals and online help
- Safer products

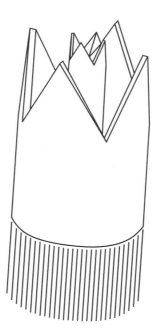

Figure 7.3. Conductors for a hermaphroditic coaxial connector. An outer, insulating sheath with four prongs, similar to the ones shown but with enlarged tips and matching widenings on the bottom (not shown), serve to lock the units together.

Interface designers are rarely in a position to control where in the development cycle interface design will occur and what weight will be given to its pronouncements. Where it has been given primacy, as in the Macintosh project, the results can be spectacular.

Aside from the field being relatively new, so that few practitioners have moved into higher management, another problem is that interface designers have little professional or collective clout. There is some work toward partially solving this problem by proposing educational standards and testing, but a practitioner's having a certificate is no guarantee of competence. The concern addressed here is with the other face of the problem: Assuming that a designer is competent, he or she is often required to design bad interfaces. I note with a trace of envy that doctors have legal safeguards if they wish to do right. For example, doctors can sue for wrongful termination if they are fired for refusing to follow a course of action that poses a threat to their patients. Structural engineers can seek the protection of the law if fired for being asked to violate the canons of their profession.

Interface designers work in an area in which incorrect decisions can contribute to physical injury and psychological debility. For example, excessive key- and mouse clicks in an interface can hasten the onset of or exacerbate existing repetitive stress injuries (RSI). Poor interface design can cause psychological distress. What is needed is a basis for establishing legal safeguards to protect conscientious practitioners. Another necessity is to establish some standards of practice—not interface design standards—for the profession. Measures, such as those discussed in this book and those that will be developed in the future, may allow numerical, objective benchmarks to be established. For example, a structural engineer must show that she has designed a bridge that meets codified standards requiring that it withstand a load of, say, twice the maximum expected, and a car must have less than 0.2 percent carbon monoxide emissions in its exhaust in order to be licensed. Similarly, we may be able to specify that an interface to a word processor is not acceptable if, say, it has an overall information-theoretic efficiency of less than 0.7 or an overall character efficiency of less than 0.8, with no individual feature rating less than 0.5.

Criteria might also be developed such that the average times—and number of keystrokes and graphical input device movements and clicks—to do tasks, averaged over a frequency-of-use weighted set of tasks, in a new word processor cannot exceed those of any prior or contemporary commercial product that does substantially the same task. Products that meet the criteria would receive some form of certification. The criteria would self-adjust as interface technology improves. At present, new products are often more difficult to use than older ones, but there is no way to know this until you've tried the product. Because these criteria affect productivity, and thus the bottom line, enterprise management should take great interest in them. Not only practitioners and management but also consumers would gain protection from the publication of objective standards of interface quality.

Steve Wildstrom, a writer for *Business Week,* pointed out that "computer manufacturers, and especially software publishers, often seem to believe that the requirements of the Uniform Commercial Code only apply to other people" (personal communication, October 1998). Many of the present software licenses that are unilaterally foisted on consumers do not promise even that the software will do the task for which it is advertised. Many of these documents specifically deny merchantability, the concept that the sale of a product automatically carries with it the presumption and promise that the product can do the task for which it was clearly intended. Some states in the United States have passed legislation that nullifies denials of merchantability for computer products; all sovereign powers should do so.

An interface-quality rating system, administered by an independent organization, might be of value to buyers of products that have a significant interface component. User interface design itself must not be regulated or restricted, and we must avoid guidelines that are based on specific interface mechanisms so that innovation will not be penalized, but relative performance ratings that compare the productivity of comparable products will spur designers to move in the right directions.

We must walk a fine line between making a product so novel that users experienced with conventional interfaces will feel lost, and making it so much like standard GUIs that we are failing to aid users to the best of our ability. At one extreme, we must avoid novelty for its own sake, although at the other extreme, we must not lose a valuable marketing opportunity by slavishly making our product too much like other products.

One of the oldest canards in the interface business is the one that says "Maximizing functionality and maintaining simplicity work against each other in the interface" (Microsoft 1995, p. 8). What is true is that adding ad hoc features works against simplicity. But that's just bad design. It is often, but not always, possible to increase functionality without increasing difficulty at a greater rate. Often, added functionality can be had without any added interface complexity; note the difference between interface complexity and task complexity. If the added functionality unifies what had previously been disparate features, the interface can get simpler.

"One way to support simplicity is to reduce the presentation of information to the minimum required to communicate adequately" (Microsoft 1995, p. 8). That is certainly the case, except that I'd replace "adequately" with "well." They err, however, by saying, "For example, avoid wordy descriptions for command names or messages" (Microsoft 1995, p. 8). But what is the minimum required to communicate well? Most of today's interfaces emphasize brevity at the expense of clarity. Why should we have to decipher a cryptic item marked "List" in a word processor's pull-down menu when it could say "Make Index or Table of Contents"? (Remember that a pull-down menu takes up no room from your document, because it goes away as soon as you move the cursor away from it or choose an option.) Do not confuse a clean, open look to the screen with a simple-to-use interface.

Navigation versus White Space

We seem to have a real fear of displaying data in our interfaces. We know that people quickly can find one among a few items much more quickly than they can find one among dozens: There is less to look through. But it does not follow, as some seem to think, that it is therefore better to have fewer items on each screen. If you have hundreds of items and split them up among dozens of screens, you lose more in navigation time than you gain in searching for the individual item, even if the one you seek is swimming in a sea of similar-looking items. Looking for something in long, gray lists is not always a terrible thing in an interface.

If people weren't good at finding tiny things in long lists, the *Wall Street Journal* would have gone out of business years ago. Would you rather have the stocks listed 15 to a page, each page decorated like a modern GUI screen, even given some scheme for helping you to find the right page, such as:

STOCKS	PAGE
AA–AD	1
AD–AS	2
AT–AZ	3
BA–BK	4
and so forth	

Such a scheme would be considered childish, wasteful, and a nuisance. Yet we sometimes spend more pixels on a screen in making neat, gray-shadowed borders than we do in presenting information. When a person is motivated—by interest or by salary—to refer to data, he finds long lists no problem at all. Visual designer Edward Tufte's (1983, p. 105) first three principles for displaying information are:

- Above all else, show the data.
- Maximize the data-ink ratio.
- Erase nondata ink.

All we need do is substitute *pixels* for *ink* for his advice to apply to display-based devices. A serious, professional user wants screens packed with useful stuff. Screens should be well labeled, with methods to make finding things easier and dense with the information that represents the real value of each screen. (After all, we do have a computer sitting there, and we should be making the best use of it we can.)

There are a multitude of studies on the design of displays. Many early but still useful studies are discussed in Tullis (1984). Some of the results are still valid, such as search time through a list of items is approximately 30 milliseconds per item (p. 126). Tullis's major results apply to 24-by-80 alphanumeric displays and gave a quantitative evaluation.[2] If the results were extended to today's bitmapped displays and could give a measure of target-finding time, that could be used to optimize not only single, isolated, nonwindowed displays (Tullis's restrictions) but also, in conjunction with estimates of navigation time, could lead to a more global optimization. There is almost certainly a tradeoff between screen complexity and navigational complexity, as Tullis himself noted (p. 132). The tradeoff depends on the speed and ease of navigation and how the data is structured. Where a search facility, such as LEAP, is used for a significant percentage of within-screen searches instead of visual scanning, still other measures would have to be devised. This is a lively area for further research.

In any case, following the popular white-space-makes-for-readability philosophy of screen design to its logical conclusion would teach us that there should only be one item of data on any screen. Thus, the user will always be able to detect it visually with an irreducible minimum of effort.

Having improved many products by decreasing the number of screens and increasing the information on each of the remaining screens—improving the logic of the design to achieve the reduction—I have come to believe that, in almost all commercial software, we have erred on the side of too little data per screen.

The best way to differentiate your product's interface is to make it work. A well-written and cogent argument for the importance of interface issues, directed in large part to management, is *The Invisible Computer* (Norman 1998).

---

2. Tullis's measures did not look at content quality but only layout. It is possible to construct counterexamples, that is, displays that rate highly on his measures but which are difficult to use.

EIGHT

Conclusion

*One began to sympathize with the dog whose muzzle is
removed at the end of a prolonged Muzzling Order, and who
does not quite know what to do with himself.*

—C. G. Grey *(in Jane's* All the World's Aircraft *1919)*

If you start with the goal of making interfaces as simple
as you can, taking account of our limitations and exploiting our abilities,
there are two things you have to do. One is to understand what we can and
cannot do, to study the maps of human thought presented by the science of
cognitive psychology and see where they lead to the engineering discipline
of cognetics. This book has followed one major highway from the map, one
that leads from research into the division of abilities between our cognitive
conscious and our cognitive unconscious, to an understanding that we have
but one locus of attention and a recognition of the central nature of habit
formation in how we react to various interface methodologies. We also learn
that individual differences are small when dealing with habituation, in contrast to the large differences between individuals in other regards.

From the science, we learn that modes, long recognized as undesirable, are at the heart of some of the most vexing irritants in current

computer interface paradigms. Any complete cure requires that an interface be modeless and is enhanced by as much monotony as we can design in. The uniformity among individuals is exploited. Productivity is improved by our being able to spend less time doing a task, and this observation leads to the interface version of the classical time-and-motion study, the quantitative GOMS analysis. GOMS leads to a feel for what details make interfaces slow and fast to use and leads to the question of how fast and efficient an interface can be and to the need for quantitative measures of efficiency.

Having gone down the road of understanding human capabilities, we then look at our present computer equipment and how we use it, finding a small set of elementary actions and methods that apply to a broad and varied landscape of applications. This uniformity can also be exploited.

We are led by our studies in an unfamiliar direction that turns out to be a shorter path to usability than the standard methods provide. Fast search methods combine with the elimination of unnecessary mechanisms, such as file names and URLs, hierarchical file structures, and applications, to allow us to take speedy shortcuts. The ZIP allows us to fly over the terrain, to see more, and to get there more quickly. We have also taken a few side paths, for example, to see how cables can be made easier to use.

This book has many lacunae; for example, I am sure I have missed prior work that I should have known about, and I may have failed to correctly attribute to their originators ideas that were not my own. Parts of this book lay out areas where, had I the resources, I would have performed experiments to test my conclusions and guesses. Please consider these areas as invitations for research.

Thank you for having read this book and for joining me on a quest for more humane interfaces. Where our journey has crossed untrodden ground, I may have taken a wrong turn here and there. Nonetheless, I am convinced that my compass is a good one and that my overall direction is correct.

Starting from what we know of human cognition, we have been led to fundamental changes in the design of human-machine interfaces. Nothing less will do.

The One-Button Mouse: History and Future

Men loven of propre kynde newefangelnesse.

—*Chaucer, "The Squire's Tale"*

I have been variously castigated and applauded for creating the one-button mouse and some of the basic methods for using it. Questions from readers of drafts of this book indicated that they thought that the way the Macintosh worked was the way that earlier mouse-driven systems from Xerox PARC worked and were curious as to the differences. This appendix describes the mouse-based systems that I saw at Xerox Palo Alto Research Center (PARC) when I was a visitor there. The even earlier use of the mouse at Douglas Englebart's group at the Stanford Research Institute (SRI) was embedded in a system that was decades ahead of its time in many ways and contained valuable ideas that have not yet been widely applied. Englebart's software, however, was often modal and was sometimes inefficient at the keystroke level.

Few users of modern personal computers remember what you had to go through to make a selection with the PARC system, as exemplified by its most popular text editor, BRAVO. Tapping each of the three mouse buttons on the PARC mice will be denoted by *L, M,* and *R* (for left, middle, and right). BRAVO did not use mouse button quasimodes.

To select a character: point to the character, *L.*

To select a word: point to word, *M.*

To select an arbitrary string of characters: point to first character, *L;* point to last character, *R.*

To select a string of words: point to first word, *M*; point to last word, *R.*

A typical mistake was using *L* and then *M*, which merely restarted the selection at what you thought was going to be the end of the desired selection. This was very frustrating, especially when the selection was large. Notice, however, that you never had to "back out" of a selection; you could always just start a new one without penalty. This was a true advance over most contemporaneous systems, which required that you use ESC or some such to cancel a selection-in-progress before you could start another.

There was an earlier editor developed, but not used much, at PARC (and of which I was unaware at the time) that used click and drag to select text. Using the notation presented in Section 3-1: To select some text, point to the top of the text, *L↓*, point to a lower point in the text, *L↑*. But this idea was not extended to other kinds of selection.

At Apple, I demonstrated how we could use one button for selections more broadly: To select any contiguous area on the screen, whether text or not, point to one corner of the region, *L↓*, and point to the other end, *L↑*. This technique came to be called "click and drag."

Other BRAVO methods were also more complex than the Mac's.

To delete text: Select text and type *d*. The problem here was that you had to be aware of the existence of a selection before you knew what typing the letter *d* would do. In the Macintosh, I chose to use the Delete key to delete text both when you are typing and when you are editing.

To insert text: Point to an insertion point, *L;* type *i;* type the new text, tap the ESC key. The ESC key took you out of insert mode. The Macintosh's design did not have an insert mode, and its method has become universal: To insert text, point and click at the desired insertion point, *L;* type new text. Instead of having an explicit delimiter to start the typing, as at PARC, you just started typing. You did not have to press ESC or anything else at the end; merely starting a new task would end the old. In BRAVO, you replaced text with this method: Select old text, type *r*, type new text, tap the ESC key. To replace text on the Macintosh: select old text, tap Delete, type new text. This design differs from the current Macintosh and Windows model, which seems simpler: To replace text, select old text, type new text.

As users have discovered, however, this often causes accidental loss of text. In the original design, which requires one keystroke more than the present method, typing is never destructive, and the text editor is, and feels, more secure; this is a lot to gain from one additional keystroke.

Unlike BRAVO and some other editors designed at PARC, on the Macintosh and, to a large extent, on subsequent systems, typing a plain letter never acts as a command. In retrospect, the improvements seem obvious, but they did not seem so at the time. My design for an interface based on a one-button mouse was refined and extended in discussions with many coworkers, most notably Brian Howard and Bill Atkinson, and, of course, many adjustments were made based on observations made during user testing and during subsequent development. Some users do have difficulty both holding down a button and simultaneously moving a graphical input device, but this is partly dependent on the physical design of the graphical input device and whether it is a mouse or another input device. In the Macintosh design, this problem was alleviated by having only one large button on the mouse, with low holding force and good tactile feedback. (Some of the recent touchpads with poorly designed buttons, especially those on portables, make dragging difficult and error-prone.) Additionally, the improvement and error reduction afforded by the elimination of modes often overweigh the pointing errors due to dragging, even with less-than-optimal graphical input devices.

What I did not see at the time is that multiple buttons on a mouse can work well *if the buttons are labeled*. If the Macintosh mouse had had multiple buttons, if the buttons had been permanently labeled, and if they had been used only for their designated functions, a multiple-button mouse might have been a better choice. A better mouse might have two buttons, marked Select and Activate, on top and on the side, a button activated by a squeezing action of the thumb. This last button would be marked Grab. Some mice at present have a wheel on top that is used primarily for scrolling. Better still would be a small trackball in that location. The mouse would control the position of the cursor; the trackball could be used, for example, to manipulate objects or to make selections from menus that float with the cursor.

APPENDIX B

SwyftCard Interface Theory of Operation

Some of the principles discussed in this book were first published in the SwyftCard manual, released in 1984. SwyftCard, which plugged into the then highly successful Apple II, was simple by today's standards. Appendix B of its manual contained an unusual feature: Along with the usual theory of operation of the hardware, it also contained a theory of operation of the software and what is probably the first appearance of a user interface theory of operation in any commercial product. In a way, that appendix was the beginning of this book. The quoted material is from the second edition (Alzofon and Raskin 1985).

> The paradigms used in SwyftCard were invented to cure a host of problems shared by almost all current systems—most of them small enough in their own right, but which taken together make learning and using conventional software far more time-consuming than necessary, and which make using computers a frustrating and annoying process.
>
> We have always wondered why, for example, you have to format disks—isn't the computer smart enough to see if a disk isn't formatted

and do it if necessary? We find cursor control keys far too slow, and when you consider the number of auxiliary commands they require (move to next/previous word, sentence, paragraph, page, move to beginning/end of line, document, file . . .) we find them too complex. The GID is only a small improvement because most of them take your hands away from the keyboard, and uses up much screen space for menus, scroll bars, and the rest of the associated GID apparatus. We are annoyed when we are put through menus instead of being able to do what we want right now, and we are puzzled by the huge number of commands in most systems. We hate disk systems that allow you to lose work through trivial human error. We are amazed that many word processors cannot keep up with human typing speed.

SwyftCard shows that with proper design all these questions and bothers—and many others that have plagued us for years—can be answered and fixed. And the system works on an inexpensive computer with only one disk drive, with minimal memory requirements. Our product does what most people need done—without an operating system, expensive price tag, or bells and whistles.

The major design principles include numerous innovations, as well as applications of what we have learned from the work of others.

1. The cursor LEAP concept, whose average time to target is about three times faster than that of the most advanced method in common use up until now: the mouse.

2. The cursor itself, whose two parts show you exactly where what you type will appear and where delete will operate. The cursor also collapses upon being moved so that you do not have to aim "one off" if you want to delete.

3. A very small set of fundamental operations that allows you to accomplish a wide range of tasks with ease.

4. The elimination of an operating system, thereby allowing all operations to be performed directly and immediately from the editor without having to go into different modes.

5. The elimination of modes in general, which makes habit formation easy because you do not have to think about what state the system is in to figure out what a command will do. This property is called modelessness.

6. Not providing many ways to do a task—again so that you do not have to think about alternate strategies when you are about

to do something. We call this principle monotony. Like mode-lessness, monotony aids habit formation.

7. The emphasis on habit formation is itself a fundamental principle of the design, and one often overlooked by other designers. We consider it important that after a brief period of learning, a user should not have to think about the system while using it.

8. The DISK command, which simplifies the usual complexities of a DOS (Disk Operating System) into one simple command. It also provides protection against most common mistakes that would cause a loss of data on other systems. The technique of making one disk correspond to one Text is what makes this command possible.

9. The emphasis on making speed of operation proportional to frequency of use (often-done tasks must be very fast, seldom-done tasks can be slow).

10. What you see is what you get—the way it looks on-screen is the way it prints on paper. (This principle was violated for underlining due to a limitation in Apple display hardware.)

11. Noun-verb design of commands. First you specify what you are going to work on (that gives you time to make sure you are right and to make corrections), then you give the order as to what to do. Some systems work the other way around, or even worse, mix the two styles.

12. It is very hard to louse yourself up or clobber something you are working on. It's not impossible, but it's hard enough to do that it is not likely to happen by chance or a momentary lapse of attention.

13. The inclusion of programming and communications within a general purpose environment, where the output is placed in the editor/retrieval environment.

14. The allowance of months of testing and reworking time in the schedule, so that purchasers of the system are not being used as test subjects.

This is only a barest sketch—the system specs run to some 50 pages—but we hope it gives you a feel for what led us to design SwyftCard the way we did.

REFERENCES

At times, I may have misinterpreted or misunderstood the intent of the works I cite. I apologize in advance for any such errors.

Accot, Johnny, and Shumin Zhai. "Beyond Fitts' Law: Models for Trajectory-Based HCI Tasks" (www.dgp.toronto.edu/~accot/Common/Articles/CHI97/chi.html, 1997).

Alzofon, David, David Caulkins, Jef Raskin, and James Winter. *Canon Cat How-To Guide* (Tokyo: Canon, 1987).

Alzofon, David, and Jef Raskin. *SwyftCard,* 2d ed. (Menlo Park, CA: Information Appliance, 1985).

Anderson, J. R. *Rules of the Mind* (Hillsdale, NJ: Lawrence Erlbaum Associates, 1993).

Apple Computer. *Inside Macintosh,* Vol. 1 (Cupertino, CA: Apple Computer, 1985).

————. *Human Interface Guidelines: The Apple Desktop Interface* (Reading, MA: Addison-Wesley, 1987).

Ashlar. *Vellum 3D Manual* (Sunnyvale, CA: Ashlar, 1995).

Asimov, Isaac. *I Robot* (New York: Bantam Books, 1977).

Baars, Bernard J. *A Cognitive Theory of Consciousness* (Cambridge, U.K: Cambridge University Press, 1988).

Business Week. "Special Report on Information Appliances" (22 Nov. 1993), p. 110.

Buxton, William. "Chunking and Phrasing and the Design of Human-Computer Dialogs," *Information Processing '86: Proceedings of the IFIP 10th World Computer Congress* (Amsterdam: North-Holland, 1986).

Card, Stuart K., Thomas P. Moran, and Allen Newell. *The Psychology of Human-Computer Interaction* (Hillsdale, NJ: Lawrence Erlbaum Associates, 1983).

Cohen, Jonathan D., and Jonathan W. Schooler, eds. *Scientific Approaches to Consciousness* (Hillsdale, NJ: Lawrence Erlbaum Associates, 1997).

Collins, Richard. *Flying* 121:10, p. 67 (October 1994).

Cooper, Alan. *About Face* (Foster City, CA: IDG Books Worldwide, 1995).

Dennett, Daniel C. *Consciousness Explained* (Boston: Little, Brown, 1991).

Dijksterhuis, E. J. *The Mechanization of the World Picture* (London: Oxford University Press, 1961).

Drori, Offer. "The User Interface in Text Retrieval Systems," *SigCHI Bulletin* 30:3 (1998).

Eriksson, H., and P. Magnus. *UML (Unified Modeling Language) Toolkit* (New York: John Wiley & Sons, 1998).

Garrison, Peter. *Flying* 121:12, p. 112 (December 1994).

————. "Drifting Off Centerline," *Flying* 122:1, p. 43 (January 1995).

Gray, Wayne D., Bonnie E. John, and Michael E. Atwood. "Project Ernestine: Validating a GOMS Analysis for Predicting and Explaining Real-World Task Performance," *Human-Computer Interaction,* 8:3, pp. 237–309 (1993).

Grudin, J. "The Case Against User Interface Consistency," *Communications of the ACM,* pp. 1164–1173 (1989).

Hewlett-Packard. *User Interface Design Rules for the New Wave Office System* (Cupertino, CA: Hewlett-Packard Personal Software Division, 1987).

Hotchkiss, B. "The Car Column," *Pacifica Tribune,* 12 Nov. 1997, p. 14A.

Horton, William. *The Icon Book* (New York: John Wiley, 1994).

IBM. *System Application Architecture, Common User Access, Panel Design and User Interaction* (Boca Raton, FL: IBM, 1988).

Jacobson, Robert, ed. *Information Design* (Cambridge, MA: MIT Press, 1999).

John, Bonnie E. "Why GOMS?" *Interactions:* pp. 80–89 (October 1995).

Johnson, J., and G. Englebeck. "Modes Survey Results," *SigCHI Bulletin* 20:4, pp. 38–50 (1989).

Kaplan, Justin, ed. *Bartlett's Familiar Quotations*, 16th ed. (Boston: Little, Brown, 1992).

Knuth, Donald E. *Literate Programming* (Stanford, CA: Center for the Study of Language and Information, 1992).

Lammers, Susan. *Programmers at Work* (Redmond, WA: Microsoft Press, 1986).

Landauer, Thomas K. *The Trouble with Computers* (Cambridge, MA: MIT Press, 1995).

Laurel, Brenda, ed. *The Art of Human-Computer Interface Design* (Reading, MA: Addison-Wesley, 1990).

Lewis, C., and D. A. Norman. "Designing for Error," in D. Norman and S. Draper, eds., *User Centered System Design* (Hillsdale, NJ: Lawrence Erlbaum Associates, 1986).

Linzmayer, Owen. *Apple Confidential* (San Francisco: No Starch Press, 1999).

Loftus, Elizabeth F. *Eyewitness Testimony* (Cambridge, MA: Harvard University Press, 1979).

————. *Memory* (Reading, MA: Addison-Wesley, 1980).

Mackenzie, I. S. "Movement Time Prediction in Human-Computer Interfaces," in R. M. Baecker, W. A. S. Buxton, J. Grudin, and S. Greenberg, eds., *Readings in Human-Computer Interaction,* 2d ed., pp. 483–493 (Los Altos, CA: Kaufmann, 1995).

Malone, Michael S. *Infinite Loop* (Chicago: Doubleday, 1999).

Mayhew, Deborah. *Principles and Guidelines in Software User Interface Design* (Englewood Cliffs, NJ.: Prentice-Hall, 1992).

Microsoft. *The Windows Interface Guidelines for Software Design* (Redmond, WA: Microsoft Press, 1995).

Miller, George A. "The Magical Number Seven, Plus or Minus Two: Some Limits on Our Capacity for Processing Information," *Psychological Review* 63, pp. 81–97 (1956).

Moore, J. S., and R. S. Boyer. "A Fast String Searching Algorithm," *Communications of the Association for Computing Machinery* 20:10, pp. 762–772 (1977).

Norman, Donald A. "Categorization of Action Slips," *Psychology Review* 88:1, pp. 1–15 (1981).

———. "Design Rules Based on Analyses of Human Error," *Communications of the ACM* 26:4, p. 255 (1983).

———. *The Psychology of Everyday Things* (New York: Basic Books, 1988).

———. *The Invisible Computer* (Cambridge, MA: MIT Press, 1998).

Penrose, Roger. *The Emperor's New Mind* (London: Oxford University Press, 1989).

Raskin, Jef. "Looking for a Humane Interface: Will Computers Ever Become Easy to Use?" *Communications of the ACM* 40:2, p. 98 (Feb. 1997).

———. "The Quick-Draw Graphics System." Ph.D. diss. (State College, PA: Pennsylvania State University, 1967).

———. "FLOW: A Teaching Language for Computer Programming," *Computers and the Humanities* 8:4 pp. (July 1974).

———. "Computers by the Millions," *SIGPC Newsletter* 5:2 (1982).

———. "Systemic Implications of an Improved Two-Part Cursor," *Proceedings of CHI 89: Human Factors in Computing Systems,* Austin: 30 April 1989, pp. 167–170 (New York: ACM Press, 1989).

———. "Down with GUIs," *Wired* pp. (December 1993).

———. "Intuitive Equals Familiar," *Communications of the ACM* 37:9, pp. (September 1994).

Raskin, Jef, and James Winter. U.S. Patent No. 5,019,806, Method and Apparatus for Control of an Electronic Display, 1991.

Reason, James. *Human Error* (Cambridge, U.K.: Cambridge University Press, 1990).

Shneiderman, Ben. *Designing the User Interface* (Reading, MA: Addison-Wesley, 1987, 1998).

Sellen, A., G. Kurtenbach, and W. Buxton. "The Prevention of Mode Errors Through Sensory Feedback," *Human Computer Interaction* 7:2, pp. 141–164 (1992).

Shannon, Claude E., and Warren Weaver. *The Mathematical Theory of Communication* (Urbana: University of Illinois Press, 1949, reprinted 1963).

Smith, S. F., and D. J. Duell. *Clinical Nursing Skills,* 3rd ed. (East Norwalk, CT: Appleton & Lange, 1992).

Stallman, Richard. *GNU Emacs Manual,* 9th ed. (Cambridge, MA: Free Software Foundation, 1993).

Tesler, Larry. "The Smalltalk Environment," *Byte* (August 1981).

Tesler, Larry, and Timothy Mott. *Report on the Xerox Palo Alto Research Center Gypsy Typescript System* (Palo Alto, CA: Xerox, 20 April 1975).

Thomas, Lewis. *The Lives of a Cell* (New York: Viking Press, 1974).

Tognazzini, Bruce. *Tog on Interface* (Reading, MA: Addison-Wesley, 1992).

Tolkien, J.R.R. (Douglas Anderson, ed.) *The Annotated Hobbit* (Boston: Houghton Mifflin, 1988).

Tuftc, Edward. *The Visual Display of Quantitative Information* (Cheshire, CT: Graphics Press, 1983).

Tullis, Thomas S. "Predicting the Usability of Alphanumeric Displays," Ph.D diss., Rice University, 1984.

de Unamuno y Jugo, Miguel. *The Tragic Sense of Life,* Chapter 9 (1913).

Weinberg, Gerald M. *The Psychology of Computer Programming* (New York: Van Nostrand Reinhold, 1971).

INDEX

Note: An online index is available at www.awl.com/cseng/. Search on the keyword "Humane."

This book is published as part of ACM Press Books—a collaboration between the Association for Computing (ACM) and Addison Wesley Longman. ACM is the oldest and largest educational and scientific society in the information technology field. Through its high-quality publications and services, ACM is a major force in advancing the skills and knowledge of IT professionals throughout the world. For further information about ACM, contact:

ACM Member Services
1515 Broadway, 17th Floor
New York, NY 10036-5701
Phone: 1-212-626-0500
Fax: 1-212-944-1318
E-mail: ACMHELP@ACM.org

ACM European Service Center
108 Cowley Road
Oxford OX4IJF
United Kingdom
Phone: +44-1865-382338
Fax: +44-1865-381338
E-mail: acm.europe@acm.org
URL: http://www.acm.org

The Humane Interface *was composed in 11-point Bembo with QuarkXpress by Stratford Publishing Services of Brattleboro, Vermont. Karen Savary designed the text. Jennifer L. Collins designed the cover (with help from Aza Raskin). The text was printed on sixty-pound recycled paper by Courier in Stoughton, Massachusetts.*